D1659242

SUN ROCK

MURCIA MONACO
KLETTERN AM MITTELMEER

ISBN 3-926807-01-6

Titelbild - Cover:
Irmgard Braun in "Bengale" (6c),
Montagne de Sainte Victoire, Foto Leuchsner

Topographische Skizzen, Karten und graphische
Gesamtkonzeption: Volker Leuchsner, Christopher
Mailänder und Achim Pasold

©   by Achim Pasold und Nicholas Mailänder
        PANICO PRESS
        Golterstraße 12
        D 7316 Köngen/Neckar
        West Germany

ISBN 3-926807-01-6

Alle Rechte, insbesondere die der Vervielfältigung,
auch auszugsweise, vorbehalten.
All rights reserved.

INHALT - CONTENTS

Vorwort - Introduction	6
Zum Gebrauch - How to use the Guidebook	12
Schwierigkeitsbewertung - Grading	16
Untermenü zur Auffindung der Gebiete Subdirectory to the Areas	18
Übersichtskarte - Survey Map	20
Spanien - Spain	22
Frankreich - France	194
Foto- und Vorlagennachweis Photo and Topo Directory	362

VORWORT

Früher allenfalls Trostpflaster für vom Wetterpech verfolgte Alpinisten, wurden die Felswände des mediterranen Raums seit Beginn der achziger Jahre als Ziele von eigenständigem Wert entdeckt. Eine Fahrt zum Klettern in die Gebiete nahe der Mittelmeerküste ist heute eine populäre Alternative zum traditionellen Alpenurlaub. Die durch die weitere Anfahrt bedingten Initialkosten werden durch die Garantie, seine Urlaubstage im trockenen Fels und nicht im durchfeuchteten Zelt zubringen zu dürfen, mehr als aufgewogen. Zu diesem Einstellungswandel des Alpinpublikums dürfte die Verbreitung des Freiklettergedankens auf dem europäischen Festland wesentlich beigetragen haben. Im Zuge dieser Entwicklung wurden südlich der Alpen Führen begangen, deren internationaler Status sehr bald er- und bekannt wurde. Zudem wurde die neue Popularität des Kletterns in den Mittelmeerländern durch die Tatsache gefördert, daß der gestiegene Leistungsstandard dem ernsthaften Freikletterer eine Winterpause verbietet - das Klettern ist für viele zum Ganzjahressport geworden. Die allwinterlichen Vogelzüge der mitteleuropäischen und englischen Freiletterer nach Italien, Südfrankreich - und neuerdings auch nach Spanien - zeigen, daß viele es verstehen, Trainingserfordernis und Genuß widerspruchsfrei zu vereinbaren. Dabei dürfte die eigenartige, zwischen Sonnenrelaxen und Hochleistung oszillierende Atmosphäre im internationalen Kameradenkreis, wo das zwischenmenschliche Geschehen genauso wichtig ist wie die eigentliche Kletterei, zur zunehmenden Popularität des mediterranen Winterkletterns genau soviel beigetragen haben, wie die animalische Freude, sonnenwarmen Fels unter den Händen zu spüren, während zu Hause weiße Flocken um die Dachgiebel wirbeln.

Hätten wir gewußt, was uns blühte, als wir uns anschickten, einen Kletterführer zur Mittelmeerküste zwischen Südspanien und Monaco zu verfassen, hieltest du dies Buch jetzt sicher

INTRODUCTION

If in earlier years the crags along the Mediterranean coast were, at best, a stop gap for weathered-off aspirants to the big alpine routes, since the beginning of the 1980's they have been making the headlines in the climbing journals as full fledged areas in their own right. A sojourn to the Mediterranean has today become a popular alternative to the traditional holiday in the Alps. The higher costs of the longer journey are more than compensated for by the guarantee that the climbing holiday will be spent on dry rock and not in a soggy tent. This change of attitude lies in the growing popularity of the concept of freeclimbing on the Continent in this decade. In connection with this development many new routes were put up in Mediterranean regions that soon won international acclaim. Moreover, the rise in climbing standards no longer permits the serious rock athlete the customary hibernation period. The seasonal migrations of Central European and English climbers to Italy, Southern France, and most recently, to Spain, show that many have discovered how to combine the necessity of serious training with the pleasure principle. A particular atmosphere prevails in this cosmopolitain climbing arena oscillating between drowsy sun bathing and an excessive drive for achievement. Here the communication is as important a part of being there as the climbing itself. It is this atmosphere that has contributed as much to promoting winter climbing on the Mediterranean, as has the gut pleasure of feeling warm rock in your hands, while at home the snow is swirling around the chimney tops.

Had we fathomed what an epic we were in for when we decided that a climbing guide of the Mediterranean Coast from Spain to Monaco would be a worthwhile project, you would certainly not be holding it in your hands at the moment. For over three years we spent every holiday with pad and pencil researching the areas that seemed most worthwhile. Our criterium for the inclusion of an area, in addition to the routes

nicht in den Händen. Über drei Jahre lang waren wir im Urlaub immer mit Block und Zeichenstift unterwegs, bis wir aus den zahllos scheinenden Möglichkeiten unseres Arbeitsgebiets diejenigen herausgefiltert und dokumentiert hatten, die uns am lohnendsten schienen. Wichtigstes Entscheidungskriterium für die Aufnahme eines Gebiets war neben der Qualität des Routenangebots seine Nähe zur Mittelmeerküste. Wegen ihrer geringen Entfernung von den Hauptverkehrswegen sind die meisten aufgenommenen Gebiete schnell zu erreichen und zudem garantiert die Nähe zum Meer, daß man praktisch das ganze Jahr über klettern kann. Die Bandbreite des in diesem Buch Vorgestellten reicht vom Fünf-Züge-"Bordillo" bis zur Vierhundertmeterwand und von der Genußkletterei im vierten Grad bis zum 8b-Gelenkkiller. Einige Gebiete, die heute im Zentrum des Interesses stehen - wie z. B. Buoux - haben wir nicht aufgenommen und andere - wie die Calanques - nur am Rande behandelt. Denn unser Ziel war es, Alternativen zu den gängigen Pilgerstätten aufzuzeigen. Dabei werden einige der in diesem Führer behandelten "Neueentdeckungen" wie Cimaï, Siurana und vor allem Montanejos von Kennern durchaus in einem Atemzug mit den bekannten Wallfahrtsorten des Freikletterns genannt. Wenn in einem echten "Topgebiet", wie Siurana oder Montanejos, noch keine einheimischen Gebietsführer vorlagen, nahmen wir die meisten zu unserem Recherchiertermin existierenden Touren in dieses Buch auf. In anderen Fällen sahen wir uns, aus Rücksicht auf einheimische Autorenkollegen oder einfach aufgrund der geringeren Zahl an wirklich lohnenden Möglichkeiten, zur Beschränkung auf eine repräsentative Tourenauswahl gezwungen. In jedem Fall wird dieser Führer genug Informationen für einen auch ausgedehnten Erstbesuch eines Gebiets liefern. Um alle im Buch beschriebene Seillängen zu klettern, wird auch der petrophile Nimmersatt einige Zeit zu tun haben. Wir hoffen, bis dahin die zweite erweiterte Auflage vorlegen zu können.

Daß die Informationsmenge, die in diesen Führer eingeflossen ist, nicht ohne die Unterstützung eines wahren Heeres an

it had to offer, was the proximity to the coast, which would guarantee easy access and the opportunity to climb the year round. The choice of climbs ranges from five-move "bordillos" to 14-pitch routes of "pre-alpine" character - from grade four pleasure climbs to 8b joint killers. We have excluded several very popular areas like Buoux, or only briefly touched on others, like the Calanques. Our aim was to provide alternatives to the already well-known sanctuaries of freeclimbing. At least three of the areas we "dis-covered" - namely Cimaï, Siurana, and most notably Montanejos - are equal to the most reknowned of the climbing Meccas. In places like Montanejos and Siurana, where no local guidebooks are available, we included practically all the routes done up to press-time. In other cases, out of consideration for the authors of the local guides, or simply due to a lack of really worthwhile routes, we made a representative selection. In any case, the guide book should supply you with enough information for an extended first visit to each of the areas. Even the most insatiable petrophile should find enough here to keep him busy until we have completed the second, more exhaustive edition.

It is obvious that the fill of information that went into making this book could never have been compiled without the aid and support of an army of helpers and helpers' helpers. Without the infinite chats in bars, on belays, and during climbs, and without the topos and maps hurriedly scrawled onto any available scraps of paper, or the permission to plagiarize much of the carefully guarded information in route books, this guide could never have been completed.

Special thanks go to Francisco Allegre, Armando Ballart, Nacho Ganzedo and Jose Maria Alsina of St. Benet, Irmgard Braun, Juan Chaporro, Antonio Garcia, Martin Lochner, Pilar and Ernesto Lopez, "Chema" Ramirez Machado, Dario Rodriguez, Ignacio Sanchez, Sebastian Schwertner, Klaus Eiler, Erika Stagni, "Tigui" and Robert Wolschlag.

Helfern und Helfershelfern er- und verarbeitet werden konnte, dürfte einleuchten. Ohne die zahllosen Gespräche an Biertheken, an Standplätzen und Einstiegen, ohne die auf schmuddelige Papierfetzen gekritzelten Karten und Routenlisten und ohne die Bewilligung der Übernahme von Infos aus sorgsam gehüteten Routenbüchern wäre dieser Führer nie fertig geworden. Besonders bedanken wollen wir uns bei Francisco Allegre, Armando Ballart, Jose Maria Alsina, Irmgard Braun, Juan Chaporro, Nacho Gancedo, Antonio Garcia, Martin Lochner, Pilar und Ernesto Lopez, "Chema" Ramirez-Machado, Dario Rodriguez, Ignacio Sanchez, Erika Stagni, "Tigui" und Robert Wolschlag.

Das Panico-Zeichenteam, diesmal verkörpert durch Christopher Mailänder, Volker Leuchsner und Achim Pasold hat das Material in dankenswerter Klarheit zur Darstellung gebracht.

Ohne die selbstlose Unterstützung durch Elizabeth Klobusicky-Mailänder wäre uns die Fertigstellung des Buches unendlich schwerer gefallen.

The Panico design team consisting of Christopher Mailänder, Volker Leuchsner, and Achim Pasold gave the book its presentable form.

Without the support of Elizabeth Klobusicky Mailänder the final phase of putting together the book would have been endlessly more burdensome. Moreover, all complaints of our English friends about the Americanisms included here, should be addressed to our English speaking editor.

ZUM GEBRAUCH DES FÜHRERS

Wie wir das Problem der zweisprachigen Darstellung gelöst haben, dürfte inzwischen klar geworden sein: fast immer steht auf der linken Buchseite der deutsche und auf der rechten der englischsprachige Text. Alle 25 Klettergebiete in diesem Führer werden zuerst mit einer allgemeinen Charakterisierung vorgestellt. Außer Mitteilungen über die "Atmosphäre" beinhalten diese Textteile auch "harte" Informationen, wie die zur Gesteinsart und -qualität, den Grad der Ernsthaftigkeit der Kletterei, den Absicherungsstandard und die "Grundschwierigkeit" eines Kletterareals. Letzteres hat sich als notwendig erwiesen, da einige der aufgenommenen Gebiete für den Genußkletterer allenfalls von "olympischem" Bedeutung sind, während andere wiederum für die "Extremen" kaum der Anreise wert wären. Im Anschluß finden sich Informationen zur Anreise, den Zugängen, den Übernachtungs- und Versorgungsmöglichkeiten sowie zu den zu erwartenden klimatischen Bedingungen.

Auf den Seiten 20 & 21 ist eine Übersichtskarte über das Gesamtgebiet; wo es hilfreich erschien, haben wir den schriftlichen Zugangsbeschreibungen zu den einzelnen Gebieten Detailkarten beigefügt.

Der überwiegende Teil der Sachinformation zu den Kletterführern geht aus den Topos und Routenlisten hervor. Zur Ausschmückung der Routenskizzen haben wir Symbole benutzt, die sich an die offiziellen der U.I.A.A. anlehnen. Die Bedeutung der Zeichen wird auf Seite 14 erläutert.

Die Führen sind an den Felsen von links nach rechts durchnumeriert und in dieser Reihenfolge aufgelistet. Wenn nicht ausdrücklich anderweilig definiert, entsprechen alle Richtungsangaben der Sichtweise eines vor dem Objekt stehenden Betrachters. Will der Leser anhand der Beschreibungen zur Tat schreiten, wird es hilfreich sein zu

HOW TO USE THE GUIDEBOOK

Each of the 25 climbing areas included in this book is introduced with a presentation of the general characteristics. Here the reader will find, in addition to some observations about atmosphere, hard core facts about the quality of the rock, the seriousness of the climbs, the quality of the protection and the basic level of difficulty of an area. Inclusion of the latter proved to be essential, as some of the regions are, for Sunday pleasure climbers, at best suited as an Olympic sight-seeing tour, while others are hardly worth the detour for the more ambitious. The general characterization is followed by information about how to get there, the approaches to the climbs, camping facilities, where to get supplies, and remarks about the climatic conditions to expect.

On pages 20 & 21 you will find survey maps of the areas. Where necessary, we have added detailed approach maps to the verbal approach descriptions. Most of the essential information can be gleaned from the topos and route lists. To enhance the topos we have used symbols that roughly correspond to the offical U.I.A.A ones. They are decoded on page 14.

The routes are described from left to right on the crags. The perspective is from that of someone facing the routes, unless otherwise stated. To be able to make sense out of our directions you will often find it useful to consult the sun, moon, stars, or the hands of your watch for orientation, unless you happen to be carrying a compass.

wissen, daß "orographisch" soviel bedeutet, wie "aus der Perspektive eines abwärtsfließenden Wassertröpfleins gesehen". Oft waren wir gezwungen, in unseren Beschreibungen die Himmelsrichtungen zu bemühen, um dem Leser eindeutig mitzuteilen, wo's langgeht. Es wäre deshalb gut, wenn ihr in der Landschaft über die Möglichkeit verfügt, dies nachzuvollziehen.

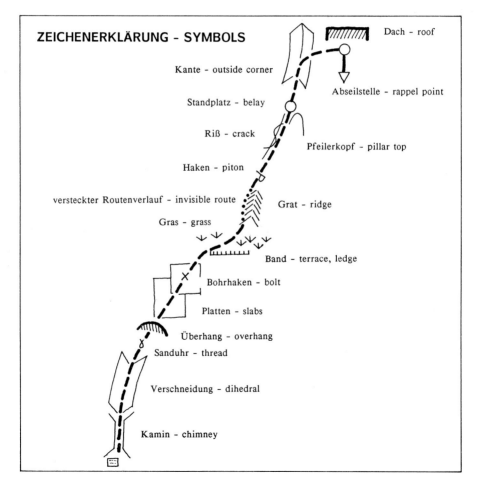

SCHWIERIGKEITSBEWERTUNG

Wir benützen in diesem Führer die französische Bewertungsskala. Diese Entscheidung hätte, nebenbei gesagt, fast zur Auflösung unseres Verlagshauses geführt ("Traditionsverächter, vaterlandsloser!"). Den Autoren schien es jedoch wenig sinnvoll, die am Ort des Geschehens übliche Meßlatte, die trotz ihrer Abstrusität funktioniert, mühselig und unzulänglich umzurechnen. Da in den Mittelmeerländern jede Gegend ihre besondere Art hat, mit der Franzosenskala umzugehen, gibt der allgemeine Vorschrieb zu den Einzelgebieten Auskunft darüber, ob hier grobe Abweichungen zu erwarten sind.

Wir haben in deutschen, französischen und englischsprachigen Publikationen Vergleichstabellen studiert. Sie erwiesen sich als hervorragendes Feld für den interessanten Forschungsbereich des Neoalpinchauvinismus. Hier unser Beitrag zur Vergleichsdiskussion:

GRADING

We have used the French grades consistently throughout the guidebook. All things considered, there seemd to us to be no rational grounds for going through wearysome and unnecessary contortions to try to impose our norm onto functioning local ratings. Since each area has its own unique interpretation of the French scale, we tried to put the particular gradings into general perspective in the general introductions to the areas, especially where they strayed far from what is normally expected of a French rating.

We have studied conversion tables for the different grading systems in German, French, and English publications. They prove to be a fruitful field for research on neo-alpinechauvisnism. Here is our contribution to the discussion:

VERGLEICHSTABELLE-CONVERSION TABLE

UIAA	FR	GB	USA
4	4-	3b	5.3
4+	4	3c	5.4
5-	4+	4a	5.5
5	4+	4b	5.6
5+	5-	4c	5.7
6-	5	5a	5.8
6	5+		5.9
6+	6a	5b	5.10a
7-	6a+		5.10b
7	6b	5c	5.10c
7/7+	6b/c		5.10d
7+	6c	6a	5.11a
8-	6c+		5.11b
8	7a	6b	5.11c
8/8+	7a+		5.11d
8+/9-	7b	6c	5.12a
9-	7b/c		5.12b
9	7c	7a	5.12c
9/9+	7c+		5.12d
9+/10-	8a	?	5.13a/b
10-	8a+	?	5.13c
10	8b	?	5.13d
10+	8b/c	?	5.14a
11-	?	?	?

DIE KLETTERGEBIETE - THE CLIMBING AREAS

1	Leiva	22
2	Sax	38
3	Puig Campana	46
4	El Ponoch & Tozal de Levante	56
5	Peñon de Ifach	66
6	Sierra de Toix	84
7	Barranco de Mascarat	92
8	Dalle d'Ola	100
9	Chulilla	104
10	Montanejos	116
11	Siurana	142
12	Montserrat	158
13	Vingrau	194
14	Mouriès	202
15	Cavaillon	220
16	Ménerbes	232
17	Montagne de Sainte Victoire	244
18	Calanques	276
19	Baou de Quatre Ouro	292
21	Cimaï	302
22	La Piade	322
23	Tourris	324
24	Baou de Saint Jeannet	326
25	La Turbie	346

① Leiva
② Sax
③ Puig Campana
④ Ponoch & Tozal de' Levante'
⑤ Peñon de' Ifach
⑥ Sierra de Toix
⑦ Barranco de Mascarat
⑧ Dalle' d'Ola
⑨ Chulilla
⑩ Montanejos
⑪ Siurana
⑫ Montserrat
⑬ Vingrau
⑭ Mouriès
⑮ Cavaillon
⑯ Ménerbes
⑰ Mont Ste. Victoire
⑱ Les Calanques d'En Vau
⑲ Le Baou de' Quatre' Ouro
⑳ Le Cimaï
㉑ Mont Coudon
㉒ La Piade'
㉓ Tourris
㉔ Le Baou de' St. Jeannet
㉕ La Turbie'

1. LEIVA

Die Sierra de Espuña erhebt sich als einsames karstiges Kalkgebirge südwestlich von Murcia und gipfelt im 1278 Meter hohen Felsgrat der Leiva. Ihre Südwand hatte für die Entwicklung des spanischen Felskletterns eine ähnliche Bedeutung wie die Ostwand der Fleischbank in der alpinen Geschichte der nördlichen Kalkalpen. Die Vielzahl von steilen Rissen durch die feste, bis knapp 200 Meter hohe Kalktafel lädt förmlich ein zur Besteigung. Die Kletterer, die sich in dieser "voralpinen" Wand seit Beginn der siebziger Jahre die Klauen geschärft hatten, sollten die Entwicklung des Kletterns auf der Iberischen Halbinsel dann während der nächsten Dekade maßgeblich beeinflussen. So geht die spärliche Absicherung in den klassischen Leivaführen vor allem auf die Verantwortung der Gebrüder Gallego sowie auf die Konten von Juan Carillo, Miguel Canovas, Mariano Lozano und Felix Gomez. Es ist ratsam, in ihren Wegen, von denen heute noch einige auf eine vollständige freie Begehung warten, immer mit Klemmkeilen gerüstet unterwegs zu sein. Die Vegetation in den Wänden wirkt nur selten störend, sondern dient, wie im Verdon, zur meist sehr willkommenen Sicherung. In den letzten Jahren wurde in den Klassikern mit Sanierungsmaßnahmen begonnen, so daß sie in ihrem Sicherheitsstandard bald den modernen Baseclimbs des Gebiets angeglichen sein werden. Trotz der Schönheit und Großzügigkeit der rund 70 Leivaklettereien ist das Gebiet nicht annähernd überfüllt. Die wenigen Leute, die man hier trifft, Kletterer wie vernünftige Menschen, sind von einer ausnehmenden Freundlichkeit. Dies trifft besonders auf die Familie zu, die das Casa Forestal La Perdiz bewirtschaftet, wo man im schütteren Kiefernwald schön zelten und gut essen kann.

The Sierra de Espuña arises as a rugged limestone plateau to the southwest of Murcia. It culminates in the 1278 meter high rocky ridge of Leiva.

Its south face plays a role in Spanish climbing which parallels that of the east face of the Fleischbank within the alpinistic history of the Northern Alps. The 200 meter limestone wall abounds in steep vertical cracks that literally invite an ascent. Those climbers who, in the 1970s, cut their teeth on this "pre-alpine" face, were to have a significant influence on the development of climbing on the entire Iberian Peninsula in the decade to follow.
Thus the Gallego brothers, Juan Carillo, Miguel Canovas, together with Mariano Lozano, and Felix Gomez, are responsible for the rather sparse pro in the Leiva classics. It is advisable to carry a good assortment of nuts on their routes, some of which are still awaiting a first free ascent. The vegetation on the face does not detract from the climbing. On the contrary, the bushes and trees, like in the Verdon, often lend themselves as belay anchors. In recent years the local climbers have begun restoration measures on the old pro in the classics, so that one can soon expect a standard of bolting equal to the modern baseclimbs of the area.

In spite of the beauty and expansiveness of the climbs in Leiva, the area is never crowded. The few people one encounters here, whether climbers or more reasonable humans, are decidedly friendly. This holds particularly true for the family with the concession to the Casa Forestal La Perdiz. At their house you can eat well and camp nearby in the profuse pine forest.

ANFAHRT UND ZUGANG

Von Murcia auf der N 340 in Richtung Almeria bis Alhama de Murcia. In der Innenstadt von Alhama findet sich ein Schild mit der Aufschrift "Sierra Espuña/Mula". Sechs Kilometer hinter Alhama nach links abbiegen in den "Parque Natural de Sierra Espuña". Nach weiteren sechs Kilometern gelangt man zu einer Abzweigung, die mit "La Perdiz" beschildert ist. Hier endet für uns die Teerstrecke. Beim unübersehbaren ehemaligen Sanatorium Esquela Hogar verzweigt sich die Schotterstraße. Der linke Abzweig führt zur Casa Forestal La Perdiz. Der rechten Abzweigung folgend gelangt man nach ca. zwei Kilometern direkt unter die Wand. Von hier sind die Einstiege in fünf bis zehn Minuten zu erreichen.

ABSTIEG

1. Auf der ins Übersichtstopo eingezeichneten Abseilpiste 3 X 45 Meter hinunter.

2. In westlicher Richtung über die Hochfläche, bis am Ende des Wandabbruchs ein Couloir nach Süden hinunterführt. Auf Steigspuren hinab, bis sie nach rechts aus der Rinne heraus- und ansteigend wieder zum Wandfuß zurückführen (ca. 15 Minuten).

ÜBERNACHTUNG

Zeltmöglichkeiten mit Wasser und öffentlichen Toiletten findet man gratis beim Casa Forestal La Perdiz.

APPROACH

From Murcia take the N 340 toward Almeria to the town center of Alhama de Murcia. Here follow the sign Sierra Espuña/Mula. 6 kilometers behind Alhama turn left toward the Parque Natural de Sierra Espuña. 6 kilometers further you reach a fork marked La Perdiz. This is the end of the paved road. The gravel road from here leads to the former sanatorium Esquela Hogar and forks again. The left branch leads to the Casa Forestal de Perdiz. If you take the right fork you come directly to the crag after two kilometers. From here it is 5 to 10 minutes' hike to the climbs.

DESCENT

1. Rappel as shown in the survey topo, 3 x 45 meters.

2. Walk over the plateau in a westerly direction to the end of the drop-off until you reach a gully leading down southward. You descend a faint trail until it leads you right out of the gully and ascends back to the base of the wall.

CAMPING

Tent sites with water and sanitary facilities are available free of charge at the Casa Forestal La Perdiz.

SUPPLIES

Groceries can be bought in Alhama. The tortillas at La Perdiz and the rabbit paellas can be highly recommended.

VERSORGUNG

Einkaufsmöglichkeiten in Alhama. Wasser in La Perdiz. Sehr empfehlenswert sind die Tortillas und die Hasenpaella in La Perdiz.

BESTE ZEIT

Aufgrund der geographischen Ausrichtung ist das Klettern während der Sommermonate in Leiva nicht üblich. Die Hauptsaison dauert von September bis Mai. Allerdings können die kalten Winde aus dem Landesinnern einen Aufenthalt im Hochwinter unangenehm gestalten, da sie im Januar die Temperaturen an einigen Tagen bis unter den Nullpunkt absinken lassen.

WEITERE INFORMATIONEN

Jose Andreu Correas,
LEIVA, GUIA DE ESCALADAS
Club Montañero de Murcia,
Plaza de Santo Domingo, 15-2 -D
30008 Murcia

BEST SEASON

Because of its geographic location climbing in the summer months in Leiva is not common. The best time is from October to April. Nonetheless, on some winter days, the cold winds from the interior can add a bitter touch to your sojourn.

FURTHER INFORMATION

Club Montañero de Murcia,
LEIVA, Guia de Escaladas
Plaza de Santo Domingo, 15-2-D
30008 Murcia

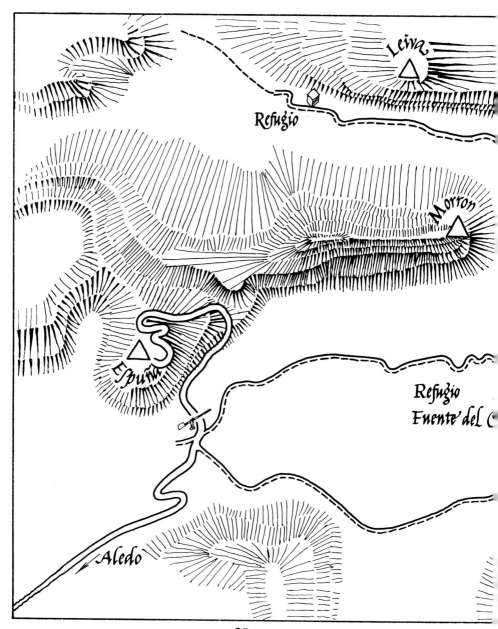

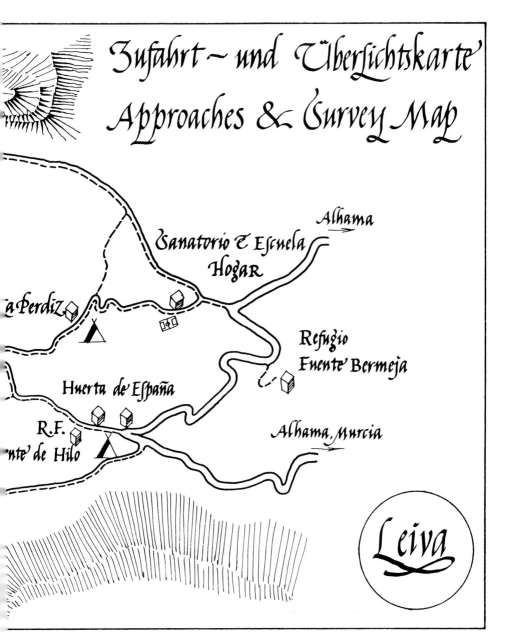

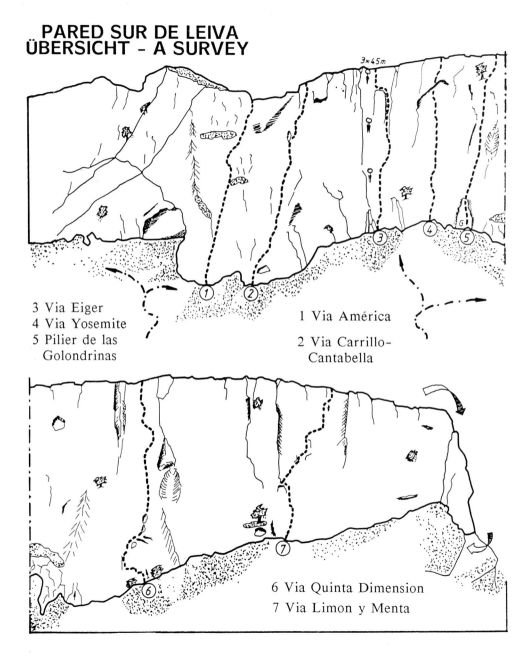

VIA AMERICA
5 SL, 5, nicht eingerichtet, not equipped, Keile bis Hex 9, nuts to Hex 9

1. Einstieg direkt am Schriftzug "América". Gerade empor über H zu SP auf Bändchen (40 Meter, 5).
2. Schräg rechts aufwärts zu Riß, der zu Stand bei Türmchen an der Pfeilerkante führt (40m, 4+ und 5).
3. Über markanten Block, der Pfeilerkante folgend, zu SP auf kleinem Absatz (30m, 3+ und 4.
4. Nach links an Gufel vorbei zu Baum im Kamin. Dieser wird bis zu seinem Ende verfolgt und dann nach rechts verlassen. Über gestuftes Gelände zu SP auf Absatz (40m, 3 bis 4).
5. Über Pfeiler und kleine Verschneidung zu Baum und gerade empor zum Gipfel (50 m).

1. The start is marked "América" Straight up (pitons) to a small terrace (40 meters, 5).
2. Diagonal right to a crack which leads to a belay near a small tower on the arete of the pillar (40 m, 4+ and 5).
3. Go up obvious blocks following the edge of the pillar to a belay on a small ledge (30 m, 3+ and 4).
4. Go up left past a niche to a tree in a chimney and exit right. Continue over broken rock to a belay on a terrace (40 m, 3-4).
5. Climb a pillar and a small corner to a small tree, then go straight to the top (50 m 3+).

Dies ist die lohnendste der ganz leichten Touren.
This is the best of the easy routes.

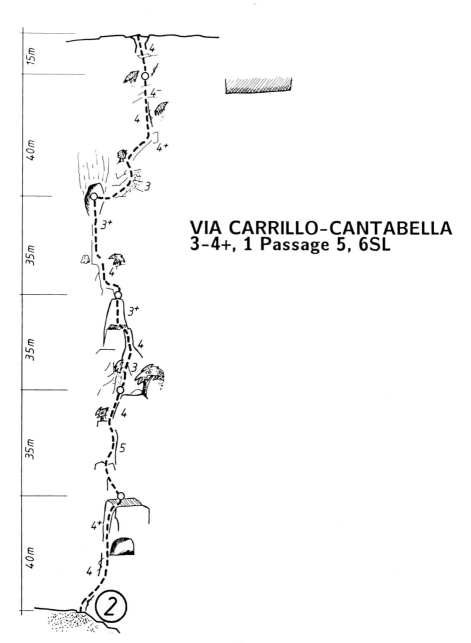

VIA CARRILLO-CANTABELLA
3-4+, 1 Passage 5, 6SL

SECTOR EIGER

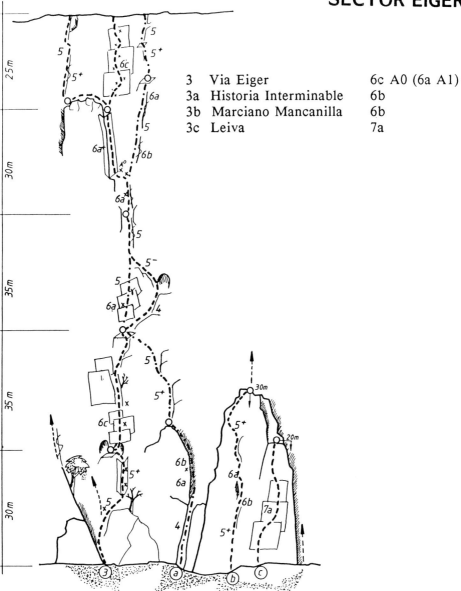

3   Via Eiger   6c A0 (6a A1)
3a Historia Interminable 6b
3b Marciano Mancanilla   6b
3c Leiva   7a

SECTOR DE LAS GOLONDRINAS

5 Pilier de las Golondrinas	6c, (6a A1
5a Fisura Snoopy	6c
5b Al Que Eyacula Dios le Ayuda	6b

VIA YOSEMITE
6c (1.SL) & A?, 4SL

Nach Erkenntnisstand Januar 87 ist nur die 1. SL saniert. Sie bietet sehr schöne Wandkletterei an kleinen Griffen. Der Rest sieht nach Abenteuer aus ... überhängende Wand- und Rißkletterei mit einem eindrucksvollen Abschlußdach. Die Sicherung dürfte antik bis nicht vorhanden sein.

By January 1987 only the first pitch had been modernized. The rest looks adventure-some ... overhanging face and crack climbing topped off by an impressive roof. The protection up there looked quite antique.

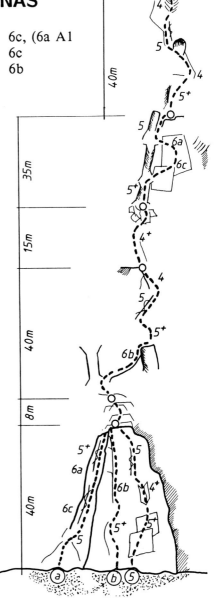

weber

Ein weicher Schuh für „harte Sachen"

Herstellung und Vertrieb: **WEBER, 7300 Esslingen, Bahnhofstr. 19**

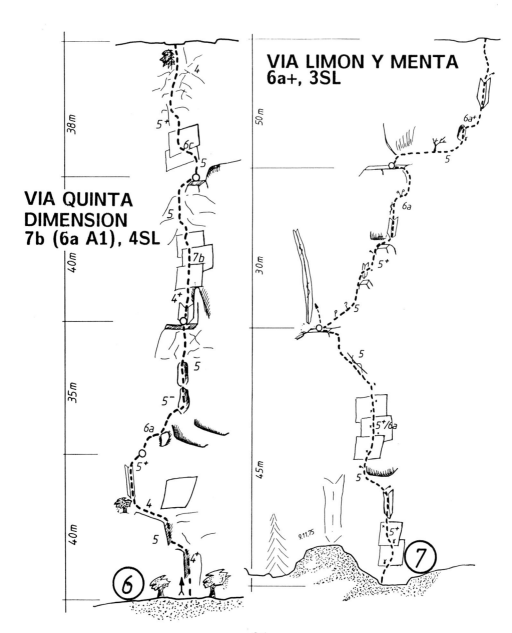

Biwakschachtel

FACHGESCHÄFT
für Bergsport und Wanderartikel

- Wir nehmen uns Zeit für Sie und beraten Sie gerne und ausführlich

- Wir testen selbst die von uns geführten Ausrüstungsgegenstände in der Praxis und geben unsere Erfahrungen weiter

- Für Insider Alpin-, Touren- und Langlauf-Ski der Marke Sohler

- Ausrüstung die unser Standard-Sortiment nicht beinhaltet, besorgen wir Ihnen schnellstens

- Eigene Ski-Werkstatt

- In enger Zusammenarbeit mit der Alpin- und Bergwanderschule Oberstdorf vermitteln wir Berg- und Wandertouren

MANFRED SCHMITT · Hauptstraße 144
Tel. (0 61 31) 68 73 26 · 6500 Mainz-Mombach

Mo. 15.00 – 18.30 · Di. – Fr. 9.00 – 13.00 u. 15.00 – 18.30
Sa. 8.30 – 13.00

2. SAX

Das Klettergebiet bei Sax mag manchem frustrierten Pilger zum Jesus de Villena den Tag noch retten. Denn nur knapp 10 Kilometer von der Geburtsstätte des klebrigen Schuhwerks findet der Kletterer in der Sierra Cabrera einen 60 Meter hohen Miniaturberg, dessen UIAA-Garantie-würdiger Kalk Kühle gewährend nach Nordosten ausgerichtet ist. Wer sich gern zwischen dem 5. und 6b. Grad bewegt, kann hier einen der genußvollsten Tage seiner Kletterkarriere verbringen. Mögen sich an den Wochenenden ein bis zwei Seilschaften in den Wänden anhäufen, so ist man unter der Woche garantiert alleine. Die meisten Wege sind mit neuen Bohrhaken ausgerüstet, Angsthasen werden jedoch auf ein kleines Klemmkeilsortiment nicht verzichten wollen.

ANFAHRT UND ZUGANG

Von Alicante auf der N 330 44 Kilometer in Richtung Madrid bis Sax. An der 1. Kreuzung im Ort links ab in Richtung Salinas. Nun schlägt man sich durch bis zur "Calle Honduras" (3. Straße südwestlich der Burg), die sich nach ca. 100 Metern in zwei Schotterstraßen gabelt. Man wählt die schlechtere rechte und folgt ihr in westlicher Richtung, wobei eine von Süden nach Norden aufgespannte Starkstromleitung als Orientierungshilfe dient. Der Kletterfelsen liegt am orographisch linken Hang des Tals, durch das der Strom nach Norden strebt.

The climbing area near Sax might well save the day for the sole-searcher frustrated by an attempted pilgrimage to Jesus of Villena. A mere 10 kilometers from the birthplace of sticky shoes the contrite seeker will discover in the Sierra di Cabrera, a 60 meter high mini-peak whose rock quality is worthy of a UIAA seal of approval. The climber of grades 5 to 7 will here experience one of the most enjoyable days of his career. If, on weekends, the cliffs may be overflowing with two to three parties, during the week one is sure to climb in friendly solitude. Most of the routes are equipped with new bolts. More cautious souls are advised to bring a small rack of nuts as well.

APPROACH

From Alicante take the N 330 toward Madrid for 44 kilometers till you reach Sax. Turn left at the first intersection in the village (follow the signs for Salinas). Townwhack to "Calle Honduras" (three blocks southwest of the castle) then continue on another 100 meters until the road forks. Take the right fork (the worse of the two dirt roads). Continue in a westerly direction using an obvious system of electrical wiring running in a north-southerly direction for orientation. The cliffs are located on the westerly slope of the valley through which the electricity flows north.

CAMPING

Usually the climbers in Sax are one day visitors based on the coast. Camping is tolerated by the locals. However, running water is non-existent anywhere near the cliffs.

ÜBERNACHTUNG

Normalerweise operieren die Kletterer in "Sax" von einem Stützpunkt an der Küste aus. Wildes Campieren wird geduldet, wenn man den Platz nicht als Müllhalde hinterläßt. Allerdings war in der näheren Umgebung des Klettergebietes kein fließendes Wasser aufzufinden.

VERSORGUNG

In Sax sind Grundnahrungsmittel käuflich zu erwerben.

BESTE ZEIT

Wegen seiner geschickten nordöstlichen Ausrichtung kann man in Sax das ganze Jahr über klettern: im Sommer sind die Nachmittags- und Abendstunden vorzuziehen, im Winter kratzt man am besten zusammen mit der Sonne die Kurve oder legt einen Zahn zu.

WEITERE INFORMATIONEN

Die zuverlässigsten Informationen, weil die einzigen, hältst du in den Händen.

SUPPLIES

Groceries are available in any number of small stores in Sax.

BEST SEASON

Because of the northeasterly positioning of the cliffs, one can pretty well climb the year round in Sax. In summer you will want to start climbing in the late afternoon and continue on into the evening. In winter you will probably want to leave with the sun or pick up on speed after the sun disappears over the horizon.

FURTHER INFORMATION

This is as much as you get.

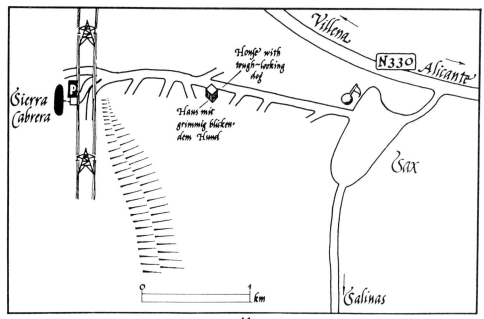

"SAX"
NORDOSTWAND - NORTHEAST FACE

1a	Direkteinstieg zu "1" Direct start to "1"	5
1	"1"	4
2	"2"	5+
2a	Direkteinstieg zu "2" Direct start to "2"	6a
2b	Überhang Direkt Overhang direct	6a-
3	"3"	5
4	"5"	5
5	"7"	5
6	"10"	6b A1
7	"11"	6b
8	"16"	6a+
9	"14"	5+
10	"15"	5

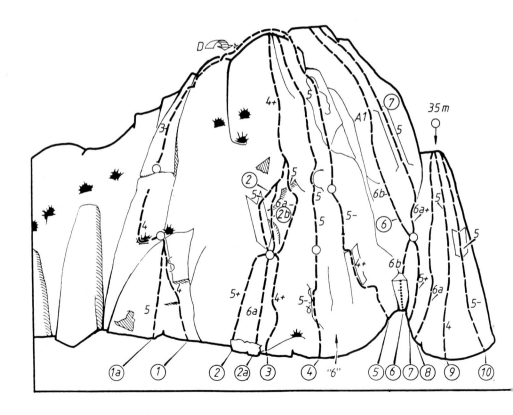

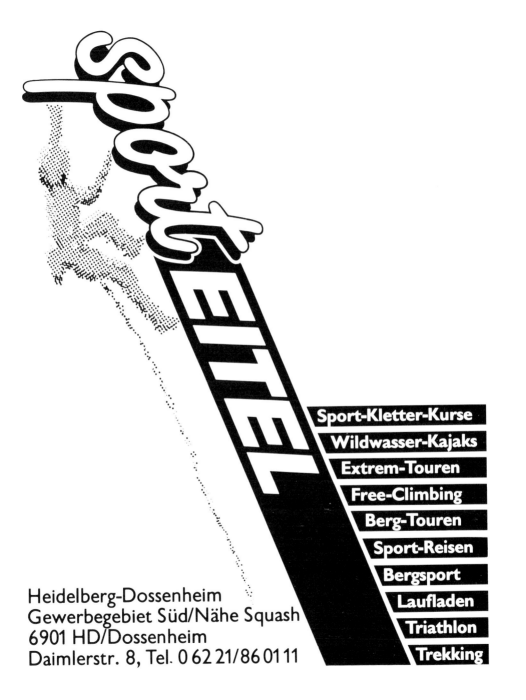

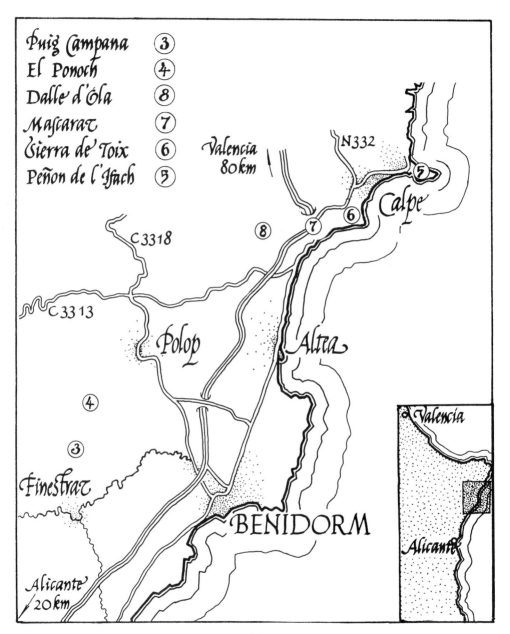

3. PUIG CAMPANA

Der Puig Campana erhebt sich in der Sierra Aitana, nur wenige Kilometer landeinwärts von dem Holiday-Jahrmarkt Benidorm. Es ist erstaunlich, daß man in der Nachbarschaft von kilometerlangen Körpergrills, UFO-Diskos und Riesenrädern nicht nur wunderschöne Klettertouren, sondern auch Stille findet. So stiegen wir an einem Ostersonntag als zwei einsame Seilschaften im festen Karrenkalk der Südwand des Berges, nur drüben am Südpfeiler war noch ein spanisches Team unterwegs. Alle Kletterrouten am Puig Campana führen nicht auf den 1410 Meter hohen Haupt- sondern nur dem sechzig Meter niedrigeren Südwestgipfel entgegen.

Aber nur auf einer der hier beschriebenen Führen, nämlich auf dem Zentralen Südpfeiler (Espero Central) duchsteigt man den gesamten Steilabbruch bis zu einem Felszacken unterm Südwestgipfel. Von hier gelangt man auf markiertem Pfad hinunter in die Südrinne des Hauptgipfels. Nur wenige Leser werden durch diese und über den anschließenden Südwestrücken des Hauptgipfels noch ca. 300 Höhenmeter zum höchsten Punkt hinaufschnaufen wollen (ca. eine Stunde vom Ausstieg). Die "Via Julia" und die "Diedro Gallego" münden schon relativ weit unten auf den "Espero Central". Terra Firma wird erreicht, entweder indem man den Aufstieg über diesen fortsetzt oder westlich auf den Abseilrouten auskneift. Die "Via Diedres Magics" steigt auf einer Schulter aus, die in die rechte (östliche) Hälfte der Südwand eingelagert ist. Von hier seilt man, teilweise entlang der Route und teilweise im Abstiegssinne links von ihr, auf den Boden hinunter.

ANFAHRT UND ZUGANG

Man verläßt die Autobahn bei der Ausfahrt Benidorm. Nun erst dem Schild "Polop" folgen und dann nach Finestrat abbiegen. Dortselbst angelangt, folgt man dem Schild "Font de Moli". Ca.

The Puig Campana is a part of the Sierra Aitana group situated only a few kilometers inland from the tourist fair Benidorm. It is astounding that a mere 10 kilometers away from the human grill on the beach, the zoo in the discos, and the crowds in the amusement parks, one can find not only excellent climbing, but also solitude. On one Easter Sunday, very busy on most other crags, there were four of us on the entire south face - on a limestone of impeccable quality. The climbs on Puig Campana do not lead to the summit, but towards the antecima, some 60 meters lower.

Only one of the routes described, namely, the South Central Pillar ("Espero Central") ascends the entire face and leads to a rock protrusion under the southwest summit. From here go to a marked path leading to the south gully of the main summit. Probably only few readers will want to ascend the some 300 vertical meters from the exit of the route over the southwest ridge to the main peak (roughly an hour from the end of the climb). The "Via Julia" and "Diedro Gallego" finish relatively low on the "Espero Central." You regain terra firma either by continuing on up the pillar or rappeling off to the west. The "Via Diedres Magics" ends on the shoulder which is inset into the right (eastern) section of the south face. From here rappel partly down the route and partly to its left (looking downward) to the ground.

APPROACH

Take the Benidorm exit from the freeway. At first follow the signs to Polop till you reach the sign for Finestrat and turn uphill there. In Finestrat, follow the signs to Font de Moli. Some 150 meters after the well take the road that branches left. Continue about 500 meters to the parking spot across the bridge of a canal built to divert the waters from flash floods. From here take the gravel road in a northeasterly direction to the start

150 Meter hinter dem Brunnen die linke Abzweigung wählend, erreicht man nach ungefähr einem halben Kilometer eine Parkmöglichkeit jenseits der Brücke über einen Sommergewitterflutwellenentschärfungskanal. Von hier nordnordöstlich der Schotterstraße folgend über den Rücken empor zum rot markierten Normalweg auf den Puig Campana. Man folgt dem Pfad, der am linken Hang des Rückens emporführt, bis 50 Höhenmeter oberhalb seiner auffälligen Abschlußkuppe. Von hier quert man horizontal zu den Einstiegen der Südwand (ca. 45 Min. vom Parkplatz, 300 HM, 770 ü.NN).

Um zum Süd*pfeiler* zu gelangen, quert man unter der Südwand auf einem breiten Band nach links (W) bis zu dessen Ende (Steinmann). Nun linkshaltend über eine 10 Meter hohe Wandstufe empor und in den großen Geröllkessel zwischen dem SW-Grat und dem Südpfeiler. Der Einstieg befindet sich im rechten oberen Eck des SW-Wandkessels (Steinmann). Von Steinmann zu Steinmann sind es 60 Höhenmeter.

ABSTIEGE

1. Vom Südpfeiler:
   Am besten folgt man nach dem Ende der Schwierigkeiten dem Grat noch ca. 100 Höhenmeter weit, bis er an den Gipfelaufbau des Vorgipfels anstößt. Von hier auf breiten bewachsenen Bändern nach rechts (Steinmänner) um dann schräg über eine Wandstufe ansteigend (eine Stelle 3-) auf einen markierten Weg zu gelangen, der in die Südrinne hinunterführt (ca. 45 Minuten vom Ausstieg).

2. Von den Ausstiegen der "Via Julia" und der "Diedre Gallego":
   Entweder wird über den Südpfeiler weitergestiegen und hinab ins Tal, wie oben beschrieben, oder über die

of the normal route (marked red) of the Puig Campana. Follow the path that leads up the left slope of the ridge till you are 50 vertical meters above an obvious shoulder. From here traverse left to the climbs on the south face (some 300 vertical meters, about 45 minutes from the parking area, 770m above sea level).

To reach the south *pillar*, traverse left (west) on a terrace under the south face to its end (cairn). Now climb leftward up a 10 meter high step to reach the lower end of the talus slope between the SW ridge and the south pillar.
The climb starts in the upper right hand corner of the basin under the SW face (another cairn). The vertical distance between cairns is 60 meters.

DESCENTS

1. From the "Esperon Central":
    Continue up the ridge another 100 vertical meters to the point where it touches the headwall of the antecima. From here, following the cairns, traverse right till you reach a steep slabby section. Diagonal up this (one spot of 3-) to reach the marked trail which leads down into the south gully (some 45 minutes from the end of the climb).

2. From the exits of "Via Julia" and "Diedre Gallego":
    Either continue over the south pillar and descend into the valley or rappel westward off the face (see descent topo, p. 54). Two 45 meter ropes are indespensible for the rappels!

3. From the exit of "Diedres Magics":
    Rappel partly down the route itself and partly east of it (see descent topo, p. 55). Take two 45 meter ropes!

Flanke westlich des Pfeilers abgeseilt. Abseiltopo auf Seite 54. Zwei 45-Meter-Seile erforderlich!

3. Vom Ende der "Diedre Magics" Abseilen teilweise auf und teilweise östlich der Route. Abseiltopo auf Seite 55. Zwei 45-Meter-Seile erforderlich!

ÜBERNACHTUNG

Normalerweise werden die Routen am Puig Campana von Stützpunkten an der Küste aus angegangen. In der Nähe des "Font de Moli" ist unbehelligtes Zelten möglich. Roman-ticker übernachten in den Ziegenhöhlen, die auf ungefähr 650 Meter Meereshöhe am Zustiegsweg liegen. Kein Wasser, viel Mond.

BESTE ZEIT

Da die hier beschriebenen Routen praktisch den ganzen Tag über der Sonne ausgesetzt sind, sind sie im Winter nur in Ausnahmefällen nicht begehbar. Im Sommer ist es ratsam, sehr früh aufzubrechen, sonst lernt man, daß die metereologischen Hindernisse beim Bergsteigen sich nicht nur auf Blitz-, Hagel- und sonstigen Niederschlag beschränken müssen.

WEITERE INFORMATIONEN

Eine Neuauflage von "SUN ROCK - Climb the Mediterranean from Malaga to Monaco" ist bei Panico Press in Vorbereitung. Dies monumentale Werk wird auf die Führen am Puig Campana erschöpfend eingehen. Bestellungen nehmen wir gerne entgegen.

CAMPING

Climbers on the Puig Campana are ordinarily based on the coast. Undisturbed camping is possible near the well. Romantics can sleep in the goat caves that are located along the approach path.

BEST SEASON

Since the routes described here are exposed to the sun most of the day, they are climbable practically the whole winter season. In summer it is advisable to get a very early start.

FURTHER INFORMATION

A new edition of "SUN ROCK - Climb the Mediterranean from Malaga to Monaco" is in the making at Panico Press. This monumental piece of climbing literature will deal extensively with Puig Campana. We are happy to take advance orders.

1 Esperon Sur Central   4
2 Via Julia   5+
3 Diedre Gallego   6a
4 Diedres Magics   5+/6a

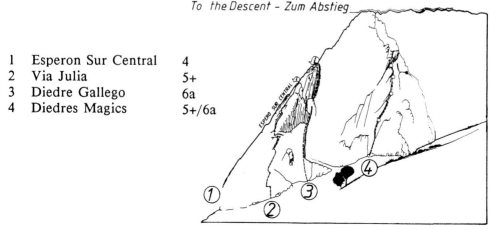

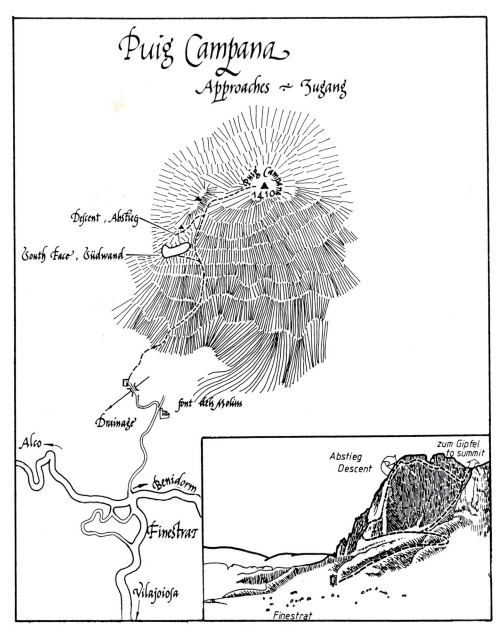

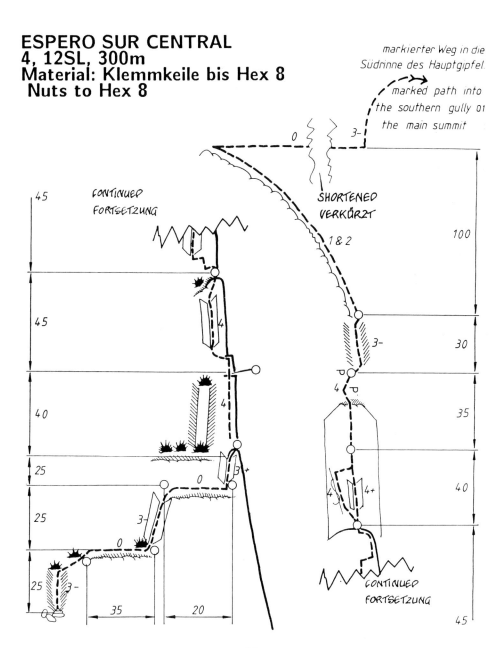

VIA JULIA
5+, 4SL, 140m
Material: Klemmkeile bis Hex 10
Nuts to Hex 10

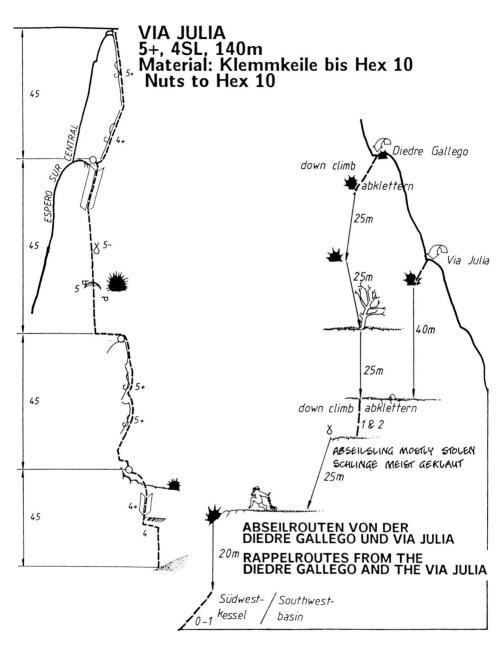

VIA DIEDRE GALLEGO
6a+ (5 A1). 6SL, 180m
Material: bis Hex 9
Nuts to Hex 9

DIEDRE MAGICS
6a-, 6SL, 140m
Material: bis Hex 9
Nuts to Hex 9

OFF ROUTE PEG
VERHAUERHAKEN

4. EL PONOCH & TOZAL DE LEVANTE

Natürlich ist es etwas gewagt, das Dreigestirn von Ponoch, Torre di Murcia und Tozal de Levante in dieses Buch aufzunehmen. Wegen ihres "alpinen" Charakters werden sie schon von den meisten spanischen Kletterern gemieden und bleiben einigen wenigen Spezialisten der Levante vorbehalten. Daß man ohne eine exakte Beschreibung oder geländekundige Führung in den riesigen, stark gegliederten Wänden so seine Probleme haben kann, durften wir am eigenen Leib erfahren. Dafür gewährt die hier aufgeführte "Valencianos-Führe" am Ponoch, wenn man sich an die Beschreibung hält, ungetrübte Kletterfreuden in exotischer Umgebung - und zwar vom Einstieg bis man wieder auf dem Boden steht. Nach der 14. Seillänge scheint es geraten, den Weg zum Gipfel nicht weiter fortzusetzen, sondern im genußvollen Zweier- und Dreiergelände nach rechts querend auf die Nordwestschulter des Berges auszukneifen. Für den Fall der Zuwiderhandlung wurden uns unsagbare Macchia-Irrfahrten angedroht.

Hat an der "Valencianos" auch noch der schärfere Genußkletterer seine Freude, so wird nur der nervenstarke Allround-Extreme der "Via de los Gomez" am Tozal de Levante etwas Positives abgewinnen können. Denn in drei Passagen dieser Führe ist man gezwungen, sich entweder psychisch oder physisch einem Material anzuvertrauen, das Leuten, die nicht alltäglich ihr Leben an ein ausgeblichenes 5-Millimeterschlingchen hängen, doch etwas "spanisch" vorkommen mag. Sind wir aber zu dieser Investition bereit, so bescheren einem diese kraftraubenden Rückschritte eine Fülle sehr moderner Situationen in dolomitenartiger Ausgesetztheit.

It is, of course, somewhat bold to include the trio Ponoch, Torre die Murcia, and Tozal del Levante in this book. Even most Spanish climbers avoid them due to their extremely "alpine" character and ascents are thus reserved for a few Levantine specialists. We found out for ourselves that one can run into problems without an exact description or an area specialist along in the highly complex walls of these mighty faces. In spite of all this, the "Valencianos" route on the Ponoch can prove to be a superb climb in exotic surroundings from beginning to end - especially if one adheres religiously to the route description. It is advisable not to continue to the summit after the fourteenth pitch, but to escape off the route towards the NW shoulder of the mountain (an interesting second and third class scramble). We were warned of onerous macchia obstacles in case we erred off route on the descent and are hereby passing on the warning!

Though the modern free climber can find pleasure in an ascent of the "Valencianos", amusement in the "Via de los Gomez" is probably reserved for the big wall expert. The climber not accustomed to entrusting his life to weather-beaten 5 millimeter slings will find the protection extremely "Spanish".

APPROACHES

From Altea take the road to Polop via La Nucia (see descent topo). Just before the bridge in Polop turn left toward the mountain and follow not the road to the Residencias La Paz, but the street to its left. It winds up to a small valley between the three mountains and a ridge parallel to them on the south. At the fork drive left to a parking spot. Descend back into the gully and walk up it till a path leads out of the dry stream bed to the start of the "Valencianos". The climb starts some 200 meters left of an obvious tower at the foot of the SE face (20

ANFAHRT UND ZUSTIEGE

Von Altea über La Nucia nach Polop. Direkt vor der Brücke in Polop nach links abbiegen, nun nicht der Straße zu den Residencias La Paz, sondern der linken Straße folgen. Sie führt in einer Links-Rechtsschleife zu einem Tälchen zwischen den Wänden der Kletterberge und einem parallel zu ihnen südlich emporziehenden Rücken. Bei der Gabelung hier nach links hinauf zum Parkplatz. Man verfolgt die Bachbett-Schotterstraßenmischung bergwärts, bis der breite Weg nach rechts aus dem Graben herausführt. Von hier leitet ein Pfad zum Einstieg der "Valencianos" empor (20 Minuten). Er befindet sich ca. 200 Meter links von einem auffälligen spitzen Turm, der der Nordostwand vorgelagert ist. Der Routenname ist am Einstieg in verblaßter roter Farbe angeschrieben.

Um zum Tozal zu gelangen, folgt man am besten den Wegspuren unter den Südwänden des Ponoch und des Torre di Murcia (nochmal 20 Minuten).

ABSTIEG PONOCH

Nicht nur was die Kletterei angeht, ist die "Valencianos-Führe" mit der "Micheluzzi" am Ciavaces zu vergleichen, sondern auch darin, daß praktisch kein Kletterer die Gipfel beider Berge mehr betritt. Wir beschreiben deshalb nur den Abstieg vom riesigen Band, das ca. 100 Meter unter dem Gipfel durch den rechten Teil der Südwand zieht. Vom Ausstieg aus dem Band (siehe Anstiegstopo) steigt man in westlicher Richtung ab bis der westliche der beiden im rechten Teil der Südwand eingelagerten Felssporne unter einem liegt. Hier gelangt das große Wasserreservoir wieder ins Blickfeld. Zuerst steigt man auf der im Abstiegssinn linken Seite des Spornes ab, folgt dann kurz der Kante und klimmt dann weiter auf der östlichen Spornseite durch eine Rinne hinab (deutliche Trittspuren). Zwei mal Abseilen (20 und 40 Meter), und man steht wieder auf dem festen Boden. Es ist ratsam, sich vor dem Einsteigen sowohl

minutes). To reach the Tozal, it is best to follow the faint trail under the south faces of the Ponoch and the Torre di Murcia (another 20 minutes).

DESCENT - PONOCH

The comparison of the "Valencianos" with the "Micheluzzi" on the Ciavaces is not limited to the climbing itself, but persists in the fact that hardly a climber goes to the summit on either one. We will describe the descent only from the large terrace which cuts across the right section of the face some 100 meters under the summit. From the shoulder where the exit ramp ends (see topo) descend westward until you are above the westernmost of the two rock spurs jutting out from the right side of the south face. Here the huge water reservoir comes into view again. At first descend the left side (facing downward) of the spur. Then stay on the ridge briefly till you can climb down a gully on the east side of the spur (traces of a trail are evident). Rappel twice (first 20, then 40 meters) till you reach terra firma. To avoid later confusion it is best to scrutinize the route itself as well as the descent before you are too close to the face.

DESCENT - TOZAL DE LEVANTE

Descend west into the gully between Tozal and Torre di Murcia. Rappel down the first steep section (some 20 meters) then climb upward 10 vertical meters diagonally east to a terrace. Traverse this till you reach a rappel. You can also get to the same rappel by looping first right then left to a steel cable which also leads to the terrace. Now rappel twice (40 meters each) to reach the ground.

über den Routenverlauf als auch über den Abstieg per Wandstudium zu orientieren, denn der Verhauermöglichkeiten sind viele.

ABSTIEG VOM TOZAL DE LEVANTE

Der Abstieg führt nach Westen hinab in die Rinne, die zwischen dem Tozal und dem Torre die Murcia nach Süden hinunterzieht. Über die erste, knapp zwanzig Meter hohe Steilstufe seilt man ab. Nun schräg (im Abstiegssinne) nach links ansteigend ca. zehn Meter auf ein Band empor, das bis zu einer Abseilstelle verfolgt wird. Hierher gelangt man auch, indem man in einer Rechts-Linksschleife absteigend ein Drahtseil erreicht, das zu der Terrasse leitet. Nun zwei Mal 40 Meter abseilend hinunter auf den Boden.

ÜBERNACHTUNG

Die meisten Kletterer am Ponoch und dem Tozal de Levante reisen von Calpe aus an, doch gibt es auch in La Nucia Zeltplätze. In der Umgebung des Zustiegsparkplatzes kann man ohne Probleme ein paar Nächte im Zelt verbringen, allerdings gibt es kein Wasser. Rechts vom Einstieg der Valencianosführe ist eine schöne Biwakhöhle.

VERSORGUNG

In Polop sind einige kleinere Läden, einen Supermarkt gibt es in La Nucia.

BESTE ZEIT

Von Oktober bis April, in den Sommermonaten ist die Hitze unerträglich.

CAMPING

Most visitors to the Ponoch and Tozal del Levante are based in Calpe. There are, however, campsites in La Nucia. You can also pitch your tent in the vicinity of the parking spot, but water is a problem. Moreover, there is a nice cave near the start of the "Valencianos".

SUPPLIES

There are several small shops in Polop and a supermarket in La Nucia.

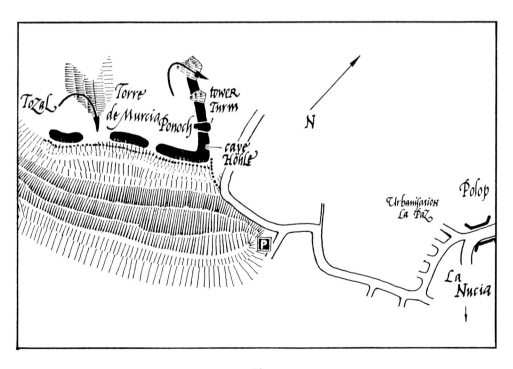

EL PONOCH
NORDOSTWAND – NORTHEAST FACE
ÜBERSICHT – A SURVEY

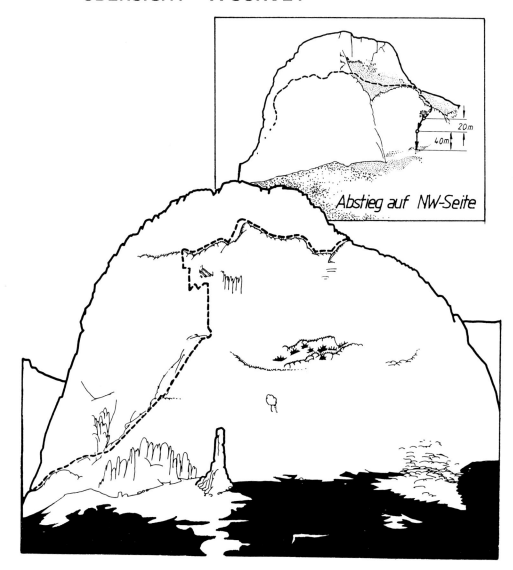

VIA VALENCIANOS
6b (5 A1), ca. 15SL, 300m,
Material: Klemmkeile bis Hex. 8
Nuts to Hex 8

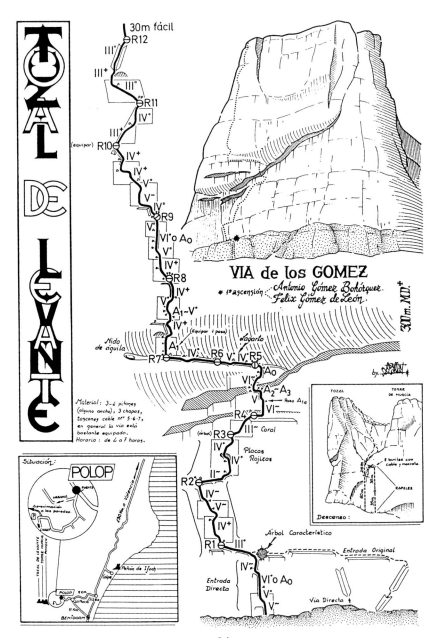

5. PEÑON DE IFACH

Vom Gipfel des Peñon de Ifach lugten die Wachen der kleinen Fischerstadt Calpe jahrhundertelang hinaus aufs Meer nach den Schnellseglern der maurischen Piraten. Tauchten die gefürchteten dreieckigen Segel am Horizont auf, trieb man die Ziegen in die Berge. Die Bauern verbarrikadierten sich mit Frau, Kind und Kegel hinter den Mauern der Burg, um ihre Haut so teuer wie möglich zu verkaufen. Blickt man heute vom Gipfel des Peñon, wird deutlich, daß andere Eroberer erfolgreicher waren als die Sarazenen. Noch immer durchziehen Ziegenpfade die schütteren Kiefernwälder. Doch bimmeln die Tiere etwas deplaziert zwischen den Bulldozerschneisen und schmucken Villen im "spanischen" Stil, die so schöne iberische Namen wie "Betty" oder "Sonnenschein" an der Frontseite aufgepinselt haben. Die Ansammlung von Häusern, die am Fuß der Felsnadel die Sandstrände säumt, würde fast ans Märkische Viertel erinnern, wäre da nicht in ihrer Mitte die aus Fertigblechteilen erstellte Stierkampfarena. Die Frage "Calpe, nein danke?" läßt sich dennoch nicht so einfach beantworten, wie das der im ersten Grausen sich wendende Gast meinen könnte.

Zumindest das Wetter der Levante dürfte fast jeden regenmüden Mitteleuropäer versöhnlich stimmen. Im Winter ist Valencia zumeist die nördliche Regengrenze, von Süden her kühlt die Sierra Nevada so ungefähr bis Murcia. Darum gelten unter den spanischen Felsgehern um Weihnachten die Klettermöglichkeiten der Levante als die einzig wirklich vor Schnee sicheren auf der gesamten Iberischen Halbinsel. Zudem sind die felsorientierten Betätigungsmöglichkeiten, die von Calpe aus unschwer erreichbar sind, durchaus beachtlich. Nach Südosten bricht der Peñon mit einer ca. 250 Meter hohen Steilwand ab, deren gelber versinterter Fels mit seinen teilweise runden Griffen allerdings nicht jedermanns Sache ist. Wer die Colodri-Wand bei Arco kennt, hat eine Vorstellung, was hier

For hundreds of years the guards of the small Spanish fishing town of Calpe peered out to sea from the summit of the Peñon de Ifach to catch sight of the swift Moorish pirate vessels. When the feared triangular sails pierced the horizon the goats were driven into the nearby mountains. The peasants withdrew behind the walls of the fortress to sell their hides as dearly as possible. Today a glance from the summit of the Peñon makes clear that other conquerors have been more successful than the Saracens. Still the goat tracks meander through the thinning pine forests. However, the bells of the animals sound displaced among yellow Caterpillars and trim "Spanish-style" villas bearing such exotic Iberian names as "Betty" or "Sonnenschein". The conglomeration of houses that disfigures the bay some thousand feet below could almost be mistaken for a teutonic architectural atrocity from the fifties - if it weren't for the corrugated iron bull ring in the middle of a dusty rectangle between shabby concrete shoeboxes.

A Christmas holiday here? But the question is not as easily answered as the visitor, turning his eyes out to sea in horror, might initially think. At least the Levantine weather might console the refugee from Central Europe or a foggy island in the North Sea. Normally the northern rain belt in winter stops at Valencia and the cool breeze from the Sierra Nevada in the south doesn't venture northward beyond Murcia. Thus, from November to February, Spanish climbers consider excursions to the sierras of the Levante (the area of the central Mediterranean coast) as the only really snow-safe trips of the Iberian Peninsula, where alpinistic satisfaction only depends on your willingness to drag a weary body off the beach. Moreover, the climbing potential of the area in the vicinity of Calpe is remarkable. The Peñon de Ifach drops off with an 800 foot wall towards the south east The style of routes here resembles that on the Colodri Wall of Arco; vertical yellow rock with rounded athletic holds along the crack connected by elegant grayrock

auf ihn zukommt. Allerdings haben die Spanier ihre Touren der modernen Entwicklung angepaßt, d.h. pensionierte Haken wurden nicht durch neue ersetzt. Die Begehung dieser Führen setzt deshalb eine einwandfreie Beherrschung des Umgangs mit Klemmkeilen oder viel Mut voraus. Links des gelben Steilabbruchs verändert sich der Fels zum verdonesken Silbergrauen, allerdings in einem Neigungswinkel, der auch für den alpinen Normalverbraucher zu bewältigen ist. Neben dem Peñon de Ifach bieten die nahe Sierra de Toix, die Mascaratschlucht und die Sierra de Bernia vor allem für Genußkletterer und Normalextreme fast unbegrenzte Möglichkeiten - von der Einseillängen-Platte bis zur 250-Meter-Wand mit voralpinem Charakter. Allerdings ist das Angebot im Achterbereich überschaubar. Hat der Felstiger die Einstiegslänge der "Sulfada" und die "Cleoplaca" in Mascarat herausgedrückt, muß er entweder zum Bohrmeißel greifen, zum Baden gehen oder nach Montanejos auswandern. In knapp einstündiger Fahrt sind zudem von Calpe aus die Ausgangspunkte für die Routen in der Sierra Aitana erreichbar, die oft schon über die voralpine Dimension hinausgehen.
Neben all diesen alpinistischen Qualitäten hat die Fremdenkolonie unter dem Peñon de Ifach noch allerlei an Annehmlichkeiten des täglichen Lebens zu bieten. Zum Beispiel kann man sich hier im Winter für runde dreihundert Mark monatlich in einer der durchaus erträglichen Siedlungen eine Villa mieten - ein ungemein komfortables Basislager für den Aufenthalt. Eher naturverbundene Climbingfreaks ziehen sich in die Hügel der Sierra de Bernia zurück, wo die Bauern bisher noch nichts gegen zeltende Bergsteiger haben. Und Campingplätze gibt's natürlich auch noch. Hat man sich erst einmal vierzehn Tage in den Bergen um Calpe herumgetrieben, wird es kaum einer bereuen, dem ersten instinktiven Fluchtimpuls nicht gefolgt zu sein. Und last but not least gibt es kaum ein Klettergebiet, das mit der gleichen Berechtigung das Gütesiegel "familienfreundlich" für sich in Anspruch nehmen könnte. Denn schon wiederholt ist es gelungen, den Frieden in leidgeprüften Familien mit kletternden Vätern in Calpe zu kitten. Oder kann man vielleicht in Rimini oder Caorle die

traverses. The Spaniards have adopted modern protection techniques here as well, that is to say, not all tottery pegs have been replaced with younger ones. In other words, a go at these routes demands dexterity with nuts or a good dose of courage. To the left of this semi-Dolomite face the rock turns gray, with an angle humane enough to permit the average alpinist an attempt at some of the routes.

In addition to the Peñon the Sierra de Toix, the Mascarat Gorge, and the Sierra de Bernia offer the pleasure climber and moderate E-grade climber a wealth of possibilities - from the single-pitch slab to an 800 foot crag with "pre-alpine" qualities. However, the spectrum of climbs in the grade eight range is limited. Those who have flashed the first pitches of the "Sulfada" and "Cleoplaca" and done most of the climbs on the Peñon will either have to get out their drills, go swimming, or exodus to Montanejos. Moreover, a mere hour's drive from Calpe there are a wealth of routes in the Sierra Aitana whose dimensions approach serious alpine character.

Besides its alpine qualities, this southern colony for winter exiles offers a spectrum of commodities for one's daily needs. For example, off season you can rent a perfectly comfortable villa for a hundred pounds a month. Winter base camp in Calpe can assume luxurious dimensions otherwise beyond the reach of most climbers' pocketbooks. Hard core nature lovers can still escape to the hills of the Sierra de Bernia. The local farmers have not yet developed an antipathy towards climbers. Not to mention the multitude of official camping sites along the coast...but demand has affected prices here heavily.

If you've managed to subdue your first impulses to flee and spent two weeks in the mountains around Calpe, you too will agree that Calpe more than deserves its quality seal as a "family-friendly" holiday spot. Not seldom - following the feud over whether to spend the holiday at the seaside or in the mountains - has the hatchet been buried in Calpe. Here both rock-starved father and sun-hungry mother can have their cake

Begehung einer herzeigbaren Kletterführe harmonisch in den familienorientierten Badetag integrieren?

ANFAHRT UND ZUGÄNGE

Auf der A 7 bis zur Ausfahrt Benisa und auf der N 332 nach Calpe, wo man sich zum Puerto durchschlägt (4 Kilometer von der Hauptstraße). Das Fahrzeug in der Nähe der Restaurants am Hafen abstellen, denn viele Leute, die näher an den Einstiegen geparkt haben, sind bestohlen worden. Die Einstiege der Routen in der Nordwand des Peñon errreicht man am besten, indem man ca. 150 Meter westlich des Restaurants "del Puerto" auf einer breiten Treppe zur Straße hinaufsteigt, die weiter oben zum Normalweg des Peñon degeneriert. Die Einstiege befinden sich in ca. 150 Meter Meereshöhe rechts des Normalwegtunnels. Für die Touren in der Südostwand folgt man zu Fuß der Straße unter den Wänden, bis deutliche Wegspuren zu den Einstiegen hinaufführen.

ABSTIEG

Auf dem Touristenpfad des Normalwegs, der von Norden kommend auf den Gipfel hinaufspiralt.

ÜBERNACHTUNG

In Calpe gibt es eine Unzahl von Campingplätzen, die allerdings in der Wintersaison geschlossen sind. In dieser Zeit sind jedoch die Appartement-Mieten auch für in Gruppen reisende Kletterer erschwinglich. Auskunft gibt gerne:
J. Morato
Agencia Immobilaria
Dr. Fleming 7
Calpe (Alicante)
(965) 83 06 00 oder 83 06 83

and eat it too...or can you think of any other Mediterranean resort where you can combine a respectable climb with an afternoon on the beach with the kids?

APPROACHES

Exit from freeway A 7 at Benisa, take the N 332 to Calpe. From the main road continue four more kilometers towards the port. It is best to park your car in view of the restaurants on the beach. Many climbers who park closer to the climbs have lost their shirts.
The routes on the north face of the Peñon are best reached by walking 150 meters west of the restaurant "del Puerto", ascending the wide stairs to a road that leads towards the Peñon and dwindles to a path, which is the normal route up the crag. The routes all begin at about 150 meters elevation to the right of the tunnel of the normal route.
For the climbs on the south face walk down the road under the face till you can take trails up to the starts of the various climbs.

DESCENT

The descent is the normal route, a trail that winds up the north side of the mountain.

CAMPING

The campsites are normally closed in winter. However, in the off-season rents for appartments are so cheap that they are within range of even the less well-endowed, especially if shared in groups.

Wer sich ins Hinterland verdrückt, sollte unbedingt den Bauern, auf dessen Grund er zu hausen gedenkt, um Erlaubnis bitten, sonst dürfen Andere den Folge-Trouble ausbaden.

VERSORGUNG

In Calpe gibt es alles, nur kein Klettermaterial. Das nächste Klettergeschäft, sehr gut ausgestattet, ist in Alicante:

K 2 Esports
Calle Belando, 12
03004 Alicante
20 65 62

BESTE ZEIT

Oktober bis April.

WEITERE INFORMATIONEN

Vicente & Juan Antonio Andres
GUIA DE ESCALADAS DEL PEÑON DE IFACH
Revista Desnivel
Apartado de Corrreos 19.083
28020 Madrid

Information is available from:
J. Morato
Agencia Immobilaria
Dr. Fleming 7
Calpe (Alicante)
(965) 83 06 00 or 83 06 03

If you plan to camp unofficially in the hinterlands,, the local farmers are usually very friendly about granting permission to camp on private property. However, they appreciate being asked.

SUPPLIES

In Calpe you can buy everything except climbing gear. The nearest climbing shop, a very well equipped one, is located in Alicante:
K 2 Esports
Calle Belando, 12
03004 Alicante
20 65 62

SEASON

October to April

FURTHER INFORMATION

Vicente & Juan Antonio Andres,
GUIA DE ESCALADAS DEL PEÑON DE IFACH
Revista Desnivel
Appartado de Correos 19.083
28020 Madrid

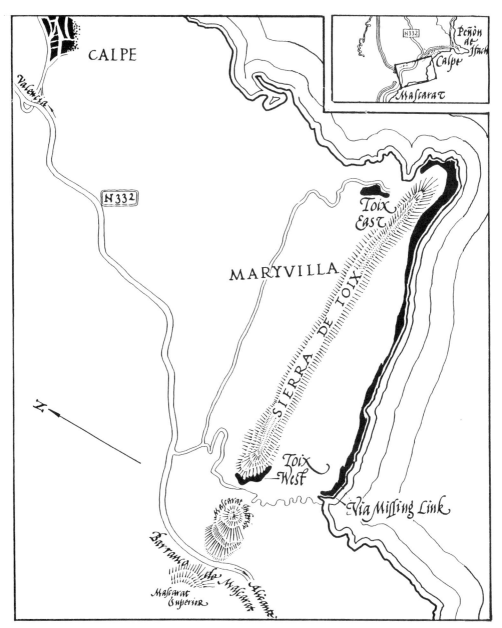

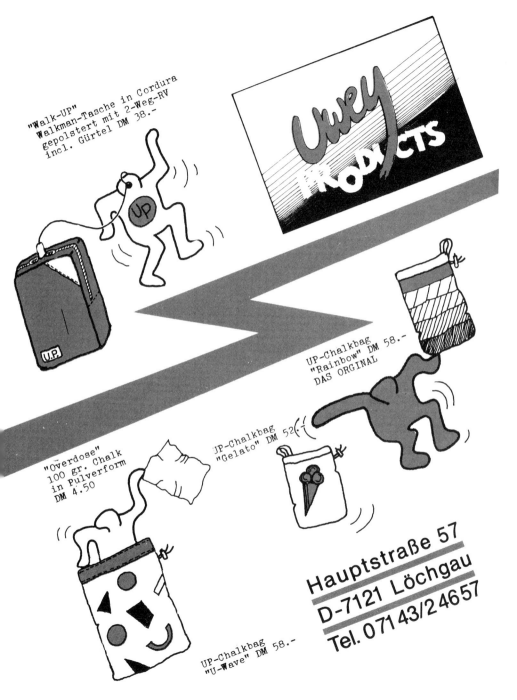

PEÑON DE IFACH
NORDWAND - NORTH FACE
ÜBERSICHT - A SURVEY

1 Verde Esmeralda   5+/6a
2 Asignatura Pendiente 6a+
3 Roxy   6b+
4 Pany   4-

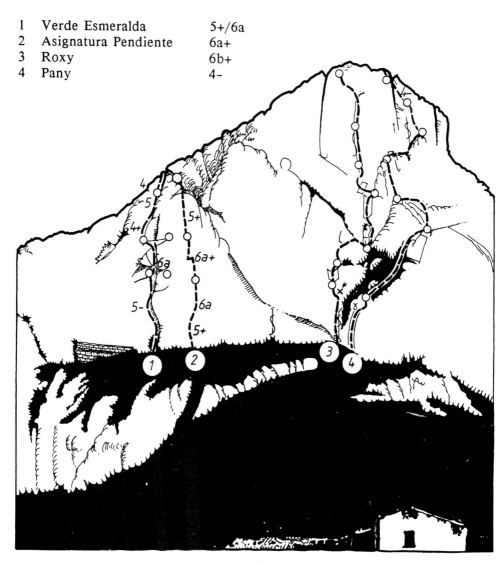

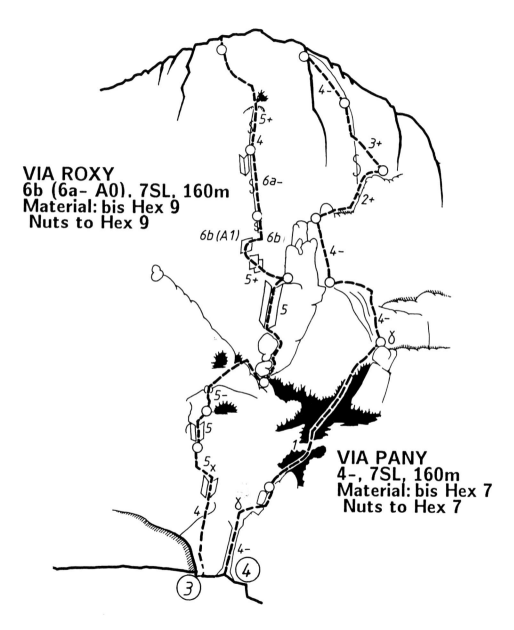

PEÑON DE IFACH
SÜDOSTWAND - SOUTHEAST FACE
ÜBERSICHT - A SURVEY

5	Via SAME	6a
6	Via Valencianos	4+
	(Weg des geringsten Widerstandes - path of least resistance)	
7	Diedro UPSA	5
8	Via Manuel	6 A1 (6a A1)
9	Via Gomez-Cano	6a+ A1 (5+ A1)
10	Via Anglada-Gallego	6b+ (5+ A1)

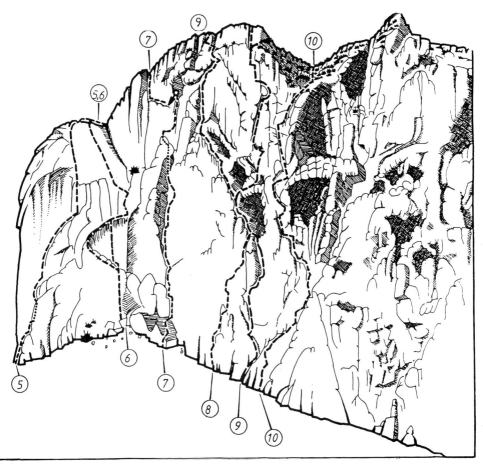

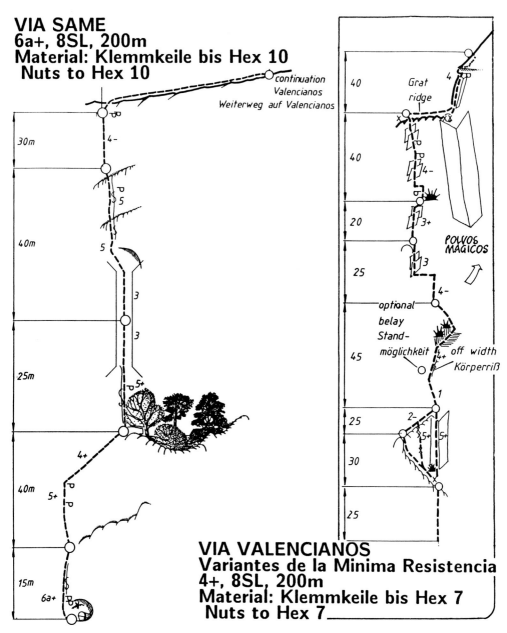

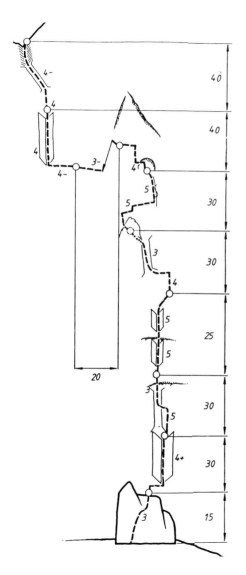
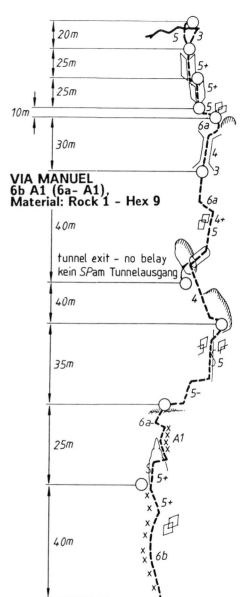

VIA GOMEZ-CANO
6a A1, 12SL, 240m
Material: Klemmkeile bis Hex 9

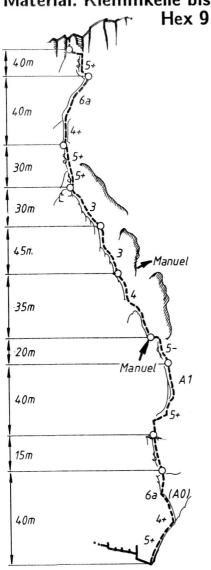

VIA ANGLADA-GALLEGO
6b (5+ A1), 9SL, 240m
Material: Klemmkeile bis Hex 8
Nuts to Hex 8

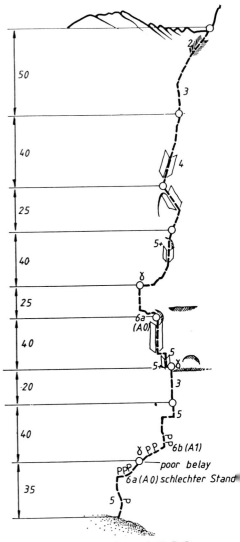

6. SIERRA DE TOIX

Die Sierra de Toix ist ein zwei Kilometer langer Bergkamm, der von der Mascaratschlucht penjonwärts zum Cap de Toix hinauszieht. Auf der Nordseite siedeln sonnenhungrige Mitteleuropäer, auf der Südseite schlummert noch ahnungslos die ursprüngliche Mittelmeerlandschaft, die abrupt hundert Meter tief zum Wasser abbricht.

In der Sierra de Toix finden sich drei Klettergebiete von recht unterschiedlichem Charakter:

Westlich, bei der Urbanisacion Maryvilla warten auf felsentwöhnte Nordländer die idealen Climbs, um nach einer langen Winterpause wieder in Fahrt zu kommen. Erika Stagni, ehemals berühmt wegen ihrer ersten Damenbegehung der Hasse-Brandler an der Großen Zinne und ihr Lebensgefährte Robert Wolschlag, genannt Pellebrosse, haben hier im steilen Karrenfels des an der höchsten Stelle über hundert Meter hohen Felsaufbaus sechzehn Wege mit Bolts versehen, die sogar weitgereiste englische Profis in Begeisterung versetzt haben.

Zweihundert Höhenmeter tiefer lauert ein ganz anderes Programm, die "Via Missing Link". Nach dem fünfzig Meter langen Einstiegsquergang direkt über dem Meer steigt man vom Schlingenstand aus frei und überhängend in zwei Seillängen hinauf zum Diagonalband.

Das dritte Toixer Gebiet ist am Ostende der Sierra gelegen. Die Wege hier sind durchschnittlich steiler als in Maryvilla und "moderner", d.h. knapper eingerichtet als drüben. Es sei geraten, die Fingerkuppen vor dem Besuch mit Benzointinktur zu verledern.

Sierra de Toix is a mountain ridge about two kilometers long that extends from the Mascarat Gorge eastward to Cap de Toix. Its northerly slopes have been urbanized by the fair-haired races. The southern slope is virgin Mediterranean countryside which plunges into the water in an abrupt drop.off. It is divided into three distinct climbing areas of differing character. The cliffs near the Maryvilla residence area are a series of slabs. Erika Stagni, who earned her reputation with the first female ascent of the Hasse-Brandler route on the Cima Grande, and her companion Robert Wolschlag, alias Pellebrosse, have equipped 16 routes here on the steep, solid crag. Some two hundred meters lower a completely different experience is on the agenda, the "Via Missing Link". You do a 50 meter traverse directly above the sea to a hanging belay. From here two overhanging pitches lead to a diagonal ramp. The third area on the Toix ridge is at the east end of the Sierra. The pro here is generally more sparse than in Maryvilla.

APPROACHES

Toix West:
From Calpe take the N 332 in the direction of Altea. Some 150 meters behind the milestone marked 139 turn left into the Urbanisacion Maryvilla. Then turn right at every fork, (a total of three times) and drive till you reach the parking spot at the cul de sac.

ANFAHRTEN UND ZUGÄNGE

Toix West:
Von Calpe auf der N 332 in Richtung Altea. Ca. 150 Meter hinter dem Kilometerstein 139 links ab zur "Urbanisacion Maryvilla". Nun bei allen Abzweigungen die rechte wählend (drei mal) zur Parkmöglichkeit am Ende der Teerstraße.

Toix Küstenfelsen:
Wie bei Toix West zum Parkplatz. Von hier auf Wegspuren in südlicher Richtung zur Bucht westlich der Küstenfelsen absteigen. Einstieg knapp links des Wassers.

Toix Ost:
Am besten wie nach Toix West nach Maryvilla, jedoch bei der 1. und 2. Abzweigung den Schildern "Supermarkt" folgen, bei der 3. Abzweigung dem Schild "Sectores C-A-F", bei der 4. links und bei der 5. rechts abzweigen.

ÜBERNACHTUNG ETC.

Siehe Peñon de Ifach.

Toix Sea Cliff:
Follow directions for Toix West till you get to the parking spot. From here take a faint path southward towards the bay west of the coastal crags. The route starts just left of the water.

Toix East:
Drive to Maryvilla following directions for Toix West. When you reach the suburb, instead of the three right turns, follow the signs to the "SUPERMARKT" for the first two forks, then the sign for "Sectores C-A-F" at the third intersection. Turn left at the fourth and right at the fifth fork of the road. This road takes you directly below the cliffs.

CAMPING, SUPPLIES, ETC.

See Peñon de Ifach

TOIX WEST
LINKER WANDTEIL – LEFT SIDE

1		5
1a		4
1b		5
2		5+/6a
3		5
4	Grün/green	6b
5	Rot/red	6a
6	Schwarz/black	6b
7		3+
8		5

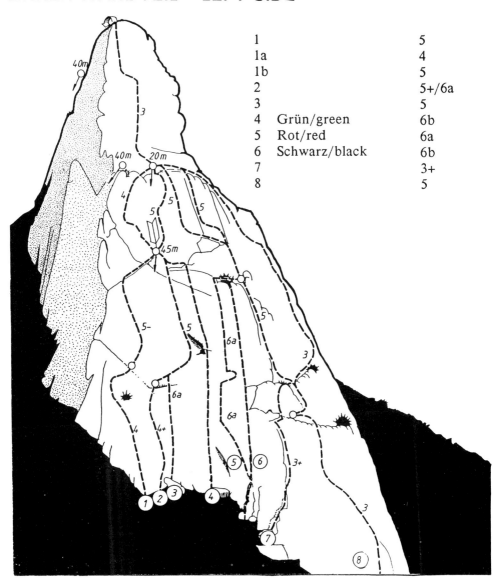

TOIX WEST
RECHTER WANDTEIL – RIGHT SIDE

9	4
10	5+
11	5+
12	5+
13	5
13a	5
14	5/5+
15	5-
16	4+

TOIX
KÜSTENFELSEN – SEACLIFFS

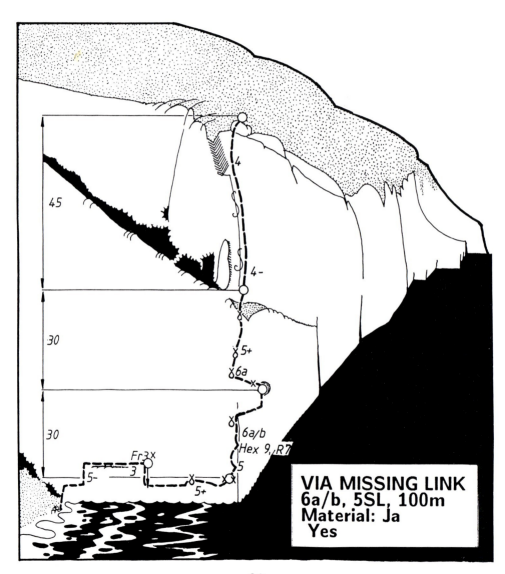

TOIX OST

1 Via de los Fakiros
2 Via la Fina
3 Via Pyramide
4 Via Yoyaba
5 Via Lloviznada

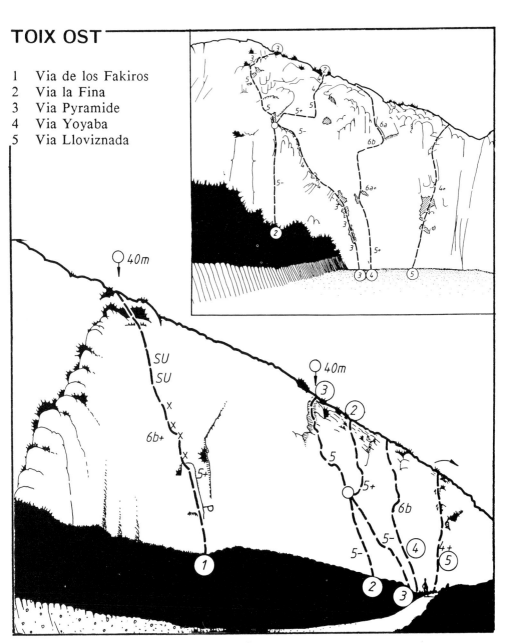

7. BARRANCO DE MASCARAT

Bei Kilometer 138 führt die N. 332 durch die "Barranco de Mascarat". Östlich erhebt sich der Mascarat Inferior, westlich der Mascarat Superior über der Schlucht, (sie trennt die Sierra de Toix von der Sierra Bernia), die von zwei eindrucksvollen Straßenbrücken überspannt wird. Die obere heißt Ponte dei Sorbisi (Seufzerbrücke), die untere ist der Ponte de los Pantalones Completos (Brücke der vollen Hosen). Wer den nun schon berühmten Pendelschwung vor- und das Geländer der Nationalstraße hinter sich hat, wird den Namen ihre Berechtigung nicht absprechen. Wer zum Klettern hergekommen ist, findet hier mit der "Via UPSA" auf den Superior und der "Via Boulder" auf den Inferior zwei "Voralpenklassiker", in der "Teta de la Novia" eine Nervenprobe für den freikletternden Mittelstand und in der "Cleoplaca" eine voll ausgegangene Superlänge für die Meisterklasse. Für die "Sulfada" kann ich keine persönliche Haftung übernehmen, die Berichte der Überlebenden rangieren von der Lobpreisung bis zur Sprengungsandrohung. Ihre erste Seillänge ist eine beliebte Workout-Arena für die Extremen. Fahrzeuge, die man in der Schlucht abgestellt hat, sind extrem gefährdet. Hier stellt sich dem, der sein Hab und Gut weiterhin im Besitz behalten will, die schwierige Aufgabe, allen Mitmenschen vorurteilslos und freundlich zu begegnen, und trotzdem sein Zeug nicht aus dem Auge zu lassen.

ZUGÄNGE

Zu den Einstiegen der "Via Boulder" und der "Sulfada" gelangt man am besten durch eine 50m-Abseilfahrt von der neuen Brücke. Man kann auch ca. 200 Meter südwestlich des alten Puente von der Straße in die Schlucht abklettern.

At kilometer marker 138, the N 332 leads through the Barranco de Mascarat. The tower to the east of the gorge is Mascarat Inferior and the peak to the west of the gorge, Mascarat Superior. They rise 200 and 300 meters respectively above the gorge which divides the Sierra de Toix from the Sierra Bernia. Two impressive bridges span the chasm, the upper one of which is called Ponte dei Sorbisi and the lower one, Ponte de los Pantalones Completos. Those who find themselves with the railing of the bridge behind them and the pendulum off the bridge before them, will have no problems understanding the reason for the names. Those who have come to climb rather than leap will find two pre-alpine classics in the "Via UPSA" on the Superior and the "Via Boulder" on the Inferior. The "Teta dela Novia" is a bold thriller for the climbing middle class and "Cleoplaca", a superb full pitch for the master. I can assume no responsibility for the "Sulfada". Reports of survivors range from hymns of praise to threats of dynamiting the route. At any rate, its first pitch provides a good workout for all aspirants. A warning to drivers who park their cars in the vicinity of the bridges: those who value their wordly possessions will be faced with the difficult task of remaining friendly and unprejudiced towards their fellow humans while simultaneously keeping a suspicious eye on their valuables.

Der Einstieg zur "UPSA" ist direkt auf der Hosenscheißerbrücke; zur "Teta dela Novia" steigt man über die erste UPSA-Länge hinauf und dann im leichten Gelände schräg nach links zum Einstieg bei Pfeil.

ABSTIEGE

Vom Mascarat Inferior steigt man über Maryvilla ab.

Den Gipfel des Mascarat Superior kann man sich sparen: auf dem großen Band unter dem oberen Wanddrittel nach links queren und auf einem Sporn zur Straße absteigen.

ÜBERNACHTUNG VERSORGUNG ETC.

Siehe Peñon de Ifach.

APPROACHES

The start of the "Via Boulder" and the "Sulfada" are best reached by rappeling 50 meters from the new bridge. One can also scramble down into the gorge about 200 meters to the SW of the old bridge from the road. The start of the "UPSA" is directly at the old bridge. To reach the "Teta dela Novia" climb the first pitch of the "UPSA" and traverse left on easy ground to an arrow at the start of the climb.

DESCENTS

Descend from Mascarat Inferior via Maryvilla.

You can omit the summit of Mascarat Superior (unless you're a peak bagger) and traverse left on the large terrace under the top third of the face, then descend to the road on a spur.

CAMPING, SUPPLIES, ETC.

See Peñon de Ifach.

BARRANCO DE MASCARAT
ÜBERSICHT - A SURVEY

1. La Teta de la Novia — 6a
2. Via UPSA — 5
3. La Sulfada — 5+/6a
4. Los Pantalones Completos — 6c+
5. Via Boulder — 5+/6a
6. Cleoplaca — 7a/b
7. Via Aurora — 5+/6a

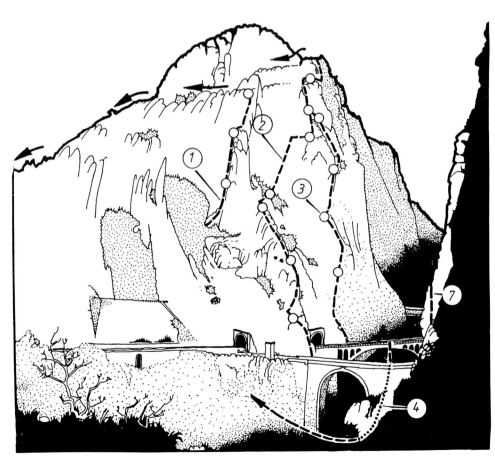

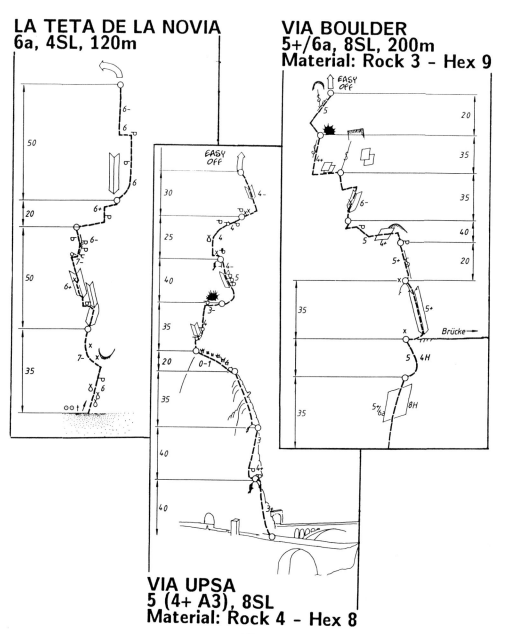

8. LA DALLE D'OLA

Die "Dalle d'Ola", knapp 40 Meter hoch und nach Süden ausgerichtet, erhielt ihren Namen im Gedächtnis an Erika and Pelles frühverstorbenen Hund. Die Platte ist ein Maryvilla für Fortgeschrittene: gleich gut abgesichert wie die Routen drüben in Toix-West, aber im Durchschnitt einen Grad schwieriger. Der Fels ist grau, steil und übersät mit Wasserlöchern. Viel Vergnügen!
Kurz vor Drucklegung erfuhren wir, daß das Land, auf dem die Felsplatte beheimatet ist, von einer Immobilienfirma aufgekauft worden ist. Hier sollen Ferienappartements gebaut werden. Bisher ist allerdings das Klettern noch gestattet.

ZUGANG

Von Calpe durch die Mascaratschlucht in Richtung Altea. Bei Kilometer 135,75 weist ein Schild nach rechts hinauf zu den Residencias Bernia. Man folgt der Straße steil bergauf, die Autobahn überquerend, bis rechterhand eine mit einer Kette abgesperrte Straße abzweigt. Hier parken und, um unsere stillschweigende Kletterbewilligung nicht zu gefährden, zu Fuß in etwa 15 Minuten der Straße folgend zur Platte.

ÜBERNACHTUNG VERSORGUNG ETC.

Siehe Peñon de Ifach.

Dalle d'Ola, a 40 meter south facing slab, was named in memory of Pelle and Erika's dog, who died an early death. The crag is a Maryvilla for the advanced. The routes are as well protected as those on Toix West, but they are, on the average, a grade harder. The rock is gray, steep, and interspersed with gouttes d'eau.

Just before press time we learned that a "developer" bought the land on wich the crag is situated and plans to build a housing development here. Climbing is, however, still tolerated.

APPROACH

From Calpe drive through the Mascarat Gorge in the direction of Altea. At kilometer 135.75 there is a sign for the Residencias Bernia. Follow this road, crossing over the freeway, till you reach a chained-off road branching off to the right. Park here, and, in order not to threaten the tolerance of climbing, walk the rest of the way up the road, some 15 minutes, to the slab.

CAMPING, SUPPLIES, ETC.

See Peñon de Ifach.

LA DALLE D'OLA

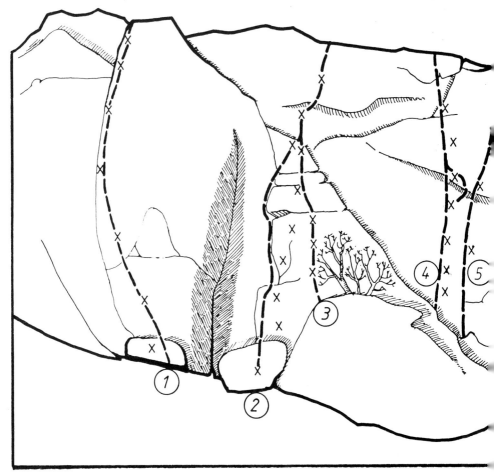

1	Blaugelb/blue-yellow	5+
2	Rotgelb/red-yellow	5
3	Gelb/yellow	5+
4	Schwarz/black	6b
5	Rot/red	6a
6	Grün/green	6a+
7	Gelb/yellow	5+
8	Creme/cream-coloured	6b
10	Rosa/pink	6a
11	Rot/red	6b/c

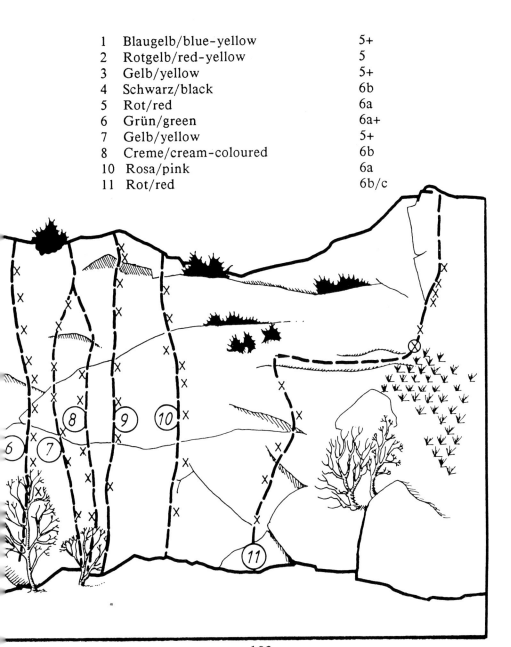

9. CHULILLA

Unter den in diesem Buch vorgestellten Klettergebieten ist Chulilla das gemütlichste. Die beschauliche Atmosphäre des verwinkelten mittelalterlichen Städtchens, das unter der alten Maurenburg über dem Turiafluß vor sich hindöst, bestimmt auch den Charakter des Routenangebots: zu den Einstiegen läuft man nie länger als zehn Minuten, der Fels ist fest, steil, löchrig und sehr gut abgesichert. Fast, als hätten wichtige Teile des Frankenjuras genug gehabt vom vielen und sauren Niederschlag und seien nach Süden ausgewandert. Ein Fehler wäre die Ortswahl auf keinen Fall gewesen, denn wenn's auch überall anders in Europa friert, regnet und mistralt, kann man in Chulilla unbeschwert klettern. Die Routenauswahl ist reichlich und reicht vom vierten bis zum neunten Schwierigkeitsgrad. Eine eifrige "normalextreme" Seilschaft hat eine Woche lang Stoff und wird sicher wiederkehren.

ANFAHRT

Auf der A 7 bis Valencia, dann auf der N 234 über Liria nach Losa del Obispo. Hier links abbiegen nach Chulilla.

ÜBERNACHTUNG

"Zeltplatz" mit Waschwasser, gratis und unbewacht, bei der "Fuente de las Pelmas" vier Kilometer vom Ortsschild in Richtung Vanacloig/Villar del Arzobispo. Trinkwasser kann an den Brunnen in Chulilla geschöpft werden. Aus den nun schon zum Gähnen bekannten Gründen sollte man das Zelten in den Orangenhainen besser vermeiden.

Of the areas covered in this guidebook Chulilla is the most good natured. The idyllic atmosphere of the sleepy medieval town tucked under an old fort built by the Moors with the River Turia meandering below also characterizes the climbs here: you never walk more than ten minutes to the routes. The rock is steep, full of pockets, and bolt protected. It's almost as if parts of the Frankenjura got tired of the frequent and acid precipitation and decided to migrate south. At any rate the choice of location would not have been a mistake. For even when elsewhere on the Continent rain, snow, slush, or the Mistral make climbing miserable, in Chulillia you can climb without suffering. The selection of routes is extensive and ranges from grades 4 to 8a. A diligent "normal E-grade" party will be kept busy for a week and will want to come back.

APPROACH

Take the A 7 to Valencia, then take the N 234 through Liria to Losa del Obispo. Turn left here to Chulilla.

CAMPING

There is an official camping site unguarded and free of cost near the "Fuente de las Pelmas" four kilometers from the edge of town in the direction of Vanacloig/Villar del Arzobispo. You can get drinking water from the fountain in Chulillia. For reasons I am reluctant to repeat, please refrain from camping in the orange groves.

VERSORGUNG

Das Einkaufsangebot in Chulilla beschränkt sich auf die Grundfuttermittel. Um über Brot, Wein Käse und Fleischwaren hinausgehende Bedürfnisse zu befriedigen, muß man mindestens bis Liria fahren.

INFORMATIONEN

In der "Bar de la Juventu" liegt ein immer aktuelles Routenbuch aus.

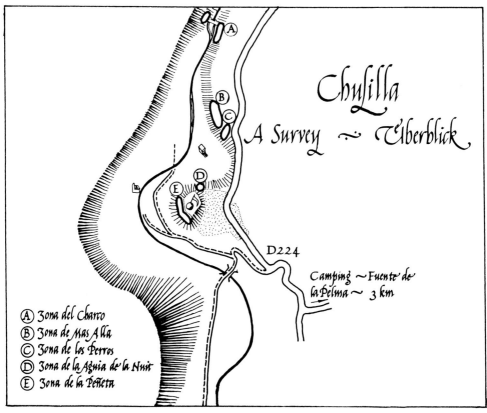

Chulilla
A Survey ~ Überblick

D224

Camping ~ Fuente de la Pelma ~ 3 km

Ⓐ Zona del Charco
Ⓑ Zona de Mas Allá
Ⓒ Zona de los Perros
Ⓓ Zona de la Aguia de la Nuit
Ⓔ Zona de la Peñeta

SUPPLIES

You can buy groceries, but not much more, in Chulilla. If your demands surpass bread, wine, meat, and cheese, you may need to drive to Liria to do your shopping.

FURTHER INFORMATION

There is an always up-to-date route book in the "Bar de la Juventu".

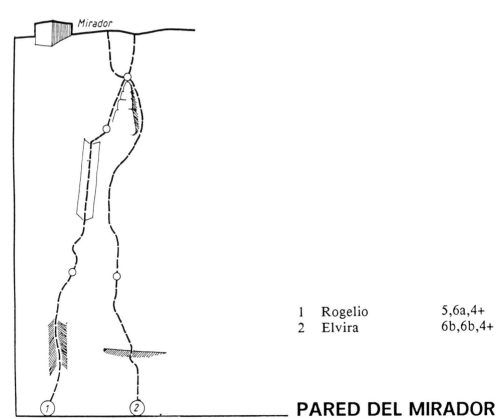

1	Rogelio	5,6a,4+
2	Elvira	6b,6b,4+

PARED DEL MIRADOR

ZONA DE MAS ALLA

1	Sourisa Vertical	6b+,5+
2	Nosferatu	6c+,6b
3	Musquito	6c
4	Valencia 8000	6a
5	Mamy on Side	6c
6	Mas Alla (3. SL)	4+
7	Tronquito	4+
8	Benimanet	6b,6b

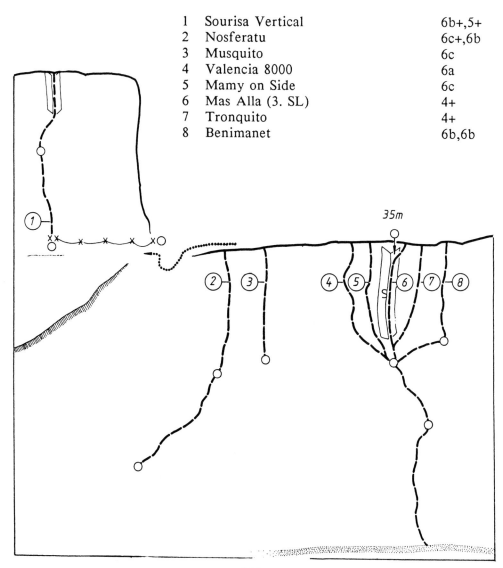

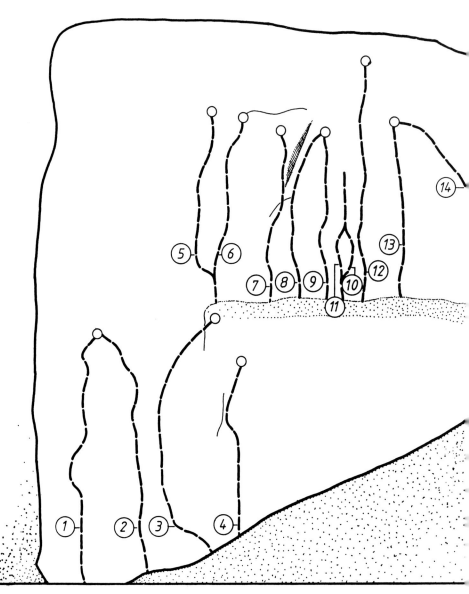

ZONA DE LOS PERROS

1a	Si Bebes no Conduzcas	7a+, 6b+
	(to the left of the arete)	
	(links vom Pfeiler)	
1	La Reina de la Seduccion	6c
2	Cequera Temporal	6a+
3	Terror Bajo el Culo	6a
4	Gefillo's Crack 6	a
5	Le Monodua	6b
6	Mujer Caliente, Verga Arrogante	5+/6a
7	Hijos de Cain	6c
8	Pelandrusca	6a
9	Ni Playa ni Ostias	6a
10	La Muerte ta Guarda	7c+/8a
11	Ta Absorbe l'Abismo	7a
12	Con el Falo como un Palo	6a/6a+
13	A Vamba Buluba	7b+/7c
14	Come Huelos	6c
15	Angel de Cuero	6b+
16	El Amo del Calabozo	6c
16a	Variante	7c+
17	Bien por mi Madre	6b
18	Spit Rambo	6c+
19	Soy une Chica Yeye	6a
20	Salome	5+

AGUJA DE LA NUIT

1 Saves que el Captus Pincha 5+
2   5+
3 La Fisura de la Nuit 5+/6a
4 Canto Gregoriano 7b

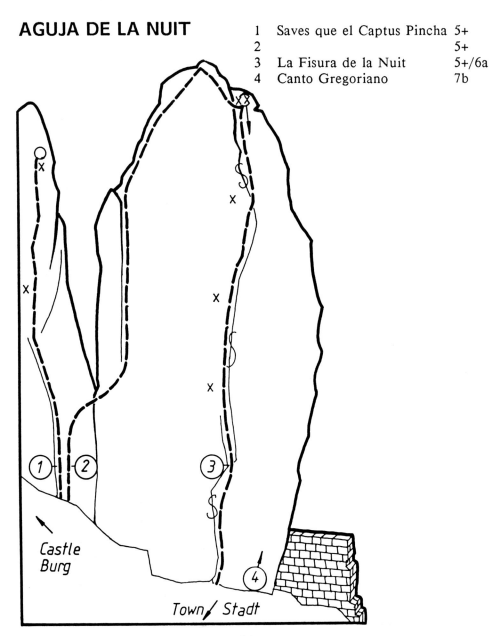

PEÑETA

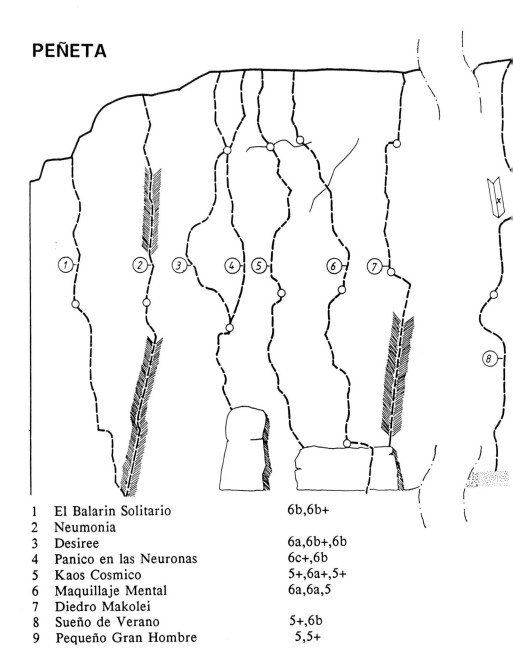

1	El Balarin Solitario	6b,6b+
2	Neumonia	
3	Desiree	6a,6b+,6b
4	Panico en las Neuronas	6c+,6b
5	Kaos Cosmico	5+,6a+,5+
6	Maquillaje Mental	6a,6a,5
7	Diedro Makolei	
8	Sueño de Verano	5+,6b
9	Pequeño Gran Hombre	5,5+

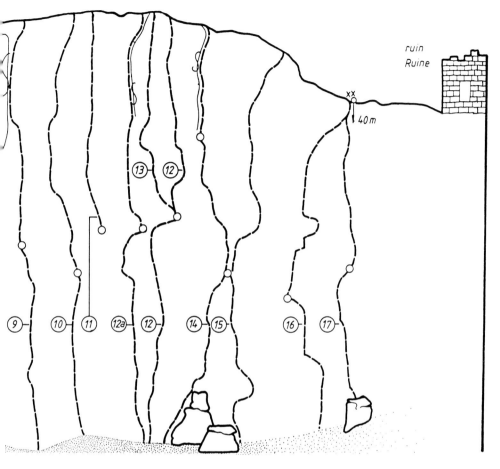

10	El Loco de la Colina	5,6c
11		
12a	Anni Hall	5,5+
12	Atzerimas	5+,6c
13	Sibringuin	6c
14	Hechizo de Luz	4+,5+
15	Amor Loco	5+,6a
16	Crisis	6a+,6b+
17	Fantasma de la Opera	6c,6b+

10. MONTANEJOS

Nur fünfzig Kilometer von der Costa de Azahar entfernt erinnert im vormaligen Thermalbad von Montanejos nichts an die Touristenströme der Küste. Die Kuranlagen um die Quellen sind verfallen, Rheumatiker und Kreislaufpatienten haben abgemagerten Hunden und einer Handvoll valencianischer Kletterpunks Platz gemacht. Die Energien ihrer Rebellion gegen den Durchschnitt verbieten ihnen den sechsten Grad - und das spiegelt sich in der Schwierigkeit der Routen in diesem Extremkletterparadies wider. Seit Beginn der achziger Jahre wurde in Montanejos eine Fülle von großzügig eingebohrten Routen mit Kletterhöhen von 5 bis hundert Metern eröffnet. Der Fels weist eine unerhört komplizierte Feinstruktur auf, mit horizontalen, diagonalen und vertikalen Rissen und Schuppen sowie Löchern und Käntchen in allen denkbaren Ausformungen. Dies fordert vom Kletterer ein hohes Maß an Wahrnehmungsfähigkeit, Kreativität und Stehvermögen (im doppelten Wortsinn), während der Rauhigkeit des Gesteins nur mit masochistischer Leidensfreude, Willensstärke oder stoischer Gelassenheit begegnet werden kann. In kaum einem Klettergebiet sagt das Wort "grifflos" mehr über die mangelnde Kraft und Geschicklichkeit des Gescheiterten aus als über die Beschaffenheit des Felses. Von vornherein sollte man auf die recht strenge Bewertung gefaßt sein, die ihre Gnadenlosigkeit bis in die oberste Etage hinein durchhält. Man zähle zur "normalen" französchen Skala ruhig einen Grad hinzu (z.B. 6a wäre anderswo schon 6b). Derzeitig befindet sich Montanejos am Beginn einer Entwicklungsphase, die sicher damit enden wird, daß man den heruntergekommenen Kurort bald in einem Atemzug mit dem Frankenjura, dem Verdon und Buoux nennt.

In the former thermal baths of Montanejos, a mere fifty kilometers inland from the Costa de Azahar, there is not a trace of the tourist masses of the coast. The bath houses surrounding the hot springs are decaying, the rheumatism and arthritis patients have given way to mangy dogs and a handful of Valencian climbing punks. The excess energies of the young rebels in their protest against the norm prohibit them from accepting anything under grade 6. And this attitude is mirrored in the difficulty of all the climbs in this paradise for the hard core extremist. Since the beginning of the 1980's a variety of climbs have been put up in Montanejos ranging from 5 to 100 meters in length and generously bolted. The rock has an intricate and complicated structure, with horizontal, vertical, and diagonal cracks, flakes, holes, and edges in all conceivable forms and sizes. This demands a high degree of perception, creativity and good footwork, whereas the rough surface of the rock can only be met with a certain masochism, willpower, or stoic equanimity. Nowhere else does the word "smooth" say more about the ability of the climber and less about the quality of the rock. Be warned of the extreme stiffness of the grading, that doesn't let up even at the upper end of the scale. If you add a degree to normal French grades you approach the ratings of other areas (6a here would be 6b elsewhere). Montanejos is at the beginning of a phase of development which will surely end in the fact that this run down watering place will become a Mecca for climbers comparable to the best Europe has to offer.

APPROACH

1. Stay on the A 7 till the exit Castellon South. Follow the N 340 to Villareal, turn right to Onda, and reach Montanejos via Vallat, El Tormo and Cirat.

ANFAHRT

1. Auf der A 7 bis Castellon Süd. Weiter auf der N 340 nach Villareal, rechts ab nach Onda und über Vallat, El Tormo und Cirat nach Montanejos.

2. Von Valencia auf der N 234 über Segorbe nach Jerica. Hier rechts ab und über Caudiel und Montan nach Montanejos.

ÜBERNACHTUNG

Wilde Zeltler werden in Montanejos verjagt.Auf dem "Camping de Conan" kann man (noch) gratis zelten, es gibt Wasser, jedoch keine Toiletten. Wollen wir eine Lavaredohüttensituation vermeiden, ist die Mitnahme eines Spatens angebracht. Im Refugio de la Maimona bieten Pilar und Ernesto um wenig Geld Matratzenlager an.

VERSORGUNG

Die "Futterbasics" gibt es in Montanejos, Exquisiteres muß eingeführt werden. Im Rifugio gibt es Puder, Kalkbeutel und Bolzen aller Größe. Neben der Hütte ist die Bar Mijares der Treffpunkt der Kletterszene. Will man abends einmal gut essen, so ist die Katakombenkneipe "La Piedraza", gleich beim Zeltplatz, nur zu empfehlen.

WEITERE INFORMATIONEN

In der Hütte liegt ein wohlgehütetes und immer aktuelles Routenbuch aus. Ernesto weiß alles: was, wo, wer, wie, nur natürlich, wie wir alle, nicht so richtig warum.

2. From Valencia take the N 234 via Segorbe to Jerica. From here turn right to reach Montanejos via Caudiel and Montan.

If you are using public transportation there is daily bus service from Valencia to Montanejos.

CAMPING

Unsupervised camping is prohibited in Montanejos and the restrictions, unlike in the rest of Spain, are strictly enforced. Camping is (still) free at the Camping de Conan where water is available, but not toilets. In order to avoid a "Lavaredo situation", it is advisable to bring a spade. Across the bridge in the Refugio de Maimona you can spend the night in Pilar and Ernesto's climbing hut for a very reasonable sum.

SUPPLIES

Ordinary staples are available on Montanejos, luxuries are not. In the hut you can buy chalk, chalk bags, and bolts of all sizes. The friendly guardians also offer generous portions of reasonably priced meals and cafe con leche by the pot. Besides the hut, the climbers gather in the Bar Mijares. If you feel like a more lavish meal, you will appreciate the unique atmosphere in the catacomb of the restaurant La Piedraza, directly adjacent to the campsite.

FURTHER INFORMATION

In the hut you will find a well-guarded and well-groomed route book.

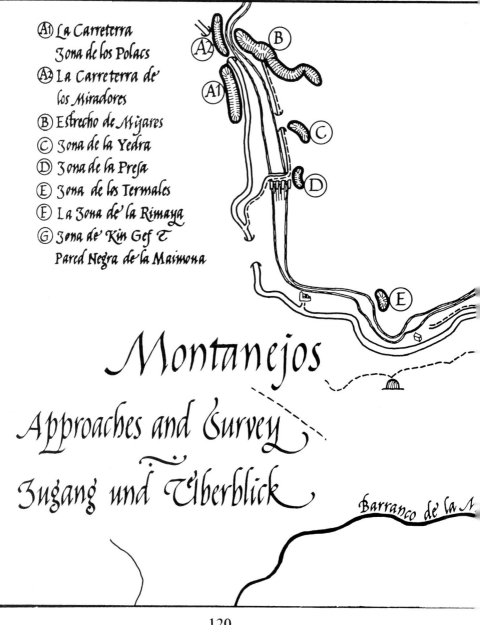

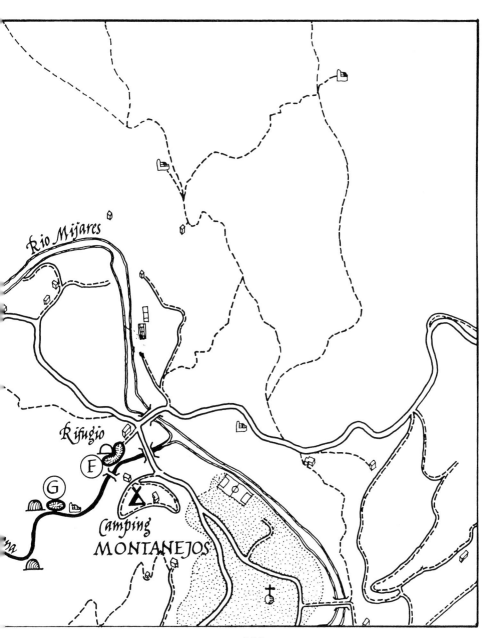

PARED DE LA CARRETERA
LA ZONA DE LA POLACA

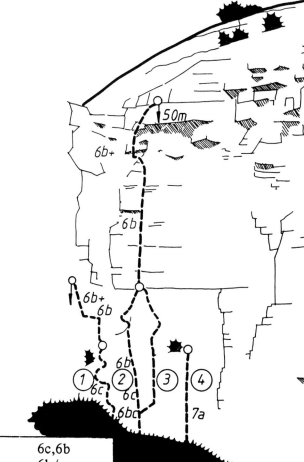

1	Loco Motoro	6c,6b
2	La Polaca Ataca	6b/c
3	Ordevas	6b+
4	Via Antiqua	7a
5	Alta Tension	6a A1
6	Delicatesem Rouge	6a+,6a,6a,6a
7	Eh Donde Vai Desgrasiato	6b+,6b,6a
8	Pelud de Caixeta	5+

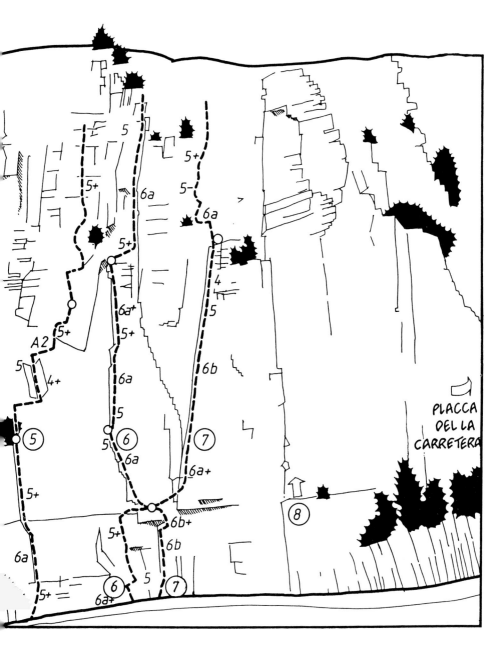

PARED DE LA CARRETERA
LA PLACA DE LA CARRETERA

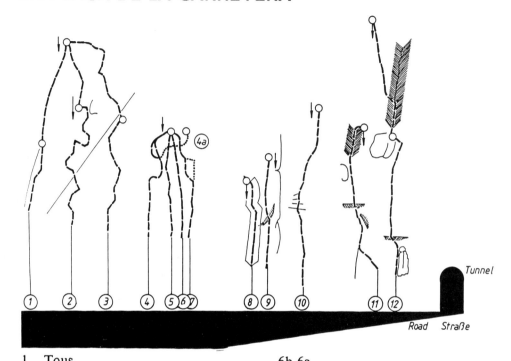

1	Tous	6b,6a
2	Oye Nena Yo Soy un Artista	6c
3	Nata y Fresas	6a,6a
4	La Agarraera	6b
4a	El Hereje	6a
5	Diabolo Grenadine	6b+
6	Ferran el Carnicero	6c+
7	La Derrota	6a+
8	Diedro Hermanos Marx	5+
9	Filomeno si te Aseguras es Menos	6a+
10	Moriras Jove	6c+/7a
11	El Mirador de Loco	6a+
12	El Baile de los Colgados	6a,5

PARED DE LA CARRETERA
LA PARED DE LOS MIRADORES

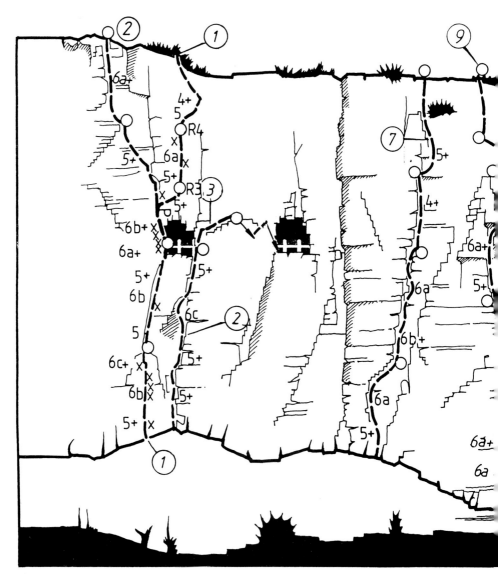

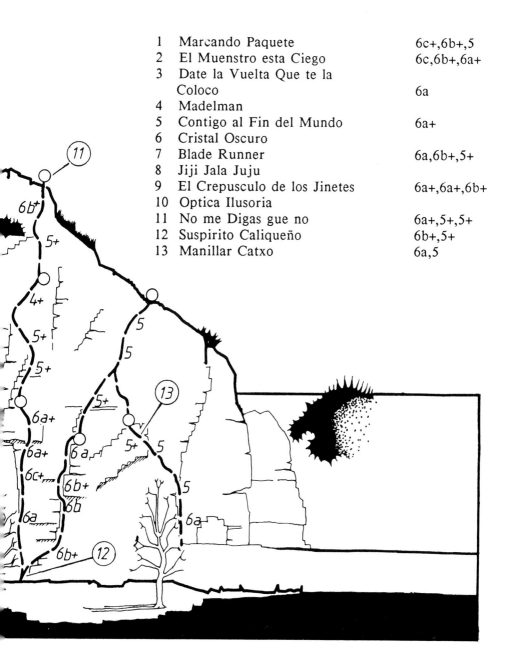

1	Marcando Paquete	6c+,6b+,5
2	El Muenstro esta Ciego	6c,6b+,6a+
3	Date la Vuelta Que te la Coloco	6a
4	Madelman	
5	Contigo al Fin del Mundo	6a+
6	Cristal Oscuro	
7	Blade Runner	6a,6b+,5+
8	Jiji Jala Juju	
9	El Crepusculo de los Jinetes	6a+,6a+,6b+
10	Optica Ilusoria	
11	No me Digas gue no	6a+,5+,5+
12	Suspirito Caliqueño	6b+,5+
13	Manillar Catxo	6a,5

EL ESTRECHO DE MIJARES

1	No me Toques que me Escito	6a+,5+,5+
2	La Broma de Satan	6a+,6b,6b+
3	Mescalina	6b
4	Sobredosis de Passion	6a,6a
5	Ser o no Ser	6b,6b+
6	Mi Padre Tiene el Sida	6b+
7	Relax	6b+,7a,7b+,6a
8a	Paralisis por Analisis	6b,6b+
8	Solo para tus Ojos	6b,6c,6c,6b
9	Solo Para tus Hijos	6c+
10	Manto Gris	5+,5 A0,6b
11	Intravenosa	7a
12	Deportes Moral	A1,A2
13	Techo Pirineos	A1
14	Directa Joaquin Blume	5+,A2
15	Garganta Profunda	A2
16	Flash Gordon	5+
17	Crispunk	6a A0,6c+
18	Escalera de los Dioses	4,5 A0,5+,6b,A2,5
19	Kyn Gefillo	6c+
20	G.P. (Jepe)	5,5,3,4,1,4
21	Vordina	7b+
22	Pelix de Guerrix	7a
23	Variante Paloma	5
24	Trilitate	4+,5+,6a
25	La vestuta Morla	7a,6a+
26	Pericondrio Tragal	5,5+,5+,4
27	Esfinge	6a,6b+,6b
28	Amanaciedo con la Casa Ardiendo	6a+

29	Aberraciones Sexuales de una Ninfomana	7b+,5+,4+
30	Anacoreta	
31	Poleo Menta	6b,6c,5+
32	Es Mucho	6c+,6c
33	Dame Veneno	6c, 6b
34	Maxima ansiedad	6b,6c,5+
35	Los Huevos de Tarancon que Duros son	6b+,6c,6b A0
36	Leonor	6c+,6a,6c
37	Viacrucis	
38	Eclipse de Luna	
39	Algebra tensorial	
40	Rasca Mama	
41	Oxido de Sobaco	6a+

ESTRECHO DE MIJARES
ÜBERBLICK - A SURVEY

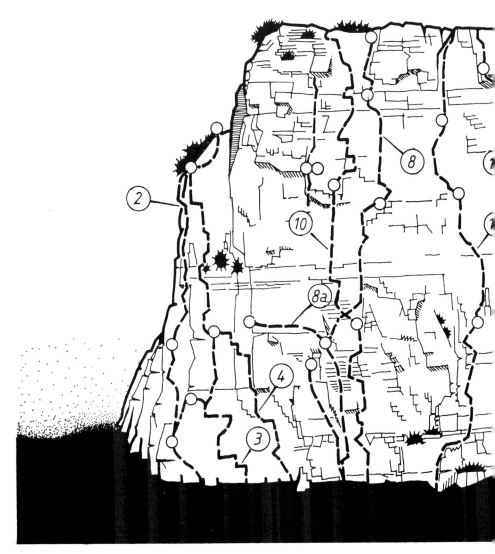

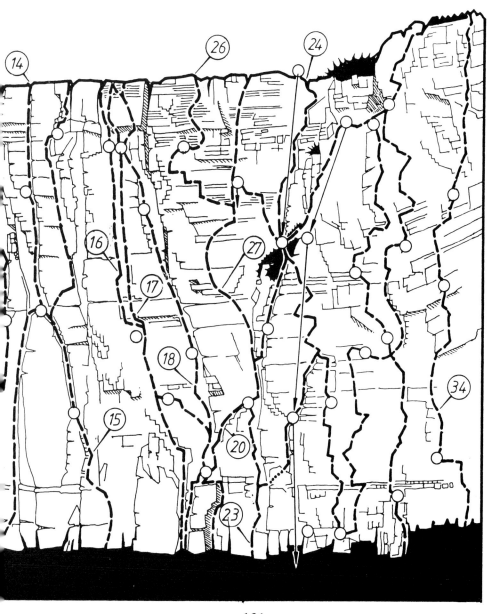

ESTRECHO DE MIJARES
LINKER WANDTEIL
LEFT SIDE

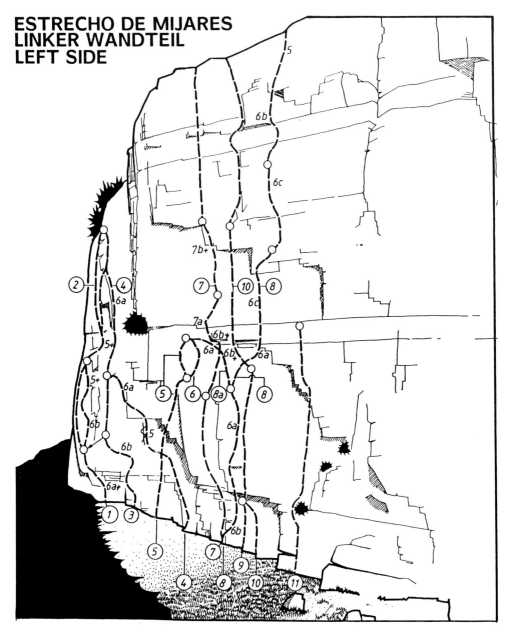

ESTRECHO DE MIJARES
RECHTER WANDTEIL – RIGHT SIDE

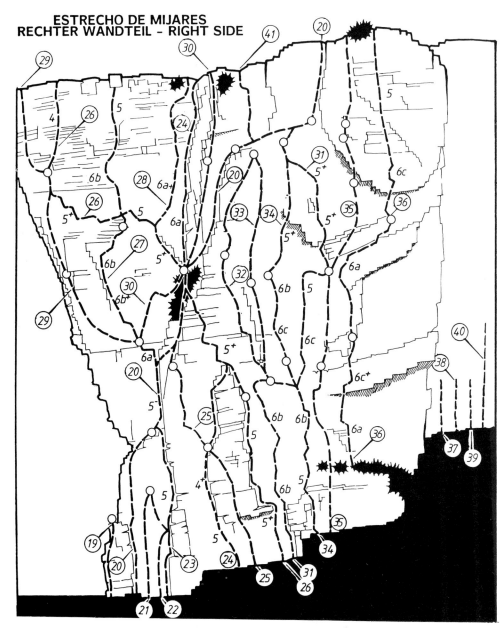

ZONA DE LA YEDRA

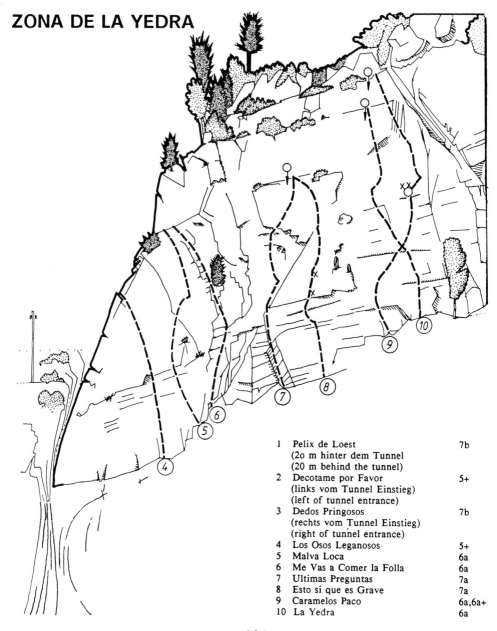

1	Pelix de Loest (2o m hinter dem Tunnel) (20 m behind the tunnel)	7b
2	Decotame por Favor (links vom Tunnel Einstieg) (left of tunnel entrance)	5+
3	Dedos Pringosos (rechts vom Tunnel Einstieg) (right of tunnel entrance)	7b
4	Los Osos Leganosos	5+
5	Malva Loca	6a
6	Me Vas a Comer la Folla	6a
7	Ultimas Preguntas	7a
8	Esto si que es Grave	7a
9	Caramelos Paco	6a,6a+
10	La Yedra	6a

ZONA DE LA PRESA

1		6c
2	Ce n'st pas l'Alpinisme	7a
3	A Ver Quien es mas Punkys	7a+
4	Escupe al Alkalde	7a
5	Boximania	6c
6	Decotame por Favor	5+

ZONA DE LA RIMAYA / ZONA DE LOS TERMALES

LA ZONA DE LOS TERMALES

1	Crucificcion	6a
2	Jimi Jazz	6a
3	No me Gustan los Hippis	6a+
4	Mama-Mia	6c
5	Fuera Bikinis	6b
6	Ca la Perdra	6c
7	La Hipotenusa	6c+

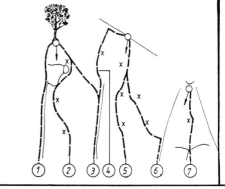

LA ZONA DE LA RIMAYA

1	Pata-Pato	6c
2	Greta Garbo	6b
3	Capitan Garfio	6c+
4	Brinwell	6c+
5	No Cal le Menestrer	7c+
6	La Sabenis-Tachenco	7a+
7	Zarza-Mora	6b

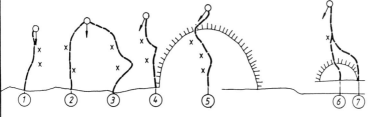

ZONA DE KIN GEF

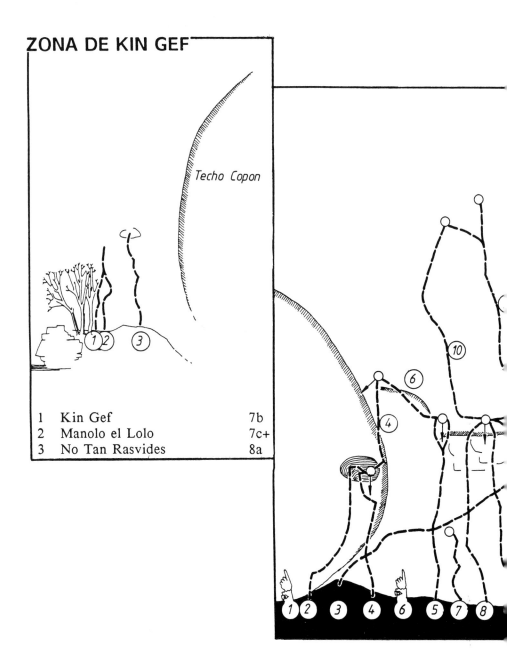

Techo Copon

1	Kin Gef	7b
2	Manolo el Lolo	7c+
3	No Tan Rasvides	8a

PARED NEGRA DE LA MAIMONA

1	Techo Copon	A2+
2	A la Vejez Viruelas	6c
3	Mister Proper	5+,5+,
4	Un Caso de Emberga-Dura	6c,7a+
5	Relaciones Sexuales con un Mosquito	7a
6	Sinbad el Marino	6c
7	El Gef de la Costa	6c
8	Canito Free	6b
9	Pa la Kaka	6b
10	Furor Uterino	6a,6a
11	Sexo, Droga y Rotpunk	6a,6a+
12	Natural Mistic	6a,5+
13	Nanas	5
14	Gozas Negro	6b
15	Fina y Segura	5,4
16	Teunch	5+
17	A Bocaos ta Mato	5

11. SIURANA

Das Zauberwort "Siurana" läßt bei Eingeweihten das Bild aufblitzen von einem Felsennest, hoch droben auf dem windzerblasenen Kamm eines Berges in Katalanien. In weiten Kehren windet sich die Schotterpiste herauf aus den Haselnußplantagen im Tal von Cornudella; auf halber Höhe duckt das Sträßchen unter den roten Überhängen einer mächtigen Sandsteinschicht hindurch, um sich dann durch tief eingeschnittene Schluchten weiter zur harten Kalkkruste der Hochfläche emporzuschlängeln. Die "Reina Mora", eine stolze Maurenkönigin, hat dafür gesorgt, daß das Städchen Siurana wenigstens zu regionaler Berühmtheit gelangt ist. Bei der "Reconquista", der Wiedereroberung der Halbinsel durch die Christen, stürzte sie sich lieber auf dem Rücken ihres Pferdes über die heute nach ihr benannte Felswand, als sich den ungläubigen Barbaren zu ergeben. Das Städtchen auf dem Berggrat hat heute fließendes Wasser, elektrisches Licht und ein paar Autos auf dem Parkplatz vor den Toren. Winters frieren die Leute im kalten Nordwestwind, im Frühling und Herbst wird das Nest zum "Geheimtip" für gewiefte Touristen, während im Sommer tagsüber die Sonne jedes Leben lähmt.

Zu Beginn der achziger Jahre begannen sich Kletterer der "klassischen" Schule für die Felsabbrüche des Hochplateaus, auf dessen südwestlichem Zipfel das Städtchen liegt, zu interessieren. Nach und nach konzentrierte sich die Aufmerksamkeit auf zwei übereinandergelagerte Felsstreifen, die sich nordöstlich der Burg, ober- und unterhalb des "Cami de la Trona" ca. 500 Meter weit am Berghang entlangziehen. Diese Felsstreifen, zwischen 8 und 30 Meter hoch, wurden zu einem Wallfahrtsort der Jünger der absoluten Schwierigkeit. Um das Setting und die Stimmung zu verstehen, führe man sich einfach folgende Formel zu Gemüte: ((Klagemauer + Weißer Stein) X 20) - Niederschlag. Wer nicht zumindest den 6. Grad draufhat, sollte einen Besuch von Siurana hauptsächlich als Sightseeing-Tour planen. Auch für den "Normalextremen" gibt es höchstens

To the initiated the magic word Siurana evokes images of a rocky citadel perched high up on the windswept ridge of a Catalonian mountain. A gravel road winds up the hill in steep, narrow curves out of the hazelnut plantations in the valley of Cornudella, the town below. About halfway up the hill the road ducks underneath the red overhangs of a sandstone stratum and then continues on up, through the deep gorges that end in the hard limestone crust of the high plateau. Here the "Reina Mora", a proud moorish queen assured Siurana at least local fame. During the "Reconquista", the reconquering of the peninsula by the Christians, she preferred a flying leap off the walls of the citadel on her horse, to captivity by the infidels. Today the village sports electricity, running water, and a few cars in the parking lot outside the gates. In winter, the cold northwest wind chills the bones of the inhabitants. In spring and autumn the village becomes the secret hang-out of informed Catalonian urbanites, whereas in summer, the sun lames any daytime activity.

At the beginning of the 80's climbers of the classical school began taking interest in the drop-offs of the high plateau on whose southwest tip the village is situated. Gradually this interest was concentrated on two rock bands to the northeast of the fortress above and below the "Cami de la Trona". The ordinary climber (<6a) will find at best two days' worth of climbing activity here, particularly on the "Can Marge". The chief customers of this open air gymnasium have naturally influenced the type of grading and the pro here. Those who still manage to flash a friendly smile while doing a 6b in Finale may find that this same grin stiffens to a grimace in a V+ in Siurana. In contrast to Montanejos, however, on towards the upper end of the scale the grading becomes more atuned to customary French ratings.

zwei Tage lang, vor allem an der "Can Marge", alpinistisches Betätigungspotential. Die Hauptkundschaft unserer Freiluftturnhalle hat naturlich auch die Schwierigkeitsbewertung und Absicherung geprägt. Leute, die in Finale im 6b-Gelände noch lächeln, sollten sich nicht wundern, wenn sich in Siurana bei V+ die Zeichen einer weniger frohen Gemütsverfassung kundtun. Keine Angst: nach oben hin nähern sich die Skalen wieder auf verflixtvertrixte Weise.

ANFAHRT

Auf der A 7 bis Reus. Von hier 7 Kilometer auf der N 420 und links ab auf der C 242 über Borges del Camp und Alforja nach Cornudella. Ca. 500 Meter nach dem Ortsausgangsschild in Richtung Albarca biegt nach rechts das Sträßchen nach Siurana ab, auf dem man nach ca. 7 Kilometer zum Parkplatz außerhalb des Städtchens gelangt.

ÜBERNACHTUNG

Direkt auf der ausgesetztesten Gratkante von Siurana unterhält der katalanische Exkursionistenverein eine Hütte, den Schlüssel erhält man in der Poststelle. Wildes Zelten wird in der Umgebung von Siurana noch geduldet. Unbedingt offenes Feuer vermeiden, Spuren von Brandkatastophen sind überall zu sehen! Es dauert Jahrzehnte, bis sich die Vegetation wieder erholt.

APPROACH

Take the A 7 to Reus. From here drive 7 kilometers on the N 420 and turn right onto the C 242 to reach Cornudella via Borges del Camp and Alforja. Some 500 meters after the town exit in the direction of Albarca, a small road turns off to the right toward Siurana. Follow this for another 7 kilometers to the parking site outside the village gates.

LODGING

The Catalonian Tourist Club has a hut situated on top of a rock pinnacle overlooking the whole arena below. The key can be obtained from the post office. Camping is still tolerated in the vicinity of Siurana, but open fires are not! Traces of forest fires are evident everywhere and the vegetation, once gone takes decades to revive.

SUPPLIES

The Bar/Restaurant Siurana serves simple meals and liquids in abundance. Anything your require in the way of nourishment beyond what you can buy in the restaurant, you will have to import.

FURTHER INFORMATION

There is a route book in the bar.

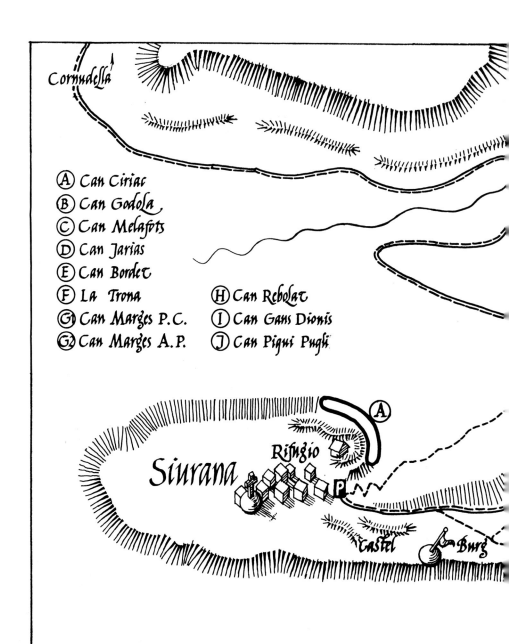

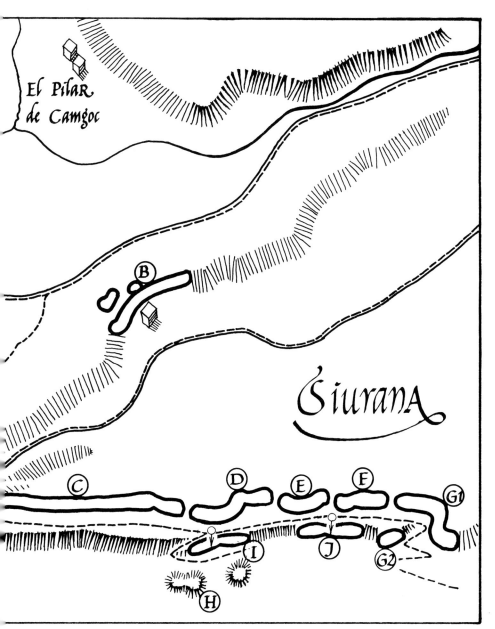

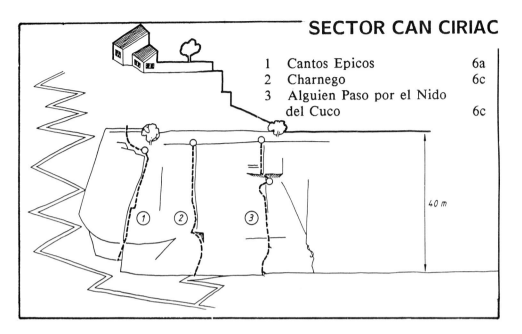

SECTOR CAN CIRIAC

1 Cantos Epicos — 6a
2 Charnego — 6c
3 Alguien Paso por el Nido del Cuco — 6c

40 m

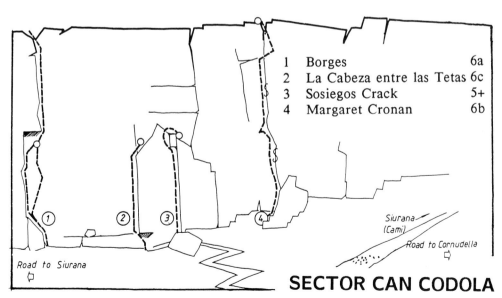

1 Borges — 6a
2 La Cabeza entre las Tetas — 6c
3 Sosiegos Crack — 5+
4 Margaret Cronan — 6b

Siurana (Cami)
Road to Cornudella
Road to Siurana

SECTOR CAN CODOLA

SECTOR CAN MELAFOTS

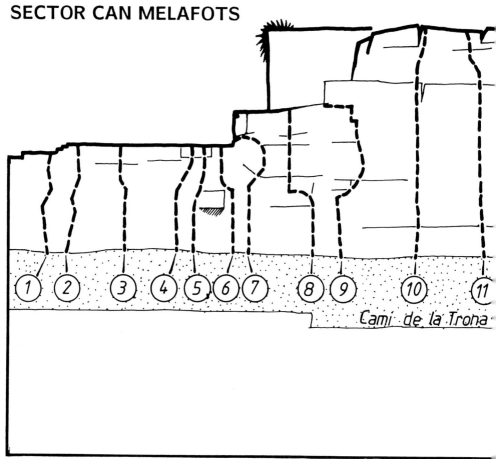

1	Per Triunfa la Canacca	6a
2	Escroto Roto	6a
3	Tan Pate el Pa con el Pate	6c
4	El Pate Tambe te te	6b
5	Todo es de Color	5+
6	Rompepechos	6b
7	Mi Primer Spit	6a
8	Ya Callate	6c
9	Ya Riete	6b

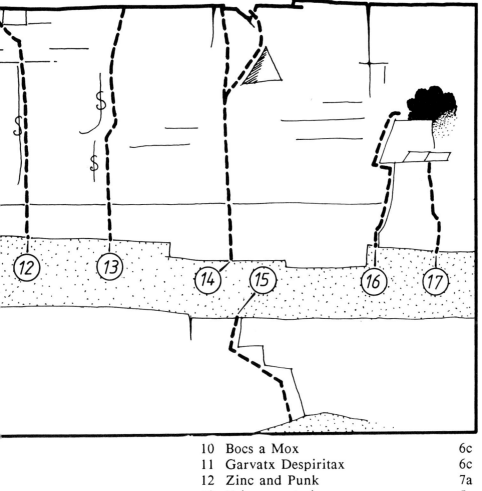

10	Bocs a Mox	6c
11	Garvatx Despiritax	6c
12	Zinc and Punk	7a
13	Trigonometeria	5+
14	Trianculo	5
15	Calsenta Motores	5-
16	De Officio: Jus Labores	6a
17	Rivet	6c

SECTOR LA TRONA

1. Que me le Photo — 6b
2. Tismol Jovillas — 4+
3. Al vostre Gust — 6b
4. Ponte a cuatro Patas y Grita como un Cervo — 5+
5. Tales of Quales — 7a

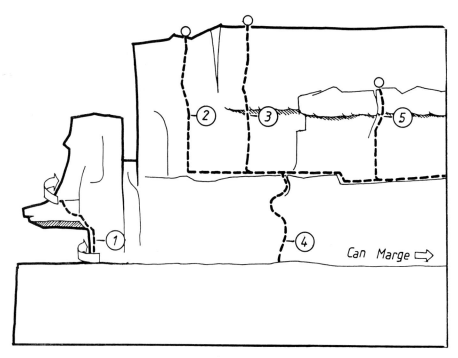

SECTOR CAN MARGES A.P.

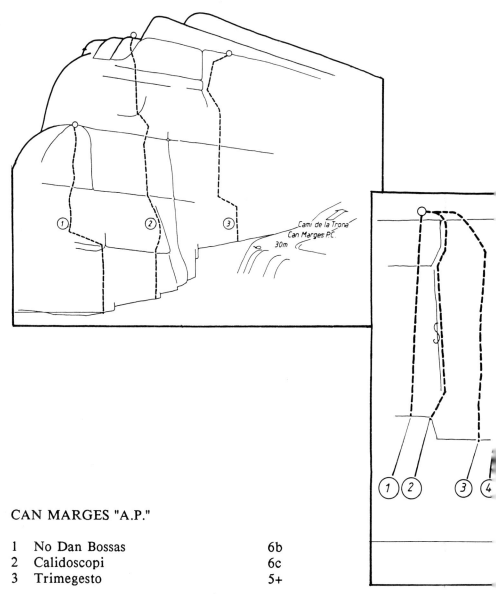

CAN MARGES "A.P."

1 No Dan Bossas   6b
2 Calidoscopi   6c
3 Trimegesto   5+

#	Route	Grade
1	Re i no Remes	6c
2	Pasatemps	5-
3	Escuela de Calor	5+
4	Fletxa	4+
5	Capricho	5
6	Spit de Boira	5
7	La Ultima del '85	5
8	Cos lo Cau	5
9	Cos que Cau	5
10	Caca Controlada	6a
11	Morron y Cuenta Nueva	6a
12	Only Tamax	6a+
13	Me Rio de Janeiro	6b+

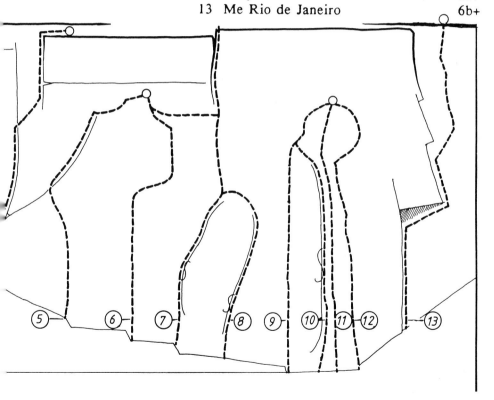

SECTOR CAN MARGES P.C.

SECTOR CAN GANS DIONIS

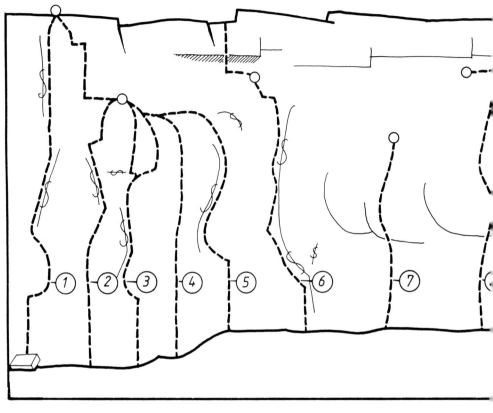

1	La Tubergolosa	5
2	Escuralamoza	6b
3	Eto e Tota	6c
4	Bsconderos Acujidos	6c
5	Eto e Diferrenfe	5+/6a
6	Hielo Gris	6a
7	Chute de Jalea	6b
8	Agonia Vaiant	6b/c
9	No Tires Tanto que te Pones Tonto	7a
10	S'ha de Badar	7a
11	Massa Temps Sense Piano	6b
12	Il n'y a pas de Fina	7b
13	Pende la Teta	7a
14	Kurt de Gandals	7a/
15	Dios Nidor	7c

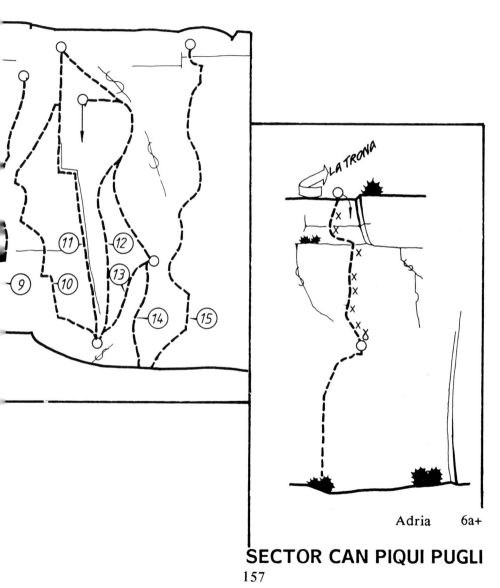

Adria 6a+

SECTOR CAN PIQUI PUGLI

12. MONTSERRAT

Der Montserrat ist sicher das traditionsreichste und bekannteste Klettergebiet der Iberischen Halbinsel. Es umfaßt ca. 40 Quadratkilometer mit über 600 Gipfeln und Nadeln. Wir beschränken uns hier auf die Beschreibung der Türme im Amphitheater von Sant Benet, oberhalb des Hauptklosters von Montserrat sowie auf die Darstellung der eher "voralpinen" Routen am Cavall Bernat, an der Pared dels Diables und an der Pared de l'Aeri. Die meisten der hier behandelten Routen weisen mehrere Seillängen auf, sind also "Klassiker" - im vierten bis 7b-ten Schwierigkeitsgrad. Am Panxa del Bisbe - dem westlichsten der großen Sant Benet-Türme - wurden auch die modernen Baseclimbs aufgenommen.

Jedoch kommen auch Leute, die das "Letzte im Fels" suchen, in dem beschriebenen Gebiet voll zu ihrem Recht. Hier einige Hinweise zu ihrer Orientierung: Die zwei wichtigsten Freiklettergebiete sind die "Zona del Camping" und die "Tochos". Die Mehrzahl der Routen des erstgenannten Gebiets finden sich entlang der "Via Crucis" und der "Via de la Santa Cueva", nur wenige Minuten vom Kloster entfernt. Die Routenverläufe sind unverfehlbar durch Petzlplatten gekennzeichnet. Informationen erhält man von April bis November beim Wart des Campingplatzes. Die "Tochos" befinden sich ca. 300 Meter unterhalb der Kletterhütte von Sant Benet, die man nach ca. halbstündigem Treppensteigen vom Kloster aus erreicht. Hier liegt ein Routenbuch aus, das immer auf dem neuesten Stand ist.

Wer glaubt, die Kletterei im Konglomerat sei eintönig und Kiesel immer ebenmäßig gerundet, ist noch nicht im Montserrat gewesen. Denn keine andere Felsart bietet solch eine Vielfalt an Griff- und Trittarten wie der montserratesische Waschbeton: scharfkantige Urgesteinssplitter, runde rote Sandsteinbollen und gerillte Karrenkalkbrocken sind fest eingebacken im harten alluvischen Zement. Und fast nirgendwo anders muß man so

Montserrat is probably the climbing area on the Iberian Peninsula that is richest in tradition and fame. It comprises an area of over 40 square kilometers with over 600 summits and needles. In this guideook we will limit ourselves to the description of the towers of the amphitheater of St. Benet, above the monastery of Montserrat, as well as a description of the some the rather alpine or prealpine routes on the Cavall Bernat, the Paret dels Diables and the Paret de l'Aeri. Most of the routes included here are several pitches long and can be considered the classics of the area, ranging from grades 4 to 7b. However, on the Painxa del Bisbe, the southeastern most of the large towers of Sant Benet, we also included the modern base climbs.

Nonetheless, those in search of the ultimate in rock need not feel short-changed in this area either. Here a few tips for orientation: The two important *freeclimbing* areas are the "Zona del Camping" and the "Tochos". Most of the routes near the campsite are along the "Via Cruces" and the "Via de la Santa Cueva", just a few minutes' walk from the monastery. The Petzl bolts wink at you from the rock to ease orientation. Information about them is available from the attendant at the camping area . The site is open from Easter until November. The "Tochos" are located some 300 meters below the Sant Benet climbers' hut. You reach the hut by climbing the stone steps above the monastery for half an hour. There is an up-to-date routebook in the hut.
Those who think that climbing on conglomerate always involves repetition of the same boring moves on uniformly rounded pebbles just haven't tried Montserrat. To the contrary, climbing on Montserrat is like a bloody geological field trip. Your right foot may be threatening to slip off a boulder of genuine sandstone, the instep of your other foot edging on a sharp crystal, while sweaty fingertips are slightly shaking in a gout d'eau of perfect Verdon quality limestone. You'll want to keep

viel Schauen, Denken und Herumstehen, bevor man vorsichtig, die Hände kaum jemals unter Kinnhöhe , die gut aufgeklappten Beine durchdrückt. Mußte man früher wegen der berüchtigten Sicherungsschrauben um sein Leben fürchten, so sind heute die meisten gängigen Führen mit exzellenten Bohrhaken saniert, so daß man fast immer mit wohligem Grausen an den runden Pfeilern hinab in die Tiefe blickt. Bisher habe ich mit niemandem gesprochen, der nicht vom Gesamterlebnis der Kletterei hier begeistert war. Es beginnt schon damit, daß man morgens aus der Eremitenhöhle kriecht um nachzuschaun, ob der weiße Zackenstreifen der Pyrenäen wieder sonnenbeschienen den Himmel vom Dunstmeer trennt. Und dann, nach Absolvierung der morgendlichen Teezeremonie, auf steilen Pfädchen durch eine der grünwuchernden Schluchten hinauf, um sich wieder einige Stunden mit einer senkrechten Denksportaufgabe herumzuplagen, ehe man sich mit dicken Armen in die Sonne legen oder bei "Nacho" in der Kletterhütte seinen Cafe con Leche schlürfen darf.

ANFAHRT

Von Barcelona auf der A 7 bis zur Ausfahrt Martorell/Montserrat. Auf der N II, bis rechts die N 150 nach Monistrol abbiegt. Von Monistrol auf der Serpentinenstraße 9 Kilometer zum Hauptkloster Montserrat.

ZUGÄNGE

1. Sant Benet

Vom Parkplatz des Klosters in südwestlicher Richtung durch das Gebäudeensemble, vorbei an der lokalen Filiale der Quardia Civil, zum Beginn des "Camino de los Hermitas". Auf ihm, endlose Stufen tretend, bis zur ersten Rechtsabzweigung (Schild). Hier rechts ab auf deutlichem Weg zur Kletterhütte von Sant Benet (25 bis 40 Minuten).

the center of gravity as close to the rock as possible, moving in dainty bridging little steps in the vicinity of "second position". If earlier the flimsiness of the old pro was cause for fear for one's life, today most of the trade routes have been so well equipped with good bolts that you can almost always let your gaze scan the rounded pillars into the depths with a shudder of pleasure. I have yet to talk to anyone who was not impressed with the quality of the total climbing experience here. It begins when you poke your nose out of one of the former hermits' caves to see whether the sugar-coated peaks of the Pyrenees are still separating the blue sunny sky from the sea of fog below. Then, following your ritual tea ceremony, you wind your way up a steep path through the green underbrush of one of the many gullies to spend some hours plaguing mind and body with a vertical crossword puzzle before you retire with swollen forearms for an afternoon in the sun or a pleasant a session of "cafe con leche" in Nacho's hut.

APPROACH

From Barcelona take the A 7 to the Mortorell/Montserrat exit. Stay on the N II till the N 150 branches right to Monistrol. From here curve up the hill 9 kilometers to the monastery.

1. Sant Benet

From the Parking lot of the monastery walk south through the building coimplex, jpast the "Guardia Civil", till you get the "Camino de las Hermitas". Takethe steep stairs of this path and stay on it until a marked path - the first fork at the top the stairs branches right to Sant Benet (25-40 minutes).

2. Cavall Bernat und Paret dels Diables

Von der Exkursionistenhütte bei Sta. Cecilia ca. 200 Meter auf der Straße in Richtung Hauptkloster bis rechts der Wanderweg Nr. 15 abbiegt. Ihm folgt man bis unterhalb der Wände. Nun gerade hinauf zu den Einstiegen (ca. 30 Minuten).

3. Paret de l'Aeri

Auf Wegspuren direkt von Sta. Cecilia (10 bis 20 Minuten).

ÜBERNACHTUNG

Die Kletterhütte von Sant Benet ist das ganze Jahr über meistens geöffnet, auf jeden Fall an den Wochenenden. Die Hütte beim Kloster Sta. Cecilia ist an den Wochenenden geöffnet. Auf dem Campingplatz beim Hauptkloster kann von der Osterwoche bis in den November übernachtet werden.

VERSORGUNG

Das ganze Montserrat-Kloster ist ein Supermarkt, billiger kauft man jedoch in Monistrol ein. In Sant Benet kann man für wenig Geld einfache Mahlzeiten erstehen.

BESTE ZEIT

Obwohl bei richtiger Routenauswahl auch im Hochsommer und Tiefwinter am Montserrat geklettert werden kann, dürften September bis November und Februar bis Mai die angenehmsten Jahresausschnitte hier sein.

2. Caval Bernat and Paret dels Diables

From the Excursionista hut near Sta. Cecilia, walk about 200 meters down the main road toward the monastery until you reach path #15 branching off toward the right. Follow it to beneath walls and scramble to the climbs from here (3o minutes from Sta. Cecilia).

3. Pared de l'Aeri

Go up a faint trail directly from Sta. Cecilia (10-30 minutes).

LODGING

1. The Rifugio St. Benet is open the year round, in winter at least weekends.

2. The campsite near the monastery is open from Easter until November.

3. The climbers' hut near Sta. Cecilia is open weekends

Monserrat

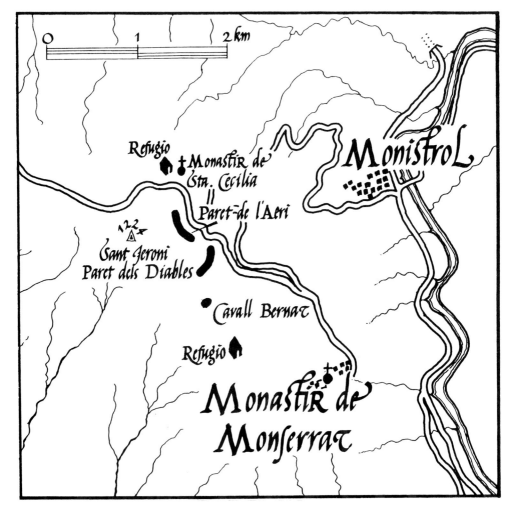

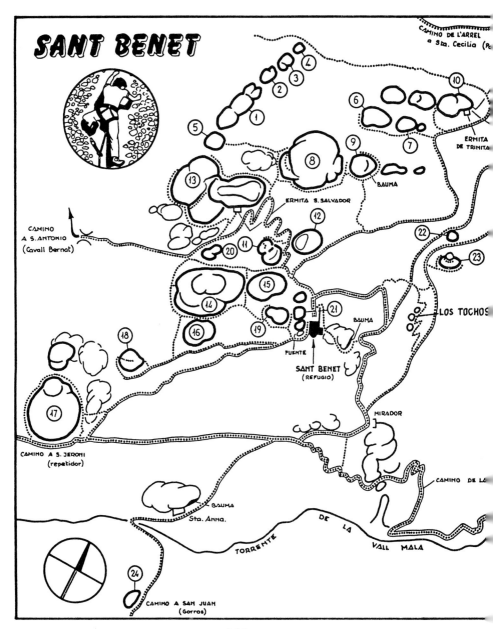

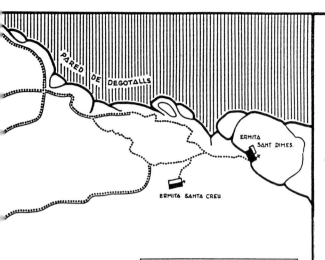

PANXA DEL BISBE
NORDWEST & WESTSEITE
NORTHWEST & WEST SIDE

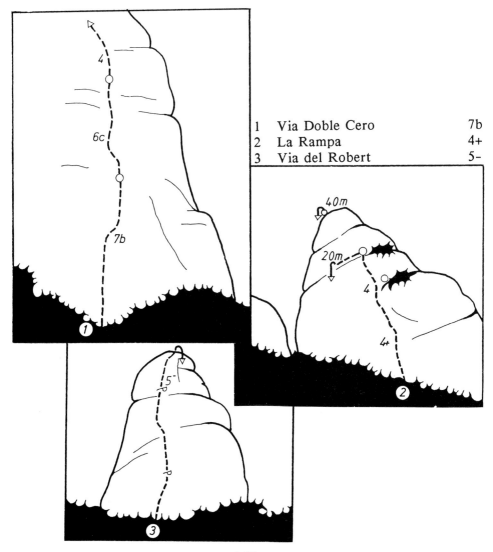

1	Via Doble Cero	7b
2	La Rampa	4+
3	Via del Robert	5-

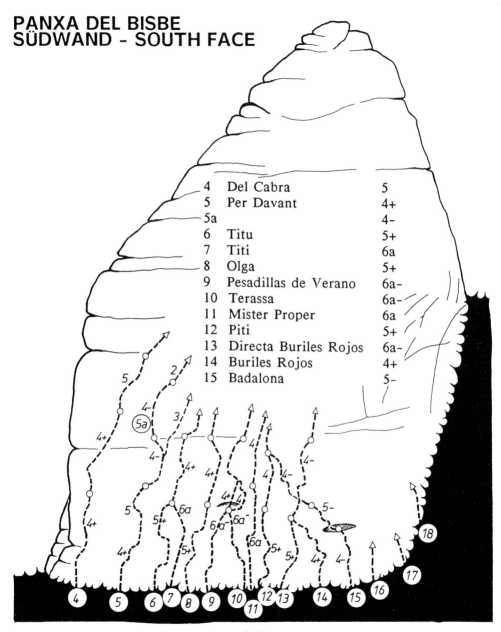

PANXA DEL BISBE
SÜDOSTWAND - SOUTHEAST FACE

16	Setze Jutges	5+
17	Metamorfosis	5+
18	Casanelles-Ludwing	6c
19	Que Monos Somos	7b
20	Au Va-Homme-Va	7c+/8a
21	Me Cago en mi Puta Vida	6b
22	La Polla Recorda	6b
23	Diedro Gris	5
24	Natura	6a

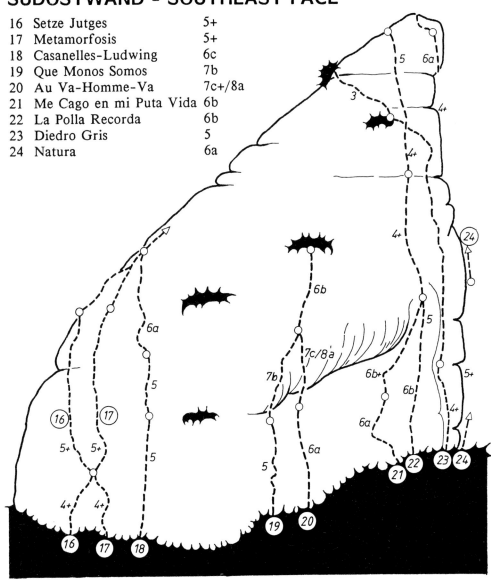

LA PRENYADA
SÜDSEITE 1 – SOUTH SIDE 1

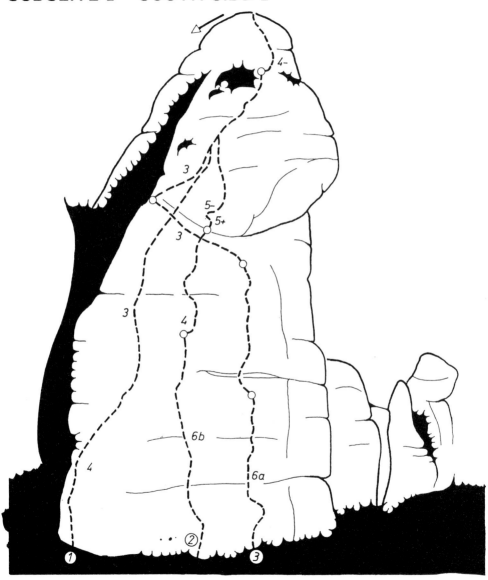

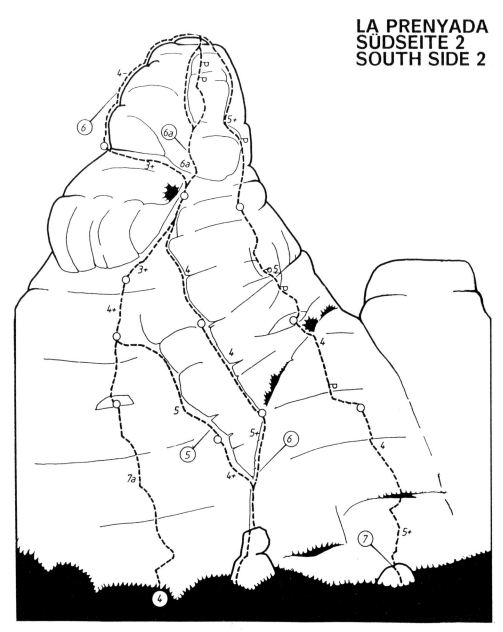

LA PRENYADA
SÜDSEITE - SOUTH SIDE
TOPO 1

1	Makoki	5-
2	Papi Mami (plaquetas)	6b
3	G.E.D.E. (plaquetas)	6a

TOPO 2

4	Monica	7a
5	Sardanyola	5
6	Gomez-Xalmat	5+ (4+ A0)
6a	Anglada-Cerda	6a
7	Baños de Sol	5+/6a

CONTRAFORT DE LA PRENYADA
SÜDWAND - SOUTH FACE

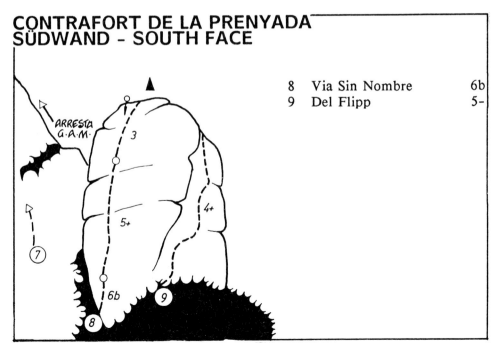

8	Via Sin Nombre	6b
9	Del Flipp	5-

CONTRAFORT & PRENYADA
NORDWÄNDE – NORTH FACES

10	Un Mundo para ellos	5
11	Chica de las Bragas de Oro	
12	Aresta G.A.M.	4+
13	Del Espejo	5-
14	Espelon Magico	5-
15	Cerda Puerco	6a

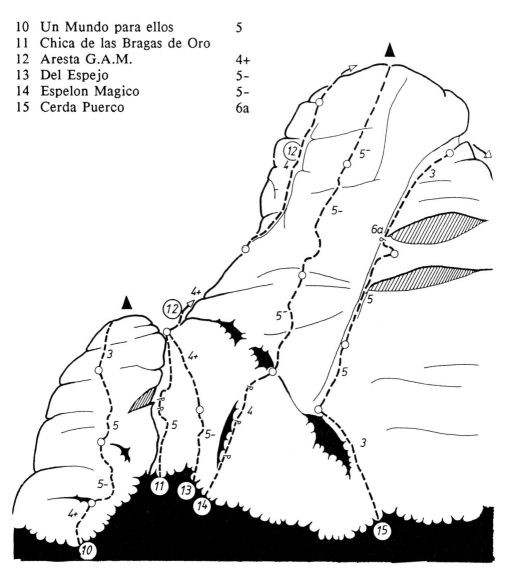

L'ELEFANT
SÜDOSTWAND - SOUTHEAST FACE

1	Laura	4+
2	Peque Mantacas (plaquetas)	5+
3	Agachate que t Han Visto	5
4	Diedro Capeta (plaquetas)	5+
5	Variante New Galactic	5+
6	Piripi-Piripa	5+ A1
7	Cerda Pokorski	6c (5 A0)
8	G.E.D.E.	6a+

L'ELEFANT
NORDWAND - NORTH FACE

9	Boy Rock	6a
10	Woman Rock	6a+
11	Inopia	6c
12	Capela Noves	5
13	Chica del Culo Gordo	5
14	Cerda-Pokorski	4+
15	Monistrol	4+

L'ELEFANT
NORDWESTWAND - NORTHWEST FACE

16	SAME	4+
17	El Muro	4+
18	Directa Julietta	5+
19	Harold Lloyd	5

L'ELEFANT
SÜDOSTWAND – SOUTHEAST FACE

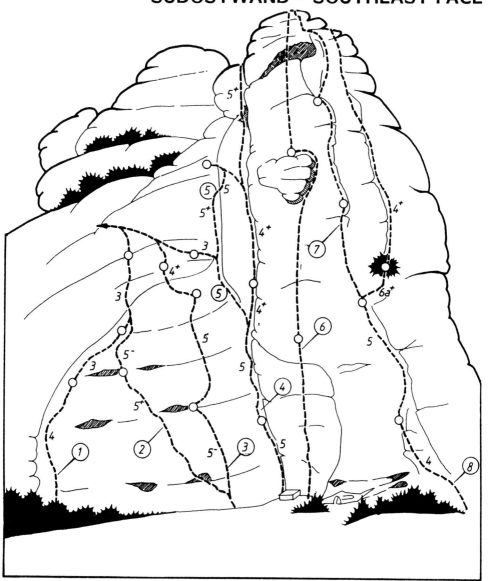

L'ELEFANT
NORDWAND – NORTH FACE

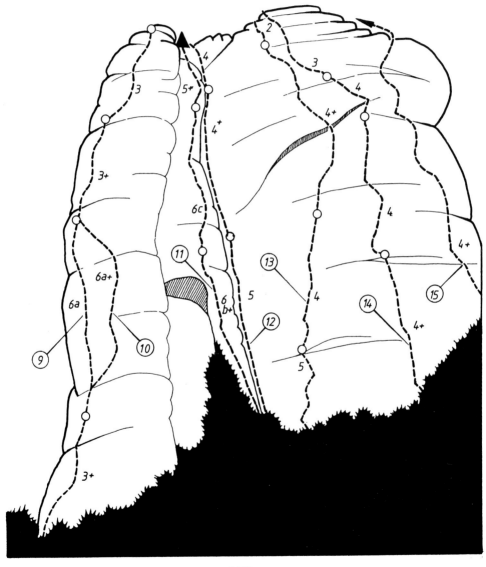

L'ELEFANT
NORDWESTWAND - NORTHWEST FACE

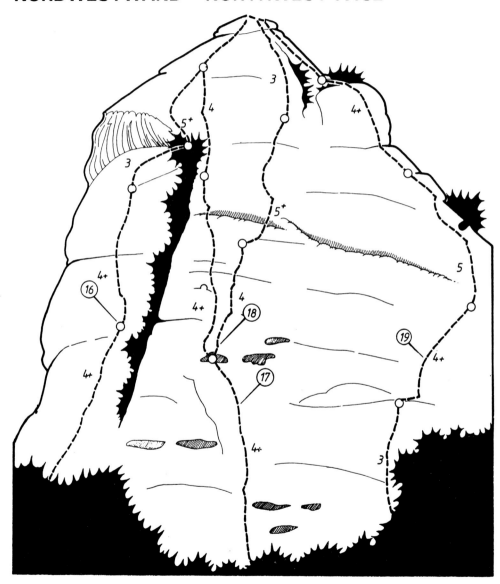

MOMIA & MOMIETA
SÜDOSTWAND - SOUTHEAST FACE

1	Brown Sugar	6b
1a		6c+
1b		6a+
2	Abre Cerveza	7a+/b-
3	Escandalo Publico	7a A0
4	Hans Extrems	4+
5	CESA	6a+
5a	Mas Guasch	6b
6	Sangre de Barrio	6c
7	Pirenaic	7a
8	Kumbaya	7a

MOMIETA
SUDOSTWAND - SOUTHEAST FACE

9	Normal	4
10	Pastel de Buitre	5+
11	Atmosfera Chunga	6c+/7a,
12	Kull de Mandrill	7a

NORDWÄNDE - NORTH FACES

13	Aresta GAM	5+
14	Dajad al Chico en Paz	7a+
15	Ha Mort la Tia	6c
16	Angel de Cuero	6c
17	Silvian	6b+
18	GAM	5+
19	Horxata de Xufa	5+

NORDWESTWAND - NORTHWEST FACE

20	Normal Route	4
21	Cistell	5
22	Castels Villena	4+
23	Codigo Neurotico	6a

MOMIA   SÜDOSTWAND - SOUTHEAST FACE

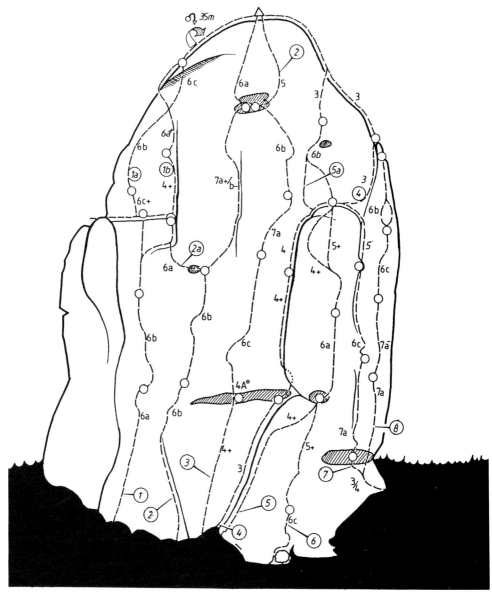

MOMIETA   SÜDOSTWAND - SOUTHEAST FACE

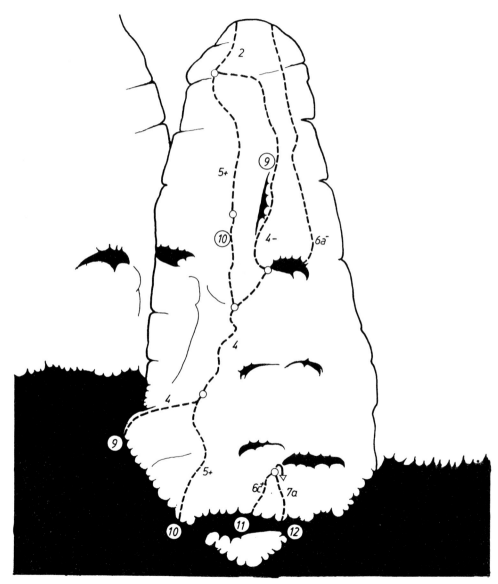

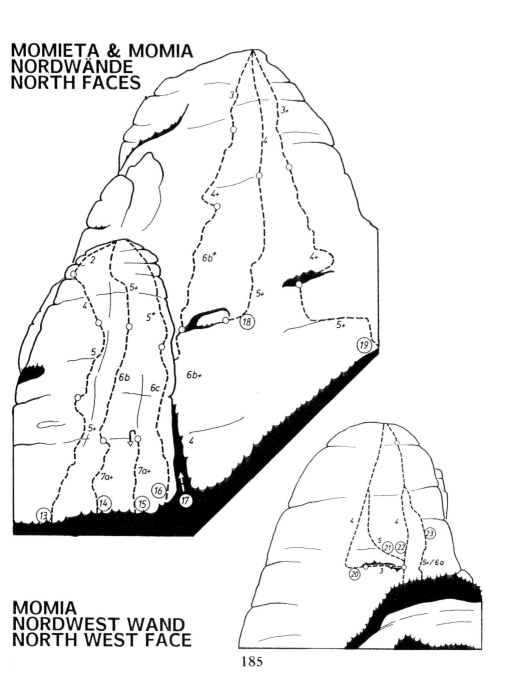

EL CAVALL BERNAT
ARESTA NORD - VIA PUNSOLA-RENIU
6a+ (5 A1), 7SL, 180m

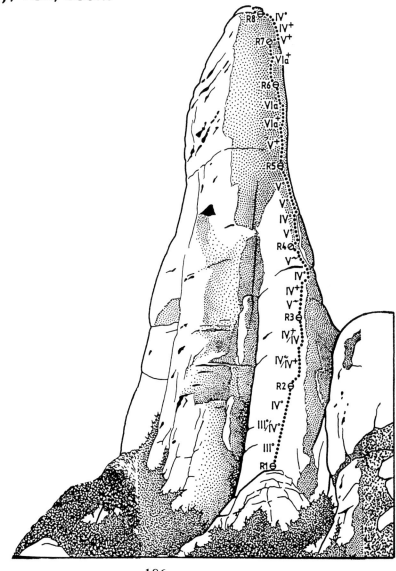

JÜRGEN BELZ

D-6900 Heidelberg 1 · Untere Straße 24
Telefon (0 62 21) 2 80 24

Alles für Berg- und Skihochtouren aus eigener Erfahrung.

Qualifizierte Beratung
umfassender Service,
sowie hochwertige Angebote.
Bergausrüstungen für jeden Zweck.

- Alle Hochtourenbindungen ständig am Lager
- Große Auswahl an internationaler Bergliteratur, Kartenmaterial und Routenbeschreibungen
- Leichtgewichtszelte aller führenden Marken
- Bergschuhe müssen passen, deshalb zum Fachmann (auch für Problemfüße)

**Ihr
Jürgen Belz**

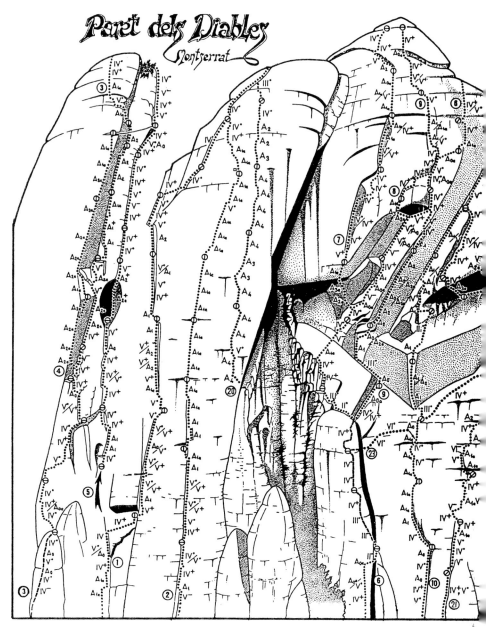

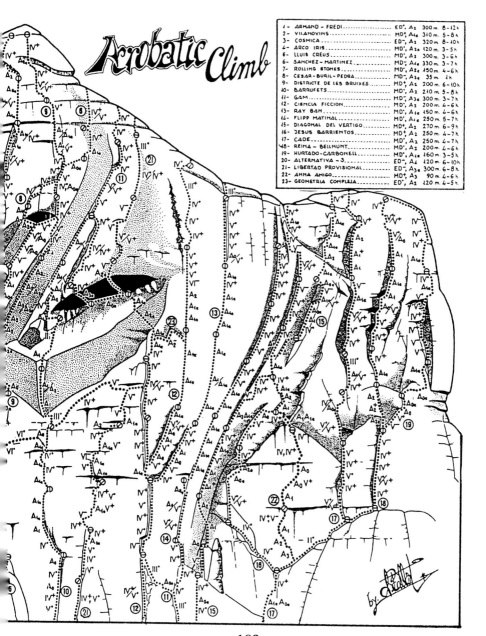

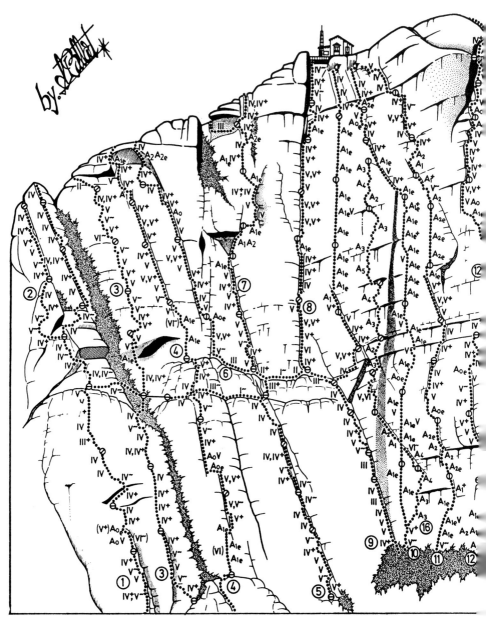

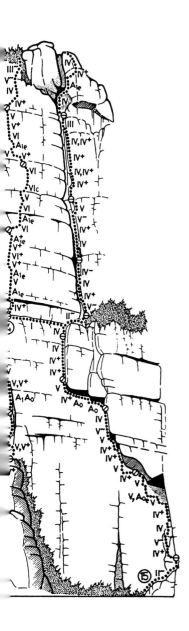

Paret de l'Aeri
Montserrat

Vias de Escalada

1- EASY RIDER .... MD⁻, A₀ₑ 300 m. 2-4 h.
2- TOPE TONI .... MD. 290 m. 4-5 h.
3- REENCUENTROS .... MD⁺-ED⁻ 300 m. 4-6 h.
4- GESAM ó TROYA .... MD⁺-ED⁻ 290 m. 5-7 h.
5- PANY - FARRERA .... BD⁺-MD⁻ 100 m. 1-3 h.
6- MAGIC STONES .... MD⁺-ED⁻ 150 m. 4-6 h.
7- ELECTRIC LADYLAND ..... MD, A₂ 160 m. 4-6 h.
8- TERRA i MAR (TIM) ...... MD⁺-ED⁻ 200 m. 4-6 h.
9- ANTONIO GARCIA .... MD, A₁ₑ 300 m. 4-7 n.
10- ANTONIO MACHIN .... MD, A₁ₑ 300 m. 4-7 h.
11- ANGLADA - CERDA .... ED⁻, A₂ 310 m. 8-10 h.
12- VALENTIN CASANOVAS ... MD⁺ A₁₋₂ 310 m. 6-8 h.
13- CADE .... MD-MD⁺ 120 m. 3-4 h.
14- OLESA .... ED-ED⁺ 160 m. 4-6 h.
15- NICOLAU-FREIXAS-BENITO . MD⁻, A₀ 320 m. 4-6 h.
16- MIRALL IMPENETRABLE .... ED, A₅ 215 m. ±25 h.

191

13. VINGRAU

Daß schon vor 300 000 Jahren die Leute wußten, wo es sich aushalten läßt, beweisen die Spuren, die der Tautavel-Mensch in einem sonnigen, windgeschützten Tal gleich nordwestlich der französischen Grenzstadt Perpignan hinterlassen hat. Verläßt man in Perpignan Nord die Autobahn und steuert hinauf in die Küstenhügel, taucht man ein in flimmerndes Grillengezirpe und betäubenden Lavendelduft. Auf Schlängelsträßchen geht's durch die weitläufigen Weinberge und verschlafenen Ortschaften, wo nur noch Kinder und Großeltern gelassen ausharren. Von heißem Kampf in steilem Fels keine Spur. Sobald nach Überquerung des Pas de l'Escale die Raffinerien an der Küste hinter der Kuppe des Sarrat de Montpeyrous versinken, wird die sanfte Kulisse urplötzlich um ein für unsereins wesentliches Element bereichert: die steilen hellen Platten und Pfeiler in der Südostflanke des Montagne de Vingrau. In den vergangenen zehn Jahren haben Kletterer aus dem Südwestzipfel der Grande Nation gut fünfzig Routen zwischen dem vierten und oberen siebten Franzosengrad erstbegangen. Das bis zu achzig Meter hohe und fast einen Kilometer lange Felsmassiv ist wie dazu geschaffen, auf der langen Fahrt nach Hispania einen Verschnauftag einzulegen. Sollten sich die Platten über Mittag gar zu sehr aufheizen, so sei geraten, es dem ältesten Menschen Europas gleichzutun. Denn nur wenige hundert Meter vom Auffindungsort unseres Vorfahren entfernt, lädt das Flüßchen Arago zu einer Abkühlungssiesta ein, die sicher keine Erfindung des 20. Jahrhunderts ist.

ANFAHRT

Von der Autobahnausfahrt Perpignan Nord nach Rivesaltes und 16 Kilometer in nordwestlicher Richtung auf der D 12 nach Vingrau. Ungefähr einen Kilometer hinter der Abzweigung nach Opoul-Perillos führt die Straße, bald nachdem man den Pas de l'Escale überquert hat, unter dem rechten Teil der

The imprints the Homo Tautavelensis left in the sunny, windstill valley just north of the French border town of Perpignan are proof that already 300,000 years ago discerning human beings knew where to seek the good life. When you leave the freeway at Perpignan North and steer towards the coastal hills you are submerged in a shrill cicada concert and intoxicated by the lavender fragrance. You wind uphill along the narrow roads through expansive vineyards and pass through sleepy towns where only pensioners and toddlers are still holding out. Nowhere a trace of the precipitous vertical forces. But as soon as you leave behind the coastal refineries and cross the Pas de'Escale you suddenly find yourself facing one significant addition to the landscape - the steep, light-colored limestone slabs of the southeast flank of the Montagne de Vingrau. In the past ten years climbers from the southwesterly corner of the "Grande Nation" have put up over fifty routes here (French 4-7c). The 80 meter high crag that extends for almost a kilometer seems to have just been made for a strategic break during the long drive south. If the midday sun heats up the slabs to warmer than your liking, follow the example of the oldest European man. For only some few hundred meters from the discovery site of our ancestor, the Arago River invites you to a refreshing midday siesta - certainly not an invention of the 20th century.

APPROACH

Take the freeway exit Perpignan North to Rivesaltes and continue in a northwesterly direction 16 kilometers to Vingrau. Roughly one kilometer after the intersection to Opoul-Perillos, the road leads over a small pass and descends directly beneath the Vingrau crags. There is a parking spot at the first hairpin curve (coming from the pass). Climbers are requested not to park elsewhere on the road, as this hinders the cumbersome

Vingrau-Wände hindurch. Parkplatz bei der ersten Serpentine (von oben gesehen). Bitte nur auf diesem Parkplatz das Fahrzeug abstellen, weil sonst die Gemüse- und Weinlaster auf dem engen Sträßchen behindert werden. Vom Parkplatz führen Zustiegspfade zu den Einstiegen. Bitte auf den Wegen bleiben, da die Vegetation es in diesem regenarmen Landstrich eh schon schwer genug hat.
Die Zustiege werden im Zusammenhang mit der Darstellung der einzelnen Sektoren beschrieben.

TECHNISCHE INFORMATIONEN

Wie die nebenstehende Karte auf den Seiten 200 & 201 zeigt, differenziert sich das Klettergebiet von Vingrau in 6 Teilareale.

Direkt über dem Parkplatz liegt, von der Straße aus deutlich sicht- und auf einem Pfädchen auch leicht erreichbar, der PILIER DES ANABOLISANTS. Die Führen hier sind steile Wand-, Platten-, und Rißklettereien.
Die Routen von links nach rechts:
- Dianabole   6a, 2SL
- Candarelle   6b+
- Le Délire   6b+
- Les Anabolisants   6b
- L'Erreur est Humaine   6b
- L'Emmental   4+/5 (ganz rechts)

Gleich rechts schließt sich der alte Übungsfels für Artif-Klettereien an. Hier sind jetzt die drei schwersten Routen des Gebiets zu finden (7b+, 7c, 7c+).

100 Meter weiter erhebt sich einer der höchsten Wandteile, die PARTIE CENTRALE, mit Routen von bis zu 3 Seillängen. Zu empfehlen sind:

supply trucks. Various paths lead from the parking site to the climbs. Please don't take shortcuts as the sparse precipitation in the area makes survival a tough process for the vegetation.
We will describe the approaches in connection with the route descriptions of the individual sectors.

TECHNICAL INFORMATION

As you can see on the map, the the climbing area of Vingrau is subdivided into six sectors.

The PILIER DES ANABOLISANTS is situated directly above the parking place and is easily reached from the path. The routes in this section are steep face, slab, and crack climbs.
From left to right the routes are:
- Dianabole   6a, 2 pitches
- Candarelle   6b+
- Le Délire   6b+
- Les Anabolisants   6b
- L'Erreur est Humaine   6b
- L'Emmental   4+/5 (far right)

Just to the right of these are the old aid routes. These have now become the hardest routes of the area (7b+,7c,7c+).

100 meters further is the PARTIE CENTRALE; the biggest crag has routes of up to three pitches on it. The best ones are:
-VDP   6a
-La Sysiphe no Piss 6a
-Le Grand Duc   6c

To the right near the street you will find well protected, technically interesting slab climbs. Between the Partie Centrale and the right sector you can grind rubber off your soles on the slabs.

You reach the SECTEUR DU PETIT DRU with its pleasant long routes by taking the path which leads north from the

- VDP 6a
- La Sysiphe no Piss 6a
- Le Grand Duc 6c

Im äußerst rechten Wandteil, nahe der Straße, warten technisch interessante und gut gesicherte Plattenklettereien. Zwischen der Partie Centrale und der rechten Zone kann man seine Sohlen in den abschmiersamen Platten verheizen.

Folgt man vom Parkplatz in der Kehre dem Wanderweg in Richtung Nordwesten über den kleinen Paß, so gelangt man zur kleinen Hütte und dem SECTEUR DU PETIT DRU mit längeren schönen Routen.
- La Lyonel 6a+, 3SL
- L'Hitre 6a/b, 3SL
- Le Pilier Rouge 4+/5, 3SL
- L'Alpsud 4+,5, 3SL
- La Dame Blanche 6a, 2SL
- Le Pilier Prat 6a/b

An der Platte direkt am Paß können wir Ihnen noch folgendes bieten:
- Fire Caca 5+/6a
- After Chèvre 6a
- 37 Grad le Matin 6b
- Le Marteau Sans Maitre 6b

ÜBERNACHTUNG & VERSORGUNG

Keep a low profile beim Zelteln und hinterlaßt keine Spuren. Die Versorgung mit Brot, Wein und Fisch ist fünftausendfach gesichert.

parking spot. This leads you over a small pass to a little climbers' hut and the Secteru du Petit Dru. Routes to try here are:

- La Lyonel   6a+, 3 pitches
- L'Hitre   6a/b, 3 pitches
- Le Pilier Rouge   4+/5, 3 pitches
- L'Alpsud   4+/5, 3 pitches
- La Dame Blanche   6a, 2 pitches
- Le Pilier Pra   6a/b

On the slab directly above the pass we can offer:
- Fire Caca   5+/6a
- After Chèvre   6a
- 37 Grad le Matin   6b
- Le Marteau sans Maitre   6b

CAMPING & SUPPLIES

Keep a low profile and leave no traces.

Bread, wine, and fish are available in unlimited quantities.

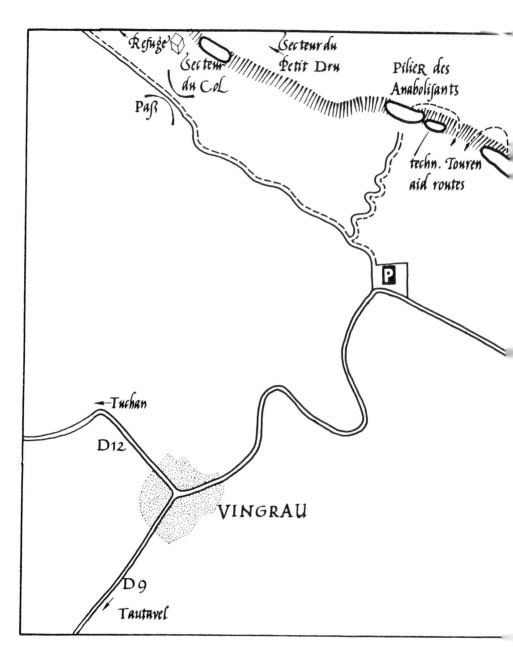

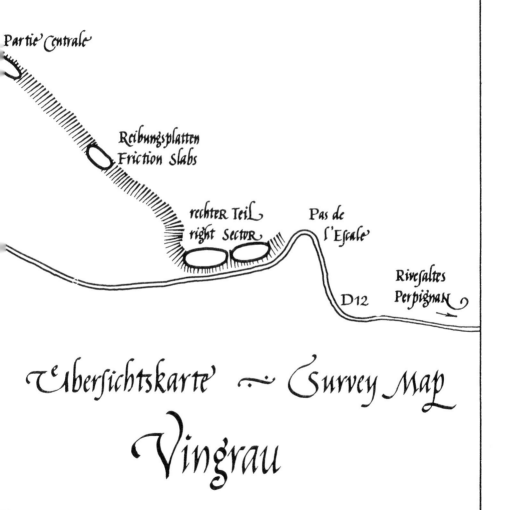

14. MOURIES

Als der französischen Hardrockszene in Buoux der Andrang barbarischer Horden aus dem Norden zuviel wurde, wichen die gestählten Profis ins Hinterland aus. Unter diesen Rückzugsgebieten ist Mouriès eine der Zugnummern. Und so werden unsere gallischen Freunde bald gezwungen sein, ihren Spürsinn erneut zu mobilisieren.
Den Felsgrat am Rande des Rhônedeltas kann man guten Gewissens als *das* archetypisch moderne Felsturngebiet bezeichnen, erfüllt es doch alle Ansprüche, die heute an ein Kletterparadies gestellt werden: guter grauer Fels, exzellente Absicherung und ein kurzer Zustieg. Die Wände sind nur ausnahmsweise höher als eine halbe Seillänge, so daß der Sichernde sich nie vom Boden wegbegeben muß, um an unbequemen Schlingenständen über der ängstigenden Tiefe herumzubaumeln. Dazu kommt, daß der Mouriès-Grat von Osten nach Westen verläuft und so, je nach Jahreszeit, die wärmende Sonne oder die schattige Kühle aufgesucht werden können. Die Nordseite bietet den Extra-Luxus, daß sie in einer saftig grünen Wiese fußt, die zum stufenlosen Übergang vom Picknick zur 7c, zur Siesta einlädt. Mouriès ist der ideale Ort, um sich nach einem "long and lonely winter" wieder Farbe und ein Lächeln ins Gesicht malen zu lassen. Hier findet man die günstigsten Bedingungen - und auch den Zwang - an seiner Technik zu feilen. Denn ohne eine saubere, vorausschauende Fußarbeit hat man trotz winterlicher Leistenübungen keine Chance. Die Platten sind so steil, daß die Fußspitzen meist unsichtbar unter einer grauen Wölbung herumtasten.
Nachdem das Klettergebiet Mouriès in einer französischen Alpinzeitschrift veröffentlicht worden war, strömten die Massen herbei. Die örtliche Bevölkerung war derartig entsetzt, daß das Gebiet sofort geschlossen wurde. Zähe Verhandlungen machten es möglich, daß heute wieder unter folgenden Bedingungen geklettert werden darf:
- die Olivenhaine der Umgebung sollten nicht betreten werden,

When the barbarian hordes from the North became too unwieldy for the French hardrock scene, the insiders fled to the hinterlands. One of the favorite retreat sites, Mouriès, is no longer the well-kept secret it was meant to be. So our Gallic friends will be forced to remobilize the their limestone geiger counters.
The rocky ridge at the edge of the Rhône delta can, in all good conscience, be labelled the archetypal modern rock gymnasium. It unquestionably has all the prerequisites of a climbing paradise - solid rock, good pro, short approach....Only in exceptional cases are the routes longer than half a pitch, so as to always permit the second a ground stance with the walkman - never a hanging belay or a glance into the dizzying depths. Moreover, the ridge runs east to west and permits a choice of sun or shade, depending on taste and season. The north facing flank offers an additional luxury - a lush green meadow at the base of the climbs where you can alternate between picnic, 7c, or siesta. Mouriès is the ideal spot to return the smile and the color to your face after a "long and lonely winter." Here you are presented with the convenient opportunity - and the necesssity - of polishing up your technique. For without foresight and decent footwork, even your winter's practice on the climbing wall won't let you cheat your way up the crag. The slabs are so steep, that your toes have to grope their way upward hidden beneath little overlaps and bulges.
After Mouriès had been publicized in a French climbing journal the crowds flocked to the new area. The local population was so shocked that the area was closed immediately. Tough negotiations made climbing possible under the following conditions:
- no trespassing in the olive groves,
- stay clear of the archeological dig,
- open fires and unsupervised camping are prohibited.

- man sollte um die archäologische Grabungsstätte einen Bogen machen,
- offenes Feuer ist untersagt und- wildes Zelten ist verboten.

ANFAHRT UND ZUGANG

Mouriès liegt an der D 17, vielleicht 25 Kilometer östlich von Arles. Die Zufahrt und der Zugang zu den Felsen ist auf den Karten auf den Seiten 206 & 207 dargestellt.

ÜBERNACHTUNG

Der Campingplatz bei Mouriès ist empfehlenswert. Das freundliche Besitzerehepaar hat ihn in einem Kiefernwald an der Mistral-Leeseite eines Hügels angelegt. Die sanitären Anlagen sind vorbildlich und die Lagereinheiten voneinander abgeschirmt.

VERSORGUNG

In Mouriès gibt es viele kleinere Läden, es lohnt sich jedoch, größere Einheiten in den Supermärkten zu Arles einzukaufen.

WEITERE INFORMATIONEN

Serge Jaulin, ESCALADES A MOURIES, Edisud, Aix en Provence 1987.

BESTE ZEIT

Wegen der günstigen Lage (wahlweise Nord- oder Südwände) kann man in Mouriès, ein wenig Leidensbereitschaft vorausgesetzt, normalerweise das ganze Jahr über klettern.

APPROACH

Mouriès is situated on the D 17 some 25 kilometers east of Arles. Directions for how to get there and to the rocks are included with the maps on pages 206 & 207.

CAMPING

The public camping spot in Mouriès is a pleasant one. The couple who owns the campground strategically situated it in a pine forest on the leeward side of a hill. The tent sites are roomy, sheltered from the Mistral, allow privacy (you don't have the sardine-can feeling of many public campsites), and the sanitary facilities are exemplary.

SUPPLIES

There are many small grocers in Mouriès. It is worth the drive to the larger supermarkets in Arles if you are in need of supplies in larger quantities

FURTHER INFORMATION

Serge Jaulin, ESCALADES A MOURIES, Edisud, Aix en Provence 1987.

BEST SEASON

Because of its favorable positioning (north and south facing climbs) you can usually climb the year round, if you're prepared to suffer a little at times.

Approach ~ Anfahrt

Approach & Survey ~ Zugang & Lage

Mouriès

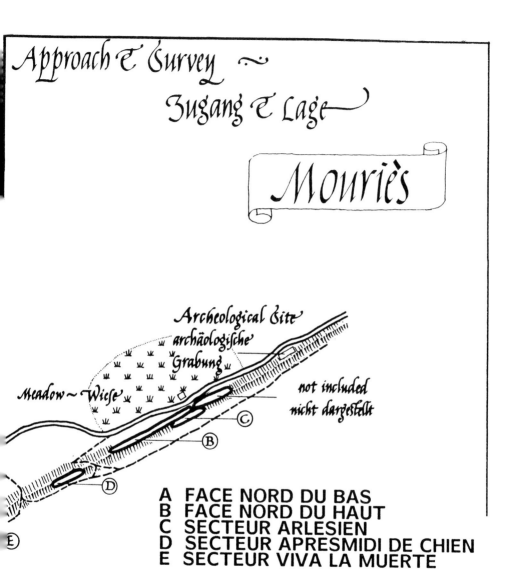

A FACE NORD DU BAS
B FACE NORD DU HAUT
C SECTEUR ARLESIEN
D SECTEUR APRESMIDI DE CHIEN
E SECTEUR VIVA LA MUERTE

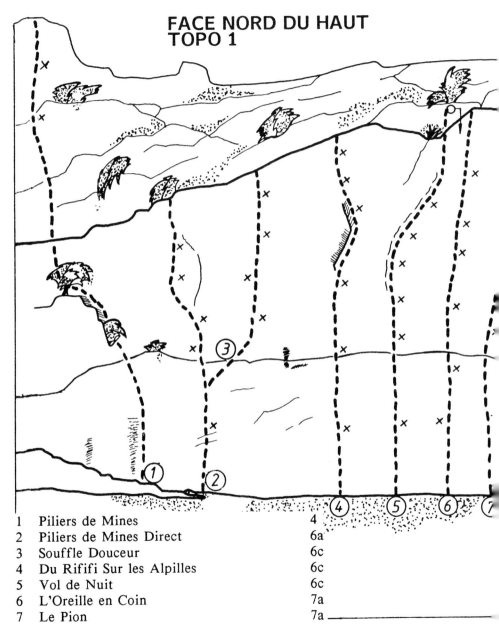

FACE NORD DU HAUT TOPO 1

1 Piliers de Mines — 4
2 Piliers de Mines Direct — 6a
3 Souffle Douceur — 6c
4 Du Rififi Sur les Alpilles — 6c
5 Vol de Nuit — 6c
6 L'Oreille en Coin — 7a
7 Le Pion — 7a

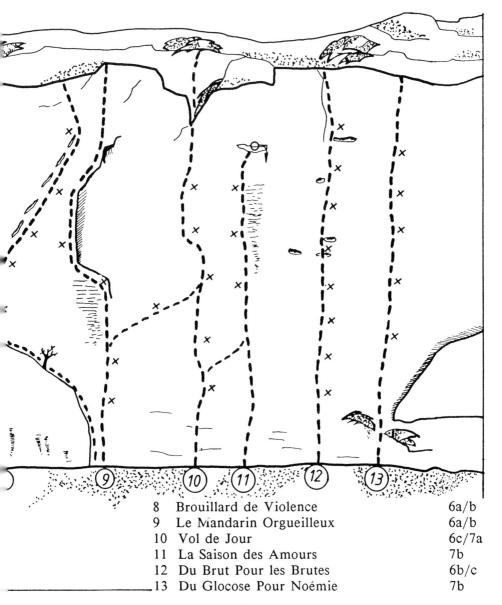

8	Brouillard de Violence	6a/b
9	Le Mandarin Orgueilleux	6a/b
10	Vol de Jour	6c/7a
11	La Saison des Amours	7b
12	Du Brut Pour les Brutes	6b/c
13	Du Glocose Pour Noémie	7b

FACE NORD DU HAUT
TOPO 2

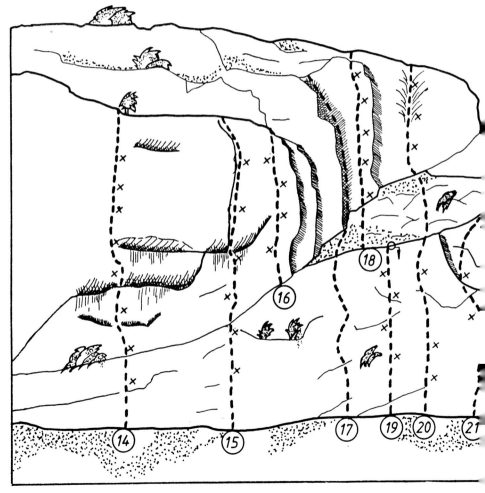

14	Un Doux Calin	7b
15	Bonjour le Soleil	5+/6a
16	Geordies on Tour	6a/b
17	Quand Tu Veux, Tu Démarres	4+
18	Erreur Médiatique	6a/b
19	Via Velpa	4
20	Méfi	4
21	Tendres Douceurs	3
22	Révolution Permanente	4+
23	Tintin au Niger	4+
24	Corbeau Solitaire	3
25	Canyon Street	5+
26	Black Out	6a
27	A Voile et à Vapeur	6c
28	Divergences	7a/+
29	Prélude à la Lune	5+

FACE NORD DU HAUT
TOPO 3

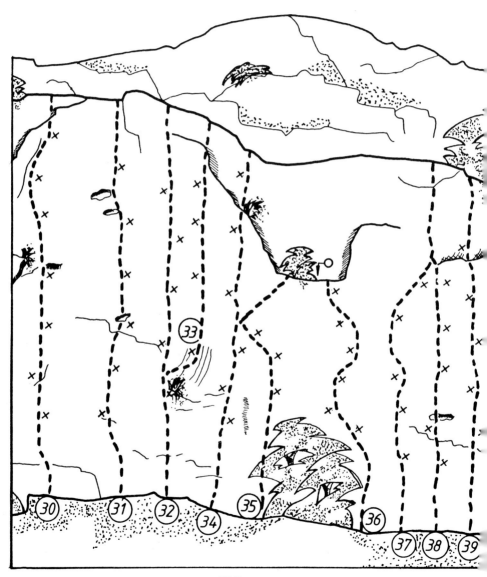

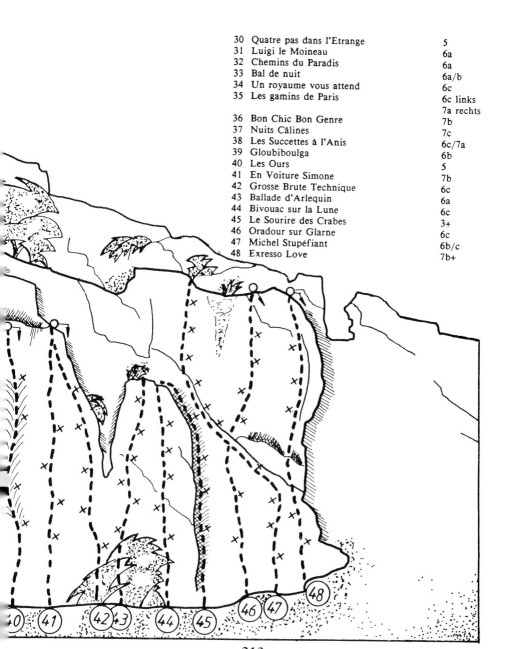

30	Quatre pas dans l'Etrange	5
31	Luigi le Moineau	6a
32	Chemins du Paradis	6a
33	Bal de nuit	6a/b
34	Un royaume vous attend	6c
35	Les gamins de Paris	6c links
		7a rechts
36	Bon Chic Bon Genre	7b
37	Nuits Câlines	7c
38	Les Succettes à l'Anis	6c/7a
39	Gloubiboulga	6b
40	Les Ours	5
41	En Voiture Simone	7b
42	Grosse Brute Technique	6c
43	Ballade d'Arlequin	6a
44	Bivouac sur la Lune	6c
45	Le Sourire des Crabes	3+
46	Oradour sur Glarne	6c
47	Michel Stupéfiant	6b/c
48	Exresso Love	7b+

FACE SUD
SECTEUR ARLESIAN

1	Fortaleza	6a
2	Escapades	5
3	Arlesian Way of Life	4+
4	Mostaganem	5+
5	Tiens Bon la Rampe	6b
6	Mariotte Bout Filtre	6b
7	Quasimodo	7a
8	Mets ton Doigt ou j'ai Mis mon Doigt	6c/7a
9	Etat d'Urgence	6b
10	S.O.S. Amor	7a

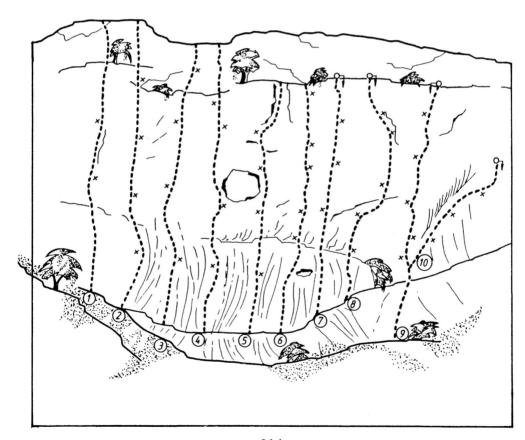

Den vauDe-Gesamtkatalog erhalten Sie im Sportgeschäft.
Oder fordern Sie ihn an bei vauDe, 7992 Tettnang 1.
Verkauf nur über den Sporthandel.

FACE SUD
SECTEUR L'APRESMIDI DE CHIEN

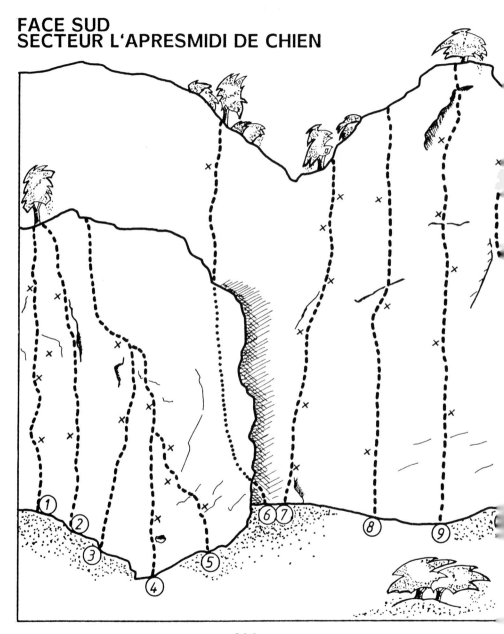

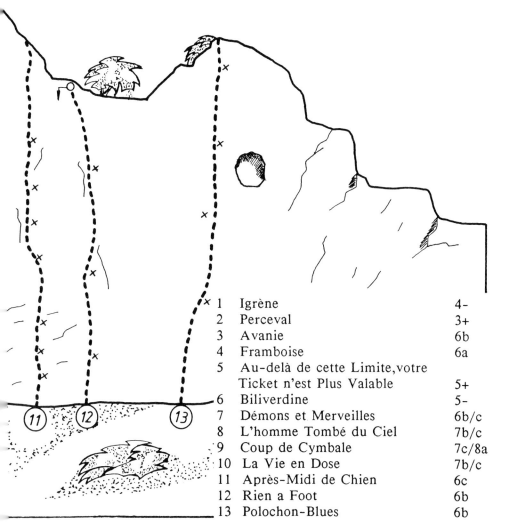

1	Igrène	4-
2	Perceval	3+
3	Avanie	6b
4	Framboise	6a
5	Au-delà de cette Limite, votre Ticket n'est Plus Valable	5+
6	Biliverdine	5-
7	Démons et Merveilles	6b/c
8	L'homme Tombé du Ciel	7b/c
9	Coup de Cymbale	7c/8a
10	La Vie en Dose	7b/c
11	Après-Midi de Chien	6c
12	Rien a Foot	6b
13	Polochon-Blues	6b

FACE SUD
SECTEUR VIVA LA MUERTE

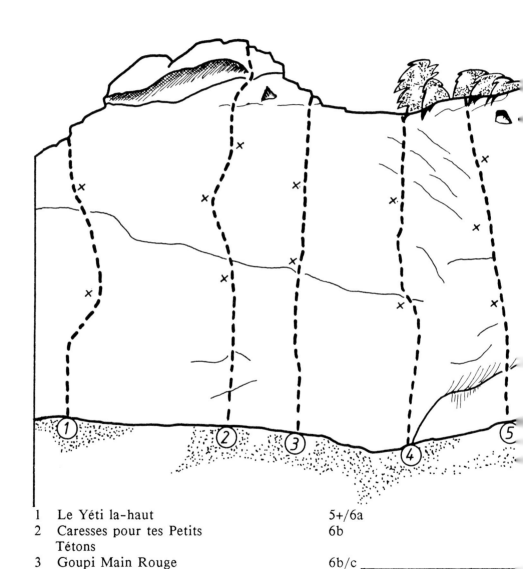

1	Le Yéti la-haut	5+/6a
2	Caresses pour tes Petits Tétons	6b
3	Goupi Main Rouge	6b/c

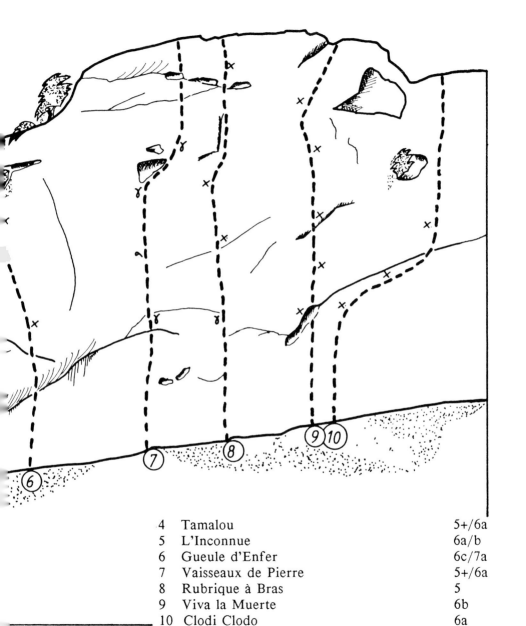

4	Tamalou	5+/6a
5	L'Inconnue	6a/b
6	Gueule d'Enfer	6c/7a
7	Vaisseaux de Pierre	5+/6a
8	Rubrique à Bras	5
9	Viva la Muerte	6b
10	Clodi Clodo	6a

15. CAVAILLON

In Cavaillon ist die Zukunft schon vorweggenommen, denn der dortige Klettergarten ist nahtlos integriert in die Sportanlagen der Stadt. Dementsprechend kurz sind die Zugangswege und abgespeckt die Griffe, wenigstens in den leichteren Touren. Wenn auch keines der modernen "Topgebiete", so ist Cavaillon doch, besonders in der kalten Jahreszeit (Südausrichtung), einen Besuch wert. Die Führen, von 4+ bis 7b, sind normalerweise zwischen 10 und 25 Meter lang, nur im Sektor "Amarcord" etwas höher. Wenn man drüben in Buoux die Fingergelenke und Unterarme gar zu sehr maltraitiert hat, kann man sich in Cavaillon an geneigten Platten regenerieren, ohne daß einem Raspelgriffe die Haut von den Fingerkuppen hobeln.

ZUGANG

Vom Ortszentrum von Cavaillon folgt man den Schildern zum Stade Municipale. Der Kletterparkplatz liegt hinter dem Stadion, 200 Meter südwestlich der Felsen.

ÜBERNACHTUNG

Die meisten in Cavaillon kletternden Ausländer werden von Apt aus operieren. Jedoch finden sich auch in Cavaillon zwei Zeltplätze. Einer liegt auf Höhe der Felsen auf dem anderen Duranceufer, der andere ungefähr einen Kilometer flußaufwärts.

BESTE ZEIT

Von Oktober bis April oder um Mitternacht.

As they are a fully integrated part of the municipal sports facilities, the Cavaillon crags are one step ahead of even most French climbing areas. The approaches are short and the holds polished, at least in the easier routes. Even if Cavaillon will never get top ratings, it is certainly worth a visit in the cold season due to its south facing position. The routes range from 4+ to 7b and are from 10 to 20 meters long (a bit higher on the "Amarcord" sector). If you need a break from the maltreatment of finger joints in Buoux you can give them a day to revive on the gently inclined slabs without the rasping edges that sheer the skin from your fingers.

APPROACH

Follow the signs for the "Stade Municipale" from the town center. The parking lot for the climbs is behind the stadium 200 meters southwest of the cliffs.

CAMPING

Most of the visitors to the crags of Cavaillon operate out of Apt. However, there are two camping sites in Cavaillon as well. One is on the bank of the Durance opposite the cliffs, the other, a kilometer upstream.

BEST SEASON

From October to April or at midnight.

Cavaillon

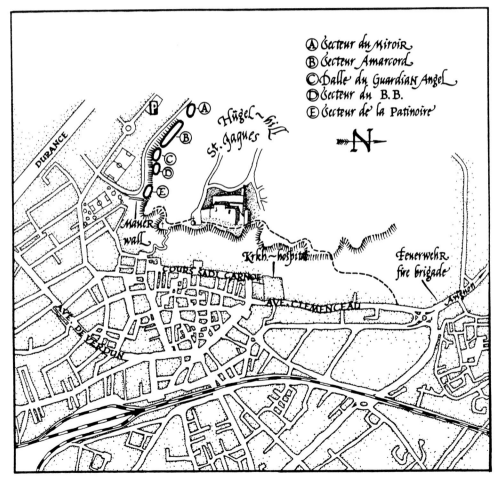

SECTEUR DU MIROIR

1. La Rouge de Gauche — 4c
2. Le Miroir — 6a/6a+
3. Lothlorien — 6b
4. Nuit d'Eclipse — 6a
5. Papillon Stone — 6c
6. Acrobatie Aérienne — 6a+

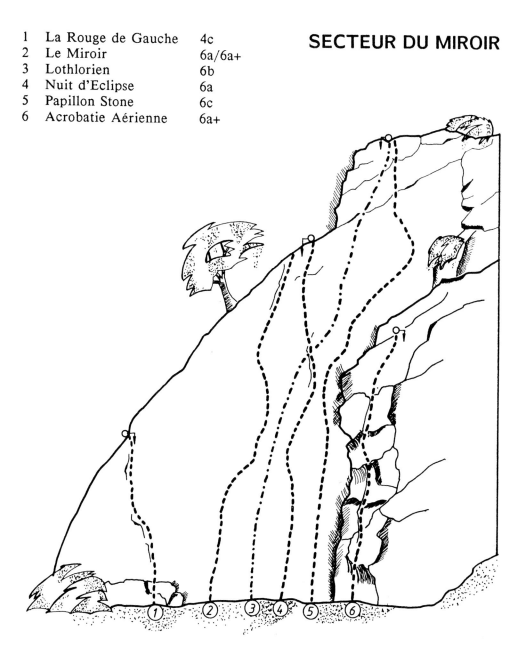

SECTEUR AMARCORD

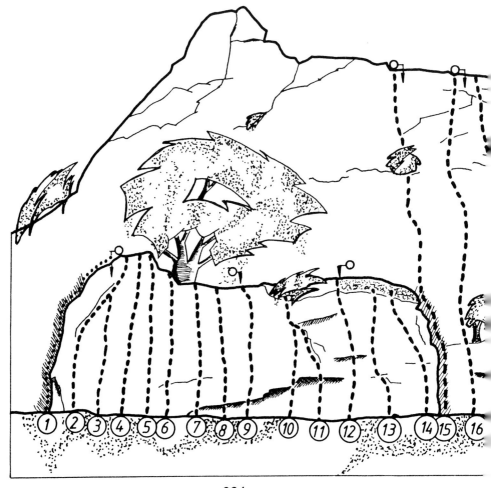

#	Name	Grade	#	Name	Grade
1	Dièdre Gris	4	14	L'Entracte	6a
2	Trident (Boulder)	6a	15	La Marrante	5+
3	Petit Pas (Boulder)	6a	16	L'Eden	4+
4	Du Bossus	5+	17	L'Elégance	5
5	Phalange	6a	18	La Fourche	5+
6	L'Onglet	6a	19	Amarcorde	5+
7	Souffrance	5	20	Du Printemps	5+
8	Du Doigt	4+	21	La Jonction	4
9	Les diables (Boulder)	6b	22	La Comique	4
10	Ernanies (Boulder)	6c	23	La Rigolade	3+
11	Tirée	5+	24	Chritalis	5+
12	Temps Modernes	5+	25	Fin Contact	7a
13	Satiricon	5+	26	Les Mutants sont parmi nous	6c

DALLE DU GUARDIAN ANGEL

1. Dance of Crapaudt — 5+
2. Take Five — 5+
3. Slick Slab — 6c
4. Enzymes Gloutons (Boulderstart) — 6a+
5. Seul Naximo Savait la Faire Danser — 6b
6. — 7b
7. Heteroclitoris — 7a
8. Guardian Angel — 6c
9. — 6c+
10. Méditérranéran Sundance — 6a

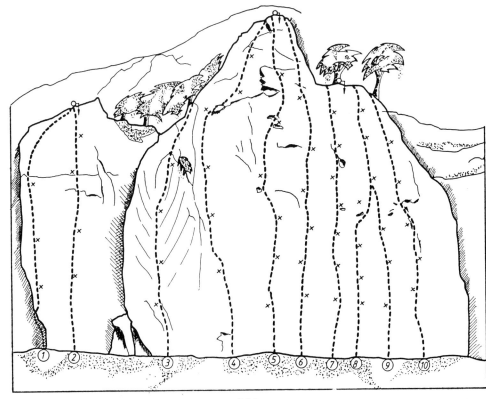

SECTEUR DU B.B.

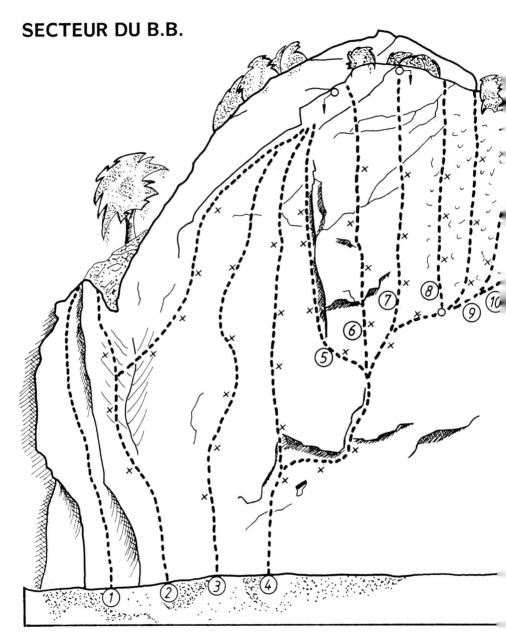

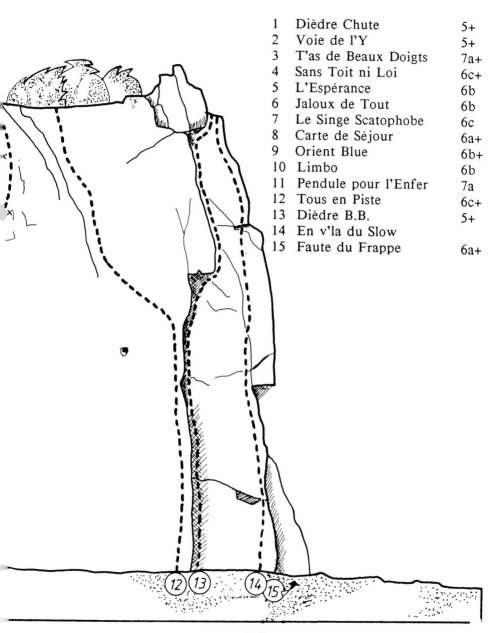

1	Dièdre Chute	5+
2	Voie de l'Y	5+
3	T'as de Beaux Doigts	7a+
4	Sans Toit ni Loi	6c+
5	L'Espérance	6b
6	Jaloux de Tout	6b
7	Le Singe Scatophobe	6c
8	Carte de Séjour	6a+
9	Orient Blue	6b+
10	Limbo	6b
11	Pendule pour l'Enfer	7a
12	Tous en Piste	6c+
13	Dièdre B.B.	5+
14	En v'la du Slow	
15	Faute du Frappe	6a+

SECTEUR DE LA PATINOIRE

1	Tortillas	?
2	12 O5	6b+
3	La Patinoire (Boulder)	
4	La Fendue	4
5	Le Coup du Père Francois	6c
6	Les Devoirs de Vacances	7a+
7	Paupières de Fièvre	7c
8	Comme des Coqs	6a

16. MENERBES

Nicht nur wenn es zu Ostern oder Pfingsten an der Styxwall gar zu heiß hergeht oder man die Gesichter im "Grünen Schlauch" und der "Crèmerie" einfach nicht mehr sehen kann, lohnt sich ein Ausflug nach Ménerbes. Das Nest liegt südlich der Straße von Apt nach Cavaillon im guten provençalischen Stil auf einem Gratausläufer der Montagnes du Luberon. Im Sommer wird auch der ehrgeizigste Felstiger in einem Cafe die beschauliche Atmosphäre dieser Kleinstadt inhalieren, bis gegen 15 Uhr die Temperaturen in dem nach Südosten orientierten Kalkstreifen der südwestlich der Stadt gelegenen Falaise de Langue d'Aze erträglich werden. Im Gegensatz zu vielen anderen neu erschlossenen Klettergebieten kommen hier auch die nicht ganz so Guten einmal voll zum Zug an den berühmten Wassertropfengriffen, während die Spitzenklasse das am Morgen Versäumte reichlich nachholen kann. Und das alles unter dem Schutz von absolut sicheren Fixpunkten; derzeitig sind die Idealisten vom M.J.C. Cavaillon dabei, alle Führen hier mit 12 mm-Schrauben abzusichern oder zu betonieren. Daß die Wandhöhe nur selten mehr beträgt als 20 Meter, ist einem in den steilen Durchstiegen oft mehr als recht, obgleich kein Kletterer etwas einzuwenden hätte, wenn jemand eine Alpenwand aus Ménerbes-Kalk hochziehen würde. Da die Falaise de Langue d'Aze auf Privatgrund liegt und die Klettererlaubnis immer an einem seidenen Faden hängt, muß unbedingt auf dreierlei geachtet werden:
- Nur Rauchen, wenn die Entzugserscheinungen es absolut notwendig machen und dann auf keinen Fall Kippen auf den Boden werfen. Die Feuerwehrleute der Gemeinde, die regelmäßig kontrollieren, bekommen sonst einen Anfall.
- An den nicht eingerichteten Routen an der rechten Seite des Felsstreifens darf nicht geklettert werden, sie wurden auf Wunsch des Grundeigentümers abgebaut.
- Nur den südlichen Zugangsweg benutzen. Er mag zwar etwas länger sein, die Erhaltung dieses schönen Klettergartens ist die kleine Zusatzmühe jedoch wert.

The detour to Ménerbes is worthwhile not only at Easter and Whitsun, when the Styxwall becomes too crowded and the faces in the "Crèmerie" all too familiar. The village is located south of the road from Apt to Cavaillon straddling the tributary ridge of the Montagnes du Lubéron. In summer even the most ambitious of climbing enthusiasts will prefer to spend the midday hours in the shade of one of the pleasant sidewalk cafes of this idyllic little town...at least till the temperatures on the southeast facing limestone band of rock just southwest of town become bearable. On the Falaise de Langue d'Aze, in contrast to many other modern French areas, even the more modest climber gets a chance to pull on the famous gouttes d'eau, whereas the extreme rock gymnast is more than compensated for his enforced rest at noon....and all this under conditions that meet the most stringent of safety standards. At present the idealists of the M.J.C. Cavaillon are in the process of equipping the routes with 12 mm bolts. For most aspirants to the routes, the fact that the walls are rarely higher than 20 meters is more than welcome, though hardly a mountaineer would complain about having longer alpine climbs of the quality of Ménerbes limestone.

Since the Falaise de Langue d'Aze is on private property observation of the rules laid down by the landowner are a prerequisite to keeping the area open for climbing.
- Smoke only when withdrawal symptoms become unbearable and, at all costs, don't discard your butts. The local firemen have been requested to do routine checkups and the landlord has been known to fly into fits of rage on discovering any trace of these reprehensible objects.
- Climbing is not permitted on the right side of the rock face. The fixed pro from old routes was removed here at the request of the owner.

ANFAHRT UND ZUGANG

1. Von Cavaillon auf der D 2 in Richtung Apt bis ca. 1,5 Kilometer hinter Robion. Dann rechts auf der D 3 nach Ménerbes.

2. Von Apt auf der N 100 bis Beaumettes und links auf der D 103 nach Ménerbes.

Und nun gemeinsam weiter: Man läßt das Ortszentrum links liegen und folgt der D 3 in Richtung Bonnieux. O,8 Kilometer nach dem Ortsausgangsschild, gleich nach dem Weiler La Peyrière, biegt rechts das Sträßchen zur Falaise de Langue d'Aze ab, auf dem man nach 1,2 Kilometern zum Parkplatz südlich der Felsen gelangt.

Vom Parkplatz auf einem Weg in östlicher Richtung bis ein Pfad steil zur Südecke ("Secteur du Coin") der Felsen hinaufführt (10-15 Minuten).

ÜBERNACHTUNG

Das Campieren und Feuermachen ist im gesamten Tal unter den Felsen streng verboten. In Bonnieux, Cavaillon und natürlich auch in Apt gibt es Zeltplätze.

- Use only the southern access. The somewhat longer approach is more than worth the extra distance to keep this idyllic niche open.

APROACH

1. From Cavaillon take the D 1 toward Apt until about 1.5 kilometers behind Robion. Then turn right on the D 3 to Mènerbes.

2. From Apt take the N 100 to Beaumettes and turn left on the D 103 to Ménerbes.

Take the D 3 toward Bonnieux (for both 1. and 2.) 0.8 kilometers after the town exit (immediately behind la Peyrère), turn right onto a small road leading to the Falaise de Langue d'Aze and drive 1.2 kilometers to the parking spot just south of the crag. From the parking spot take a dirt road eastward until a steep trail veers uphill and leads to the southern corner of the "Secteur du Coin" (10 to 15 minutes).

CAMPING

Camping and open fires are not permitted in the entire valley below the rocks. Public camping is available in Bonnieux, Cavaillon, and naturally in Apt as well.

VERSORGUNG

In Ménerbes wird zwar niemand verhungern, aber am besten kauft man in den Supermärkten in Apt und Cavaillon ein. Magnesia und neue Strümpfe kriegt ihr bei:

Sports Technic
50, Cours Gambetta
84300 Cavaillon
Tel. 90 78 03 46

Auch in Apt gibt es neuerdings ein Sportgeschäft. Es liegt an der N 100 in Richtung Avignon, fast am Ortsausgang auf der linken Straßenseite.

BESTE ZEIT

Aufgrund der günstigen Lage kann man an der Falaise de Langue d'Aze das ganze Jahr über klettern.

WEITERE INFORMATIONEN

ESCALADE A MENERBES,
M.J.C. Cavaillon -section ESCALADE,
157 Avenue General de Gaulle,
84300, Cavaillon, Tel. 90 71 65 33.

Der Führer ist bei "Sports Technic" zu erwerben.

SUPPLIES

No one will go hungry by shopping exclusively in Ménerbes, but the selection is larger in the supermarkets of Cavaillon and Apt. Chalk and stockings are available from:

Sports Technic
50, Cours Gambetta
84300 Cavaillon
Tel. 90 78 03 46

In Apt a sports shop has opened recently. It is located on the left side of the N 100 almost at the edge of town in the direction of Avignon.

BEST SEASON

Because of its favorable situation you can climb most of the year round on the Falaise de Langue d'Aze.

FURTHER INFORMATION

ESCALADE A MENERBES
M.J.C. Cavaillion - section ESCALADE -
157 Avenue General de Gaulle
8400 Cavaillon
Tel. 90 71 65 33

The Guidebook is available at "Sports Technic".

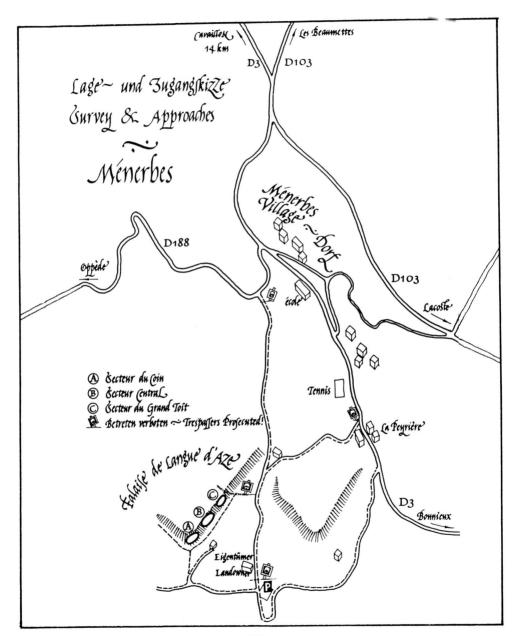

SECTEUR DU COIN

1 Projekt
2 Magic Circus   6c
3 Lecture Inachevée   6c
4 Images   7a
5 Vagabondages   6a
6 Wind and Whispering   6b+
7 A la Poursuite de Tartarin 8a
8 Secrets   6c+

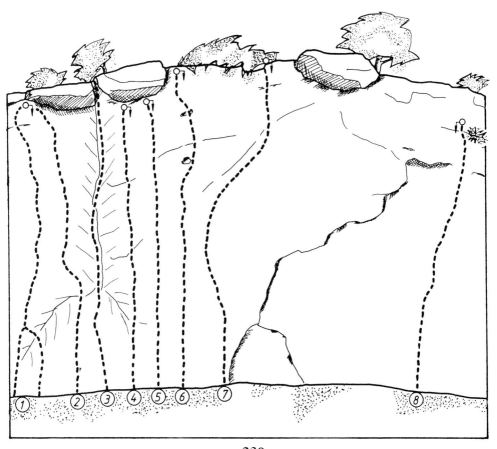

SECTEUR CENTRAL

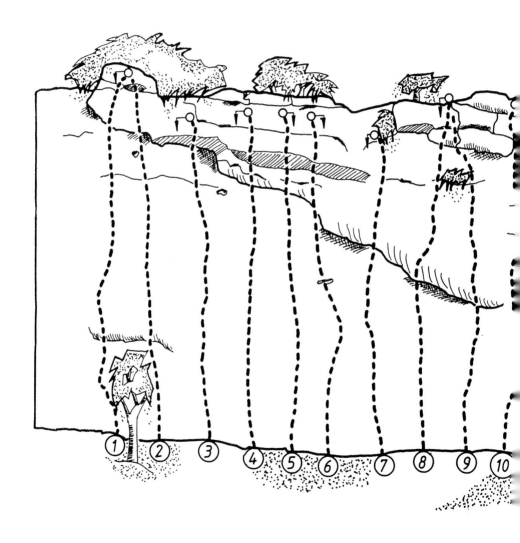

#	Name	Grade
1	Scenario Douteux	6b+
2	Scoop	6c
3	Les Objects du Délire	6c/6c+
4	Tchao - Pantin	6a+
5	La Salsa du Démon	6b
6	Coup de Théatre	6a+
7	Paquet Cadeau	6a
8	Le Dernier Combat	6a
9	Science-Friction	6c+
10	Piano Ivre	6a
11	Ça Sent la Poudre	6a
12	Aja	5
13	Elektro Soul	4+
14	Catharsis	5+
15	Le Lézard Megalomane	6a+
16	La Carambole	6a
17	Overcool Sensation	6b
18	Exercice de Style	6b
19	Psychodélice	6b
20	Paroles et Musique	6a
21	Zootalure	6a
22	Dialectichic	6a/6a+
23	La Rage Dedans	6b

#	Route	Grade
1	Le Dièdre à Loulou	5+
2	Projekt	
3	Le Cimetière des Fous	7b
4	Bras de Fer	7a
5	Programme de Choc	7a
6	Paradis pour Tous	6b
7	Grandeur Nature	6b+
8	R.E.M.	6b+
9	Regatta d'Eté	6b
10	Jeu de Scène	6b
11	Dans tes Yeux Lagon Vert	6c+
12	Nostalgie Balnéaire	6b+/6c
13	Rêve de Fan	6c

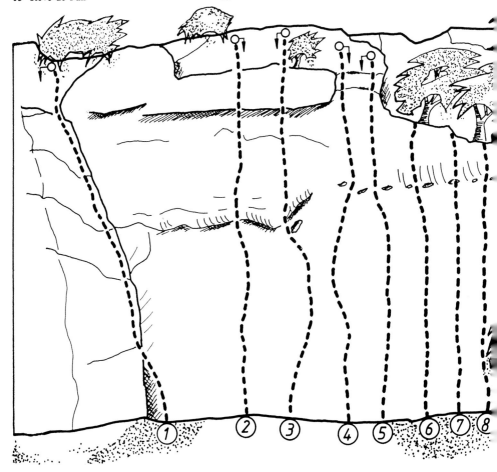

SECTEUR DU GRAND TOIT

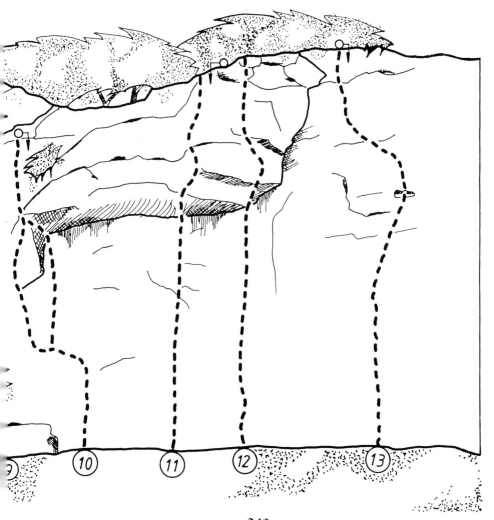

17. MONTAGNE DE SAINTE VICTOIRE

Im Vergleich mit den aufmüpfigen Nachwuchsstars Mouriès, Ménerbes, Buoux und Cimaï, ist der Montagne de Sainte Victoire ein ehrwürdiger Großvater unter den südfranzösichen Klettergebieten. Schon in den vierziger und fünfziger Jahren wurden die ersten Kletterwege in den Südwänden des zwölf Kilometer langen Grates begangen. Zu Beginn der siebziger Jahre galten die Baseclimbs in der Paroi des Deux Aiguilles, in der Fallinie des "Signal"-Gipfels, als besonders anspruchsvoll. Erstmalig in Kontinentaleuropa existierte damals am Fuße des Mont Sainte Victoire eine Kolonie von Felsbeatniks, deren Mitglieder die Platten systematisch zu erschließen begannen. Da Christian Guyomar und Bernard Gorgeon, unterstützt von Jacques Nosley und Christian Hautcoeur, ihre Routen grundsätzlich von unten erstbegingen, wurde in einer fugenlosen Platte eben nicht gebohrt, sondern geklettert. Es war kein Geheimnis, daß in manchen Schlüsselstellen in Routen wie "Le Medius", "Levitation" oder "Tamanrasset" neben den windigen, in seichte Risse gedroschenen Normalhaken, gegeneinander abgebundene Skyhooks als Sicherung herhalten mußten. Wer nicht den siebten Grad in der Platte sicher beherrschte, vermied es lieber, dreißig Meter über dem Erdboden sein Leben irgendwelchen ausgebleichten Siebenerschlingen anzuvertrauen. Wer will, kann auch heute noch Reisen in die Vergangenheit antreten, wenn auch viele Deux Aiguilles-Touren jetzt mit Bohrhaken abgesichert worden sind. Die anderen "Secteurs" des Mont Sainte Victoire (bis auf St. Ser) hinken in dieser Entwicklung hinterdrein, so daß wir uns aus Sorge um das Überleben unserer Leser, aus Solidarität mit unseren französischen Freunden und Platzgründen auf eine Beschreibung der Paroi des Deux Aiguilles beschränken. Zu unrecht werden die sehr schönen und gut gesicherten Plattenschleichereien links vom "Pas de l'Oppidum" von ausländischen Besuchern vernachlässigt, sie sind allerdings nicht unter 6a+ zu haben. Überhaupt ist die Deux Aiguilles-Wand eher ein Betätigungsfeld für die Kletterer schärferer Richtung, wenn auch nicht für

Compared with the young upstarts Mouriès, Ménerbes, Buoux, and Cimaï, the Montagne de Sainte Victoire is the venerable great-grandfather among the climbing areas of Southern France. The first climbs were put up on the south faces of the twelve kilometer long ridge as early as the 1940's and 50's. Beginning in the 1970's the baseclimbs of the "Paroi des Deux Aiguilles" below the summit of "Le Signal" ranked among the boldest on the Continent. It was here that the first colony of rock beatniks in Europe settled and began to develop the slabs systematically. Since Christian Guyomar and Bernard Gorgeon, together with Jacques Nosley and Christian Hautcoeur, never put up their routes by rappeling as a matter of principle, they simply climbed the slabs rather than bolting them. It is no secret that on the crux moves of such routes as "Le Medius", "Levitation", or "Tamanrasset", tied off skyhooks were added as pro to the flimsy pegs bashed into the shallow cracks. If you didn't feel at home in at least 6b/c faceclimbing you would have been well advised not to entrust your life to the sun-bleached slings 30 meters above ground. Today you can still take a trip into the past by climbing some of the old routes on the Deux Aiguilles, though many of them now sport modern bolts. But even with these recent improvements the entire Aiguille face is not a place for the timid. Because the other "secteurs" on Mont St. Victoire (except St. Ser) are somewhat retarded in the promotion of modern safety features, out of concern for the welfare of our readers, and out of solidarity with our French colleagues (not to mention lack of space) we are limiting our description of the region to the Paroi des Deux Aiguilles.

The elegant and fairly well protected friction slabs to the left of the "Pas de l'Oppidum" have been unjustly ignored by foreign climbers. However, they are not to be had under 6a+. Further on to the right the routes become steeper and demand well-developed forearms and impeccable footwork. Climbers of the amateur league and pleasure climbing categories will find

Leute, die vom Tremor geschüttelt werden, sobald die Sicherung unterm Knie verschwindet. Nach rechts hin werden die Führen tendenziell steiler und verlangen neben ausgefeilter Fußtechnik auch eine gut entwickelte Unterarmmuskulatur. Mover der Volks- und Genußklasse finden an den Deux Aiguilles vielleicht für zwei Tage Stoff, dann gehen sie am besten nach Puyloubier zum Meister Gorgeon, um sich die Beschreibungen von St. Ser zu holen.

ANFAHRT UND ZUGANG

Von Aix en Provence auf der D 17 über le Tholonet nach St. Antonin. Ungefähr sechshundert Meter nach dem Kirchlein sind Parkplätze links und rechts der Straße. Die Scherben überall auf dem Boden mögen als Warnung dienen, keine Wertsachen, oder noch besser überhaupt nichts, im Auto zu lassen. Auf schwarz markiertem Weg in einer Viertelstunde zu der Paroi des Deux Aiguilles.

ABSTIEG VOM "SIGNAL"

Vom höchsten Punkt wendet man sich in Richtung "Croix de Provence" und verfolgt den Rücken des Sainte Victoire-Kammes bis zum "Pas de Chat". Von hier auf Steigspuren nach Süden hinab, bis man auf den schwarz markierten Wanderweg trifft.
Gemütlicher ist es, den Gratrücken weiterzuverfolgen, bis kurz vor dem Aufschwung zum Kreuz der schwarz markierte Pfad durch eine Höhle hinabführt. Man folgt den Markierungen, das gesamte Signal-Massiv querend, hinunter zum Parkplatz.

sufficient recreation potential to sustain them for only two days or so. Thereafter, they are best advised to pay Master Gorgeon in Puyloubier a visit, to get a copy of his list of the routes on St. Ser.

APPROACH

From Aix en Provence take the D 17 through le Tholonet to St. Antonin. Some 600 meters behind the church you will find parking spots on both sides of the road. The fragments of glass scattered on the roadside should serve as sufficient reminder not to leave valuables, or better yet nothing at all in unattended vehicles. Take the path (black markers) to the Paroi des Deux Aiguilles (15 minutes).

DESCENT FROM THE "SIGNAL"

From the highest point turn toward the "Croix de Provence" and descend the Sainte Victoire ridge to the "Pas de Chat". From here turn southward and follow a faint trail which leads you to the path with the black markers. It is better to stay on the ridge from the "Pas de Chat" until you get to the black markers, which disappear into a cave before reaching the cross. Then follow the markers, traversing the entire Signal face down to the parking lot.

CAMPING

There are campgrounds in Beaurecueil and Puyloubier. The former has some of the qualities of a cage, the latter is unguarded, but situated in a pleasant pine forest. Registration off season is in the town hall.

ÜBERNACHTUNG

Zeltplätze findet man in Beaurecueil und Puyloubier. Erstgenannter ist ein Käfig, letzterer zwar praktisch ohne Bewachung aber dafür in einem Kiefernwald gelegen. Anmeldung in der Nebensaison in der Mairie (Rathaus). Daniel Gorgeon betreibt in Puyloubier eine Klettererhütte. Es ist nicht möglich, ihre Lage ohne Rechts- und Hochwertangaben zu beschreiben; man frage sich durch.

VERSORGUNG

Kleine Einkäufe sind in Puyloubier möglich. Der nächste Supermarkt und eine Anzahl guter Speiselokale findet man in Trets.

WEITERE INFORMATIONEN

Bernard Gorgeon, Christian Guyomar, Alexis Luchesi, ESCALADES DANS LE MASSIF DE LA SAINTE-VICTOIRE, PARTIE CENTRALE - LES DEUX AIGUILLES LE SIGNAL, Edisud.

In der Kletterhütte in Puyloubier verkauft Daniel Gorgeon Infos zum wiederentdeckten und gut ausgerüsteten Sektor von St. Ser. Außerdem gibt der Altmeister gern Auskunft über neue Entwicklungen an den Deux Aiguilles.

Daniel Gorgeon runs a climbers' hut in Puyloubier. The hut is easy to find by asking for directions in town, but the way there is impossible to describe.

SUPPLIES

The basics can be bought in Puyloubier. The nearest supermarket and several good restaurants are located in nearby Trets.

FURTHER INFORMATION

Bernard Gorgeon, Christian Guyomar, Alexis Lucchesi, ESCALDES DAN LE MASSIF DE LA SAINTE VICTOIRE - LES DEUX AIGUILLES, LE SIGNAL, Edisud, Edition de la Liberation, Aix en Provence.

In the climbing hut in Puyloubier Daniel Gorgeon will be happy to sell you a compilation of routes on the recently rediscovered and well equipped St. Ser sector. In addition, he cheerfully provides information about any new developments on the Deux Aiguilles.

Ste. Victoire Survey

with the topo sections as presented in this guidebook.

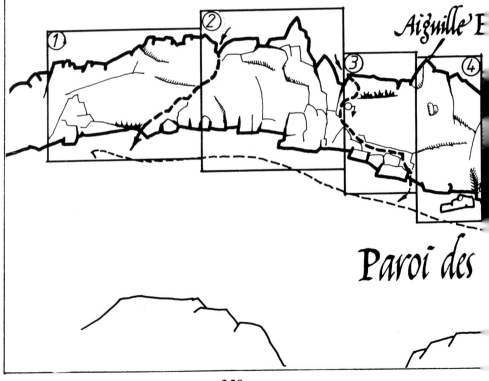

Paroi des

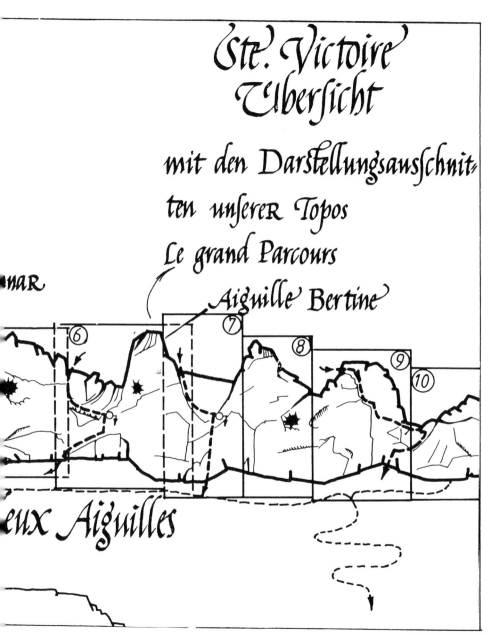

TOPO 1

#	Name	Grade
1	La Yanneck	5+
2	Dérélita	7a
3	Cornichon Délirant	7a
4	Flagrant Délire	6c+
5	Fiascosialiste	6c+
6	Choflagom	7b
7	Plus Fort que moi tu Pleures	6a; 6b/c (1 SL)
8		
9	Gnai	6c

TOPO 2

#	Name	Grade
1	Supervers & Pepperman	6b
2	La Lequer	6a
3	Miss Marple	
4	La Dédouille	7a
5	Compet ou pas, ça Pu Quand Même	7b
6	La Présence	7a
7	Escarpolettissime	7b+
8	L'Organe	7c
9	Steelfinger	7b

:shalb:

„Ideen werden sichtbar"

Druckhaus Veigele
(vorm. Kurt Munz GmbH)
Davidstr. 8/1 · 7320 Göppingen · Tel. 0 71 61 / 7 43 46
oder 0 71 61 / 6 88 58   Telefax 0 71 61 / 7 18 58

Wir drucken für Sie: Auf Ein- und Vierfarbmaschinen. Setzen mit dem Computer, reproduzieren, führen anspruchsvollste Kartonagen – sowie Papierveredelungen (auch von Hand) aus, übernehmen Verpackungen wie Versand und – empfinden Ihre Wünsche als unsere Pflicht zur Hilfe.

TOPO 1

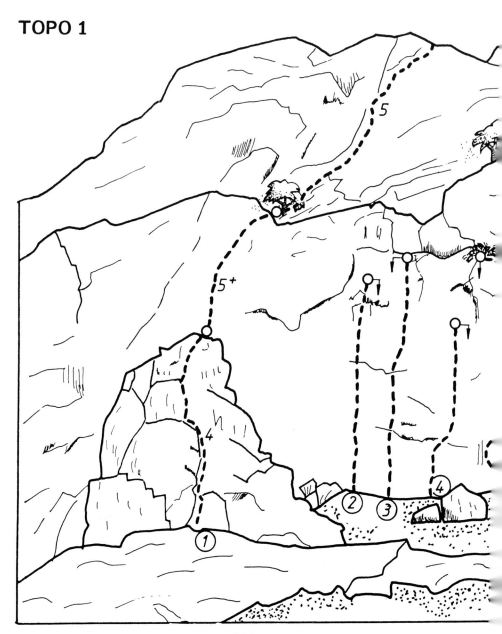

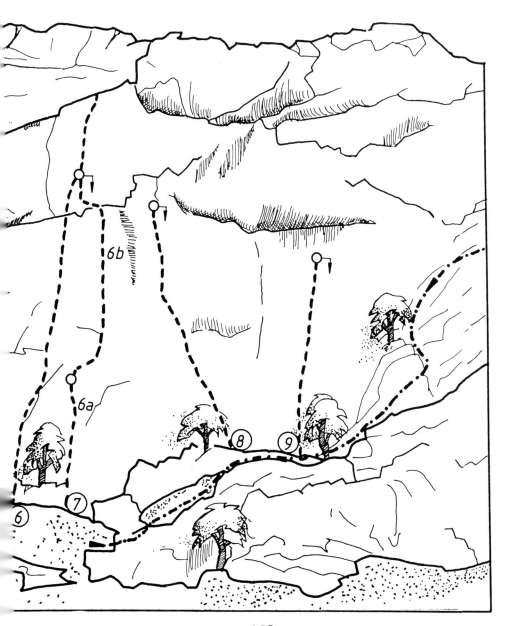

TOPO 2

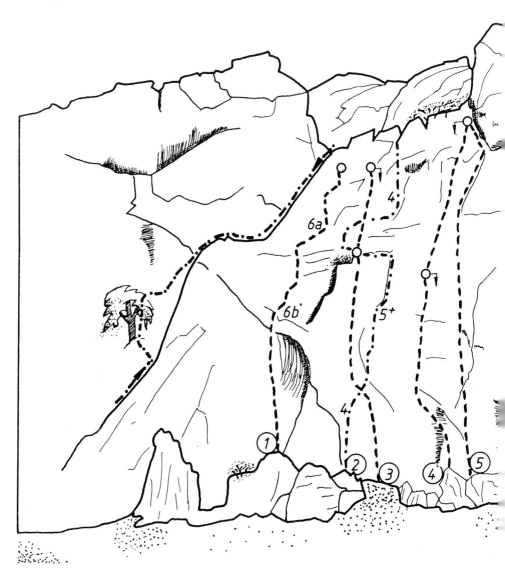

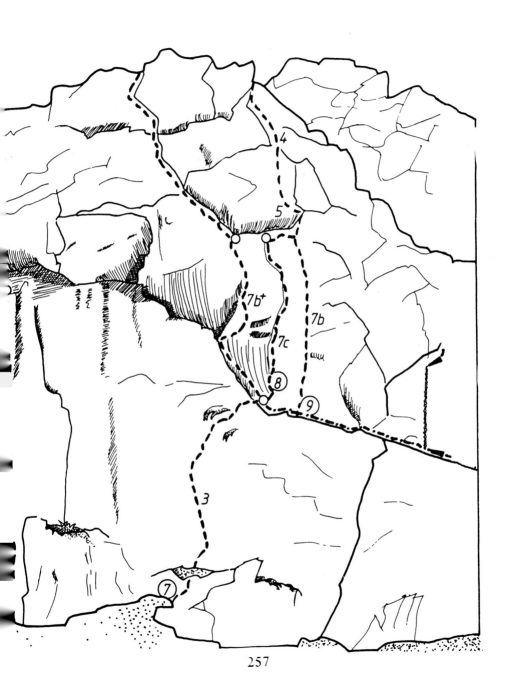

TOPO 3

1	La Mégotine	4+
2	La Croucouniaque	4+/5
3	Super-Rognures	5
4	Les Rognures d'Ongles d'Allah	3/4
5	L'Extension	5+
6	Pollution	6a
7	La Barnett	7

TOPO 4

1	Arrosoir et Persil	7b+
2	La Barnett	7a+
3	La Martine	6b/c
4	La Krishna-Dalle	7a
5	La Phial	5+
6	La Reposante	6a
7	L'Extra-Dalle	6a/b
8	La D.J.	5+/6a
9	La Fissure Brown	7b (3.SL)
10	Les Gousses d'Aulx	5+
11	Les Gouttes d'Eau	5+
12	La Pycnostyle	5+
12a	Variante	
13	Dièdre des Tordus	5+

„PFÄLZER KLETTERLADEN"

Ihr Spezialausrüster für Fels, Eis und Schnee

Fachkundige Beratung

Peter Lischer

6749 Busenberg, Hauptstraße 3
Telefon (0 63 91) 24 00

TOPO 3

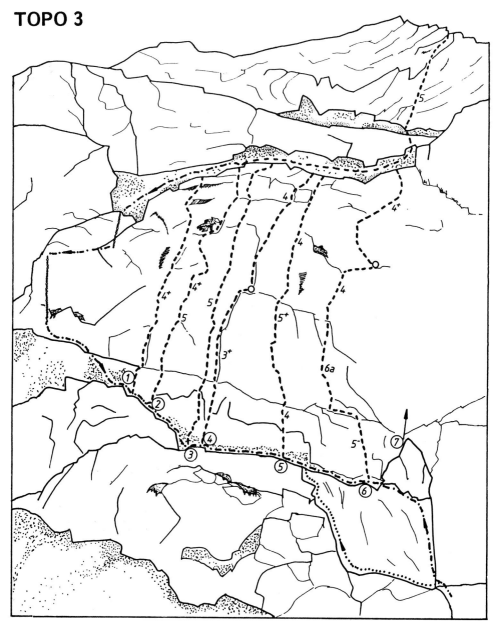

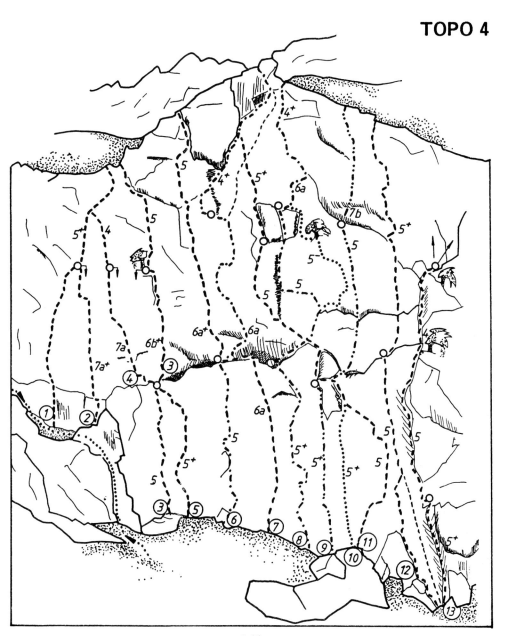

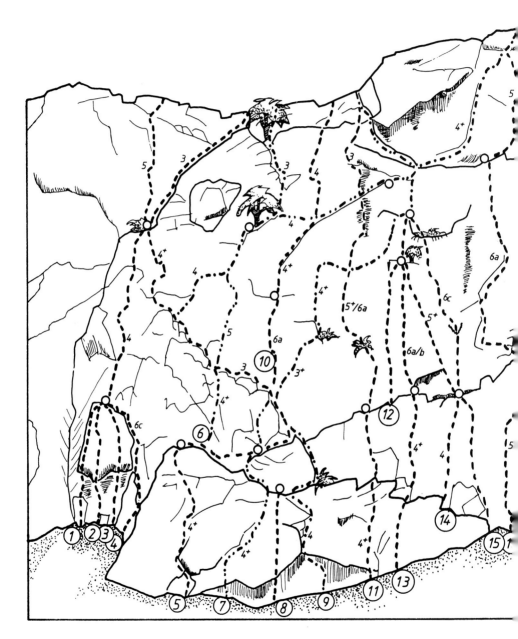

TOPO 5

#	Nom	Cotation
1	Planquez les Femmes	7a
2	Erotissimo	7c
3	Cuni Lingus	6c
4	La V.D.Q.S.	6c
5	Les Deux Ecailles	4+
6	Le Manchot Exité	4+
7	Le Boulon de Gauche	5
8	Le Retour à la Case Départ	7a
9	Le Boulon du Millieu	4+
10	La Dalle en Pente	6a
11	La Cultenud	5+/6a
12	Clitomine	6a
13	Clitomax	6a/b
14	Le Boulon de Droite	5+/6a
15	Half Gnome	6c
16	L'Antirabique	6a
17	Le Cafard Né Homme	5+
18	Le Quatre Quart	5/5+
19	Le Pouce	5+

TOPO 6

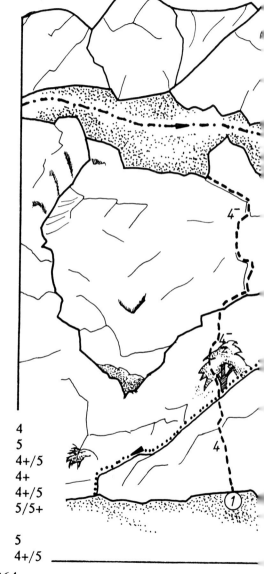

1	Les Plattes Dalles	4
2	La U.L.K.	5
3	La Deloripous Despapiers	4+/5
4	La Directe du Grand Parcours	4+
5	Le Grand Parcours	4+/5
6	Le Requiem	5/5+
7	La Pimprenelle et le Pervers Chevelu	5
8	Baskets Blues	4+/5

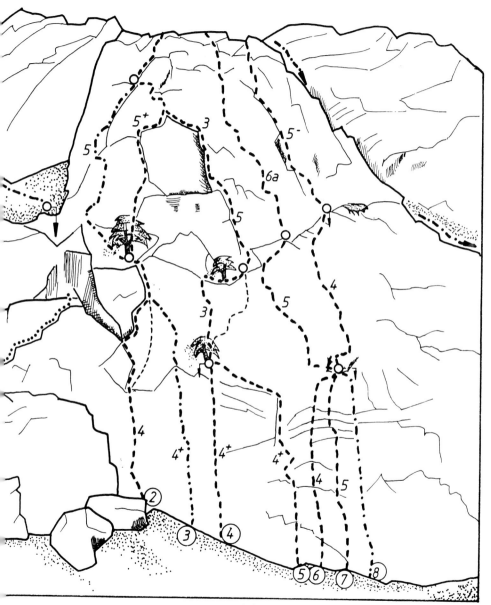

TOPO 7

1	La Psycho d'Elite	4+
2	La Dénéa Depeuf	4+
3	L'Intégrale	4+
4	La Kaspate	4/4+
5	Les Commandos	5
6	Les Masques de Pierre	4/4+
7	Les Sept	4
8	La Mouche	3+
9	La Tsé-Tsé	4+/5
10	Bestagnase Vérolique	7a
11	L'Ovni	6c

TOPO 8

1	6ème Métatarsien	6b/c
2	Directe des Aromates	5/5+
3	Les Aromates	4/4+
4	Hyper Medusée	7a
5	Hyper Medius	6c
6	Super Medius	7a
7	Niki Chagrin d'Humeur	7c
8	Le Medius	7c
9	La Lévitation	6c/7a
10	Gouroumaniak	6c/7a
11	La Pagode	6a
12	Les Fagots	5+
13	L'Inflation	6c
14	Grille Homard	6c/7a

TOPO 7

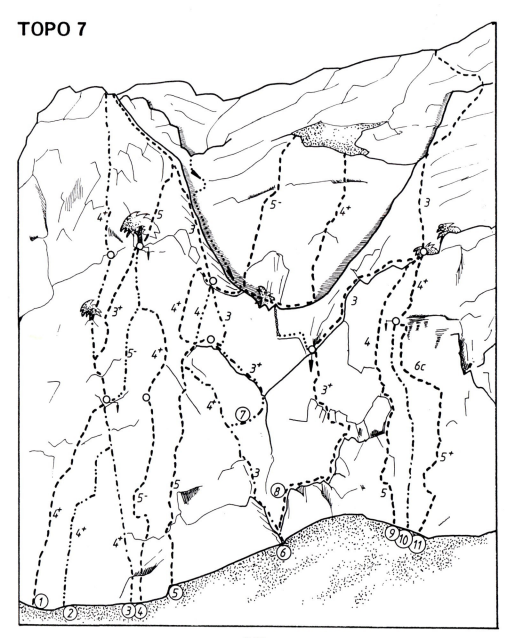

TOPO 8

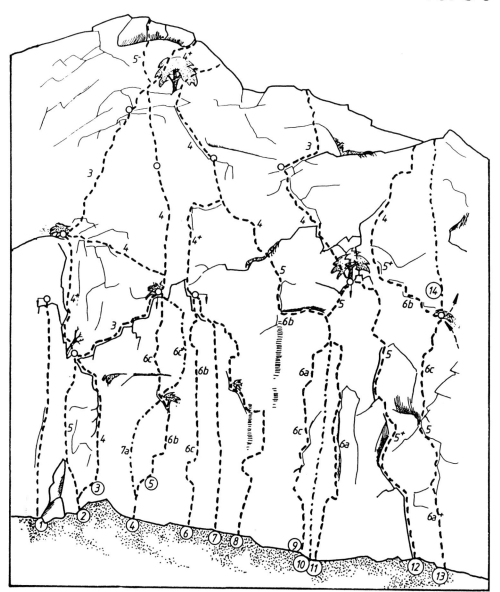

269

TOPO 9

1	Grille Homard	6c/7a
2	La Doyouspitingliche	6c/7a
3	La Gassi-Touil	6b/6b+
4	Directe Gassi-Touil	6c
5	La Spleen	6b+
6	Les Chas	5+
7	Messaline	6a+
8	Bengale	6c
9	L'Ensigienord	6b+
10	La Tamanrasset	6b+
11	Voie du Bout	7a
12	Snoupinette	6c/7a

TOPO 10

1	G.T.M.	5+/6a
2	Caravane Seraille	6b+
3	Les Crêpes Centrifuges	6b+
4	40 Vêpres Collantes	6c/7a
5	Les Crêpes Volantes	6b+
6	La Transversale	4
7	La Boule	8a+

PARAFLUGSCHULE ZILLERTAL

FLY

The Zillertal Paragliding School led by Helmut Walder (Austrian record holder 1986) provides expert instruction.

Paraflugschule Zillertal
Atlas Sportalm
A-6283 Hippach/Austria
Call: 0043/5282/3720 and 3721

IT TAKES A PRO TO SHOW YOU HOW TO GET IT UP **SAFELY!**

TOPO 9

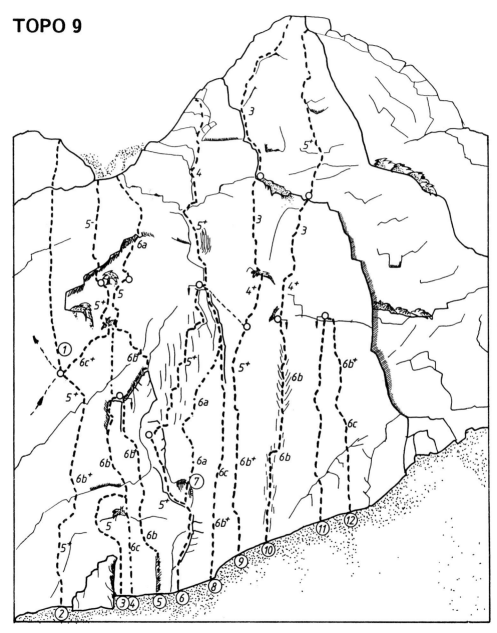

TOPO 10

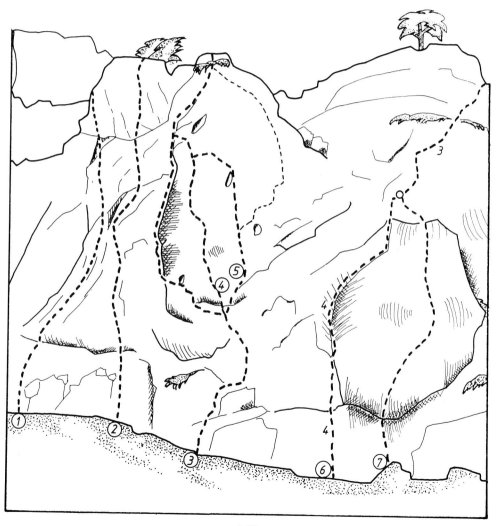

LE GRAND PARCOURS

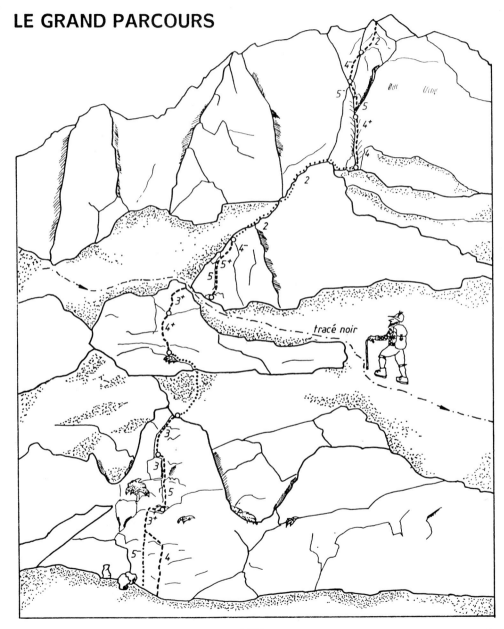

18. LES CALANQUES - EN VAU

Wir behandeln hier diesen absoluten Renner unter den mediterranen Klettergebieten bewußt sträflich, d.h. nur ganz am Rande. Funktion dieses Buches ist es, Alternativen zum schon Bekannten anzubieten und nicht, abgekaute "Leckerbissen" nochmal einzuspeicheln. Weil wir davon ausgehen, daß die meisten Leser die abgeschmierten Klassiker eh schon abgehakt haben, beschränken wir uns auf die Darstellung der noch rauhen Neueröffnungen, die man im Lucchesi-Führer nicht findet. Daß es klar ist: allein mit den in unserem Führer enthaltenen Informationen hätte nur Sherlock Holmes eine Chance, die im folgenden dargestellten Führen aufzuspüren. Unsere Calanques-Infos sind ausschließlich als Ergänzung zum Edisud-Gebietsführer gedacht. Leute, die hier das übliche Calanques-Geschwärme vermissen, seien auf die unter "Informationen" angegebene Literatur verwiesen, sowie auf einen Gewährsmann aus "einschlägigen Kreisen": "...einfach das überlegene Revier."

ANFAHRT UND ZUGANG

Damit der zitierte Herr möglichst Umsatzeinbußen verzeichnet, wähle man unter den drei Zugangsmöglichkeiten am besten die erstaufgeführte. Sie wird sich nur kurzfristig als die teuerste erweisen.

1. Man nehme eines der Ausflugsboote, die vom Hafen in Cassis in die En Vau fahren. Dies kostet zwar pro Strecke 20 Francs, erspart aber Mühe, Zeit - und Ärger mit der Diebstahlversicherung.

2. Von Cassis auf der Küstenstraße in Richtung Calanques und auf dem schwarz markierten Weg in die En Vau (45 Minuten).

The rather sparing description of this favorite among Mediterranean climbing areas is intentional. The purpose of our book is to offer new alternatives to well-known classical areas and not to rehash the existing information on popular sites. We are assuming that most of our readers are familiar with the greasy classics of the Calanques and will limit our presentation to the still unpolished new routes not described in Lucchesi's guidebook. To make it clear: by using this guidebook alone, only Sherlock Holmes would have a chance of tracking down the routes described here. Our information on the Calanques is merely intended to supplement the local Edisud guide. Those who find our omission of the usual songs of praise about the Calanques unpardonable are referred to the literature listed under FURTHER INFORMATION as well as to the remarks of the informant from pertinent circles: "...definitely a high yield territory!"

APPROACH

If you prefer to minimize the bounty of the gentleman quoted above you are best advised to use only the first of the three approaches described below. The seemingly steep price will prove to be only temporarily dear.

1. Take one of the sight-seeing boats from the port of Cassis to En Vau. The cost of 20 francs per trip is more than worth the time, energy, and harangues with the theft insurance you are later spared.

2. Take the coastal road from Cassis in the direction of the Calanques and on the trail marked in black to the En Vau (45 minutes).

3. Von Cassis ungefähr 5 Kilometer auf der N 559 in Richtung Marseille. Beim Hinweisschild zum Col de Cardiole biegt man links ab und folgt der "Rue Forestière" zum Parkplatz. In südlicher Richtung zur "Maison Forestière". Der hier beginnende rotmarkierte Weg führt in einer guten halben Stunde in die En Vau. Von dieser Zugangsmöglichkeit ist aufgrund der Diebstahlgefahr am Parkplatz dringend abzuraten!

ÜBERNACHTUNG

Man übernachtet am besten im Campingplatz von Cassis, der von April bis Oktober offen ist, oder in einem der Zeltplätze an der Straße in Richtung la Ciotat. Seit dem Brand auf dem Plateau de Castelveil kontrolliert die Polizei regelmäßig die En Vau im Hinblick auf Zeltler, die dann zur Kasse gebeten und verjagt werden. Biwakieren am Strand wird bislang noch geduldet. Wildes Zelten in der Nähe der Parkplätze und das Übernachten dort im Campingbus ist schlichtweg gefährlich.

VERSORGUNG

Supermärkte in Cassis. In der En Vau gibt es kein Trinkwasser!

WEITERE INFORMATIONEN

A. Lucchesi, ESCALADES DANS LE MASSIF DES CALANQUES - EN VAU, Edisud, 1983.

M. Lochner, TOPOS A LA CARTE, Selbstverlag Lochner, 1987.

G. Rébuffat, CALANQUES, SAINTE BAUME, SAINTE VICTOIRE, Editions Denoel, 1986.

3. Drive 5 kilometers from Cassis toward Marseille on the N 559. At the sign to Col de Cariole turn left and take the forest service road to the parking area. Go south to the "Maison de Forestère". The trail marked in red which starts here leads to the En Vau in about half an hour. This approach is least preferable due to the high incidence of theft at the parking lot.

CAMPING

It is best to camp on the campground at Cassis, which is open from April to October, or at one of the tent sites located along the road in the direction of la Ciotat. Since the forest fire on the Plateau de Castelveil there are regular police checks for campers at the En Vau, who are persistently fined and driven away. A word of caution - campers on unguarded sites, even in locked vehicles, are subject to being attacked!

SUPPLIES

There are supermarkets in Cassis. In the En Vau there is no potable water.

FURTHER INFORMATION

A. Lucchesi. ESCALADES DANS LE MASSIF DES CALANQUES - EN VAU, Edisud 1986.

M. Lochner. TOPOS A LA CARTE, Selbstverlag Lochner, 1987.

G. Rébuffat. CALANQUES, SAINTE BAUME, SAINTE VICTOIRE, Editions Denoel, 1986.

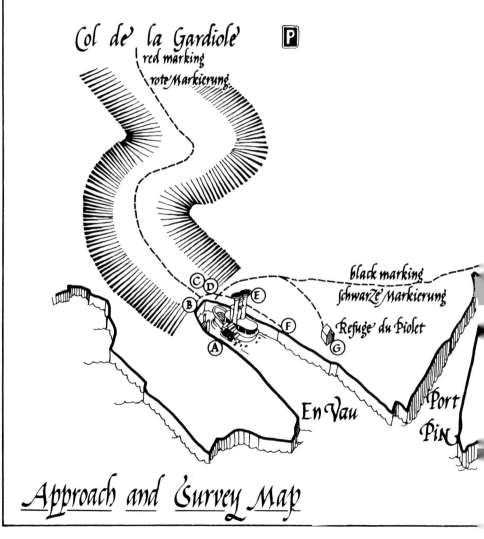

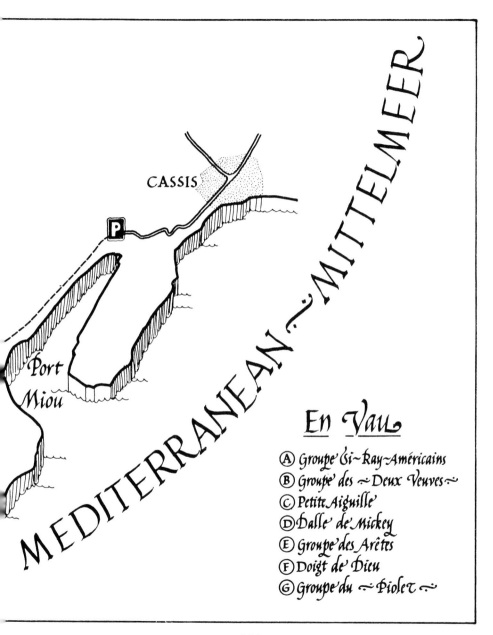

GROUPE SI-RAY-AMERICAINS

Orientierungsroute hier ist der Klassiker "Bateau Ivre" (24), der neu eingerichtet wurde. Die 1. SL ist nicht 5+/6- ist wie im Führer steht, sondern 7a+, die 2. 5+ und die 3. 7a.
In der näheren Umgebung befinden sich folgende Neutouren:

The guide route here is die classic "Bateau Ivre" (24), that has been reequipped. Pitch 1 is not 5+/6- as stated in the local guidebook, but 7a+, pitch 2 is 5+ and No. 3 7a. In its vicinity you'll find the following new routes:

- Coeur Grenadine   6b+
  am Einstieg des "Bateau
  Ivre" abseilen
  rappel from the start of
  the "Bateau Ivre"

- P 4 Connection   6c+
  vom Stand nach der 1. SL
  des B.I. gerade empor zum
  2. Stand
  straight up from the belay
  after the first B.I. pitch

- Les Rues sont Pleines   7b
  de Promesses
  zwischen B.I. (24) und
  "La Participion (23)
  between B.I. (24) and
  "La Participation" (23)
- Accroche-toi à la Vie   5+,5+,7a
                                                 5+,6a

  links von/ to the left of
  "Gamma" (22)

GROUPE DES DEUX VEUVES

1	Conan	6b
2	La Pancarte (55)	5+/6a
3	Zouzou Fafan	7b
4	Phallus	6c

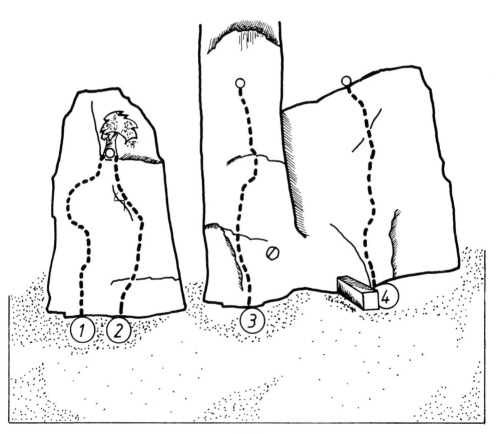

LA PETITE AIGUILLE

DALLE DE MICKEY

Am Strand links/on the beach, left side:

- Débilodrome 6b
  (SO-Seite/SE-side)
- Feluda (NW-Seite/NW-side) 6b

LA DALLE DE MICKEY

Links oberhalb der Petite Aiguille
To the left and above the Petite Aiguille

1 Extrème Gauche   6a+
2 Le Train Sauvage   7a
3 A Droite   6b
4 Troisième Sexe   6b
5 Les Passageurs du Vent 6b
6 Sale Temps pour les Nains 6c

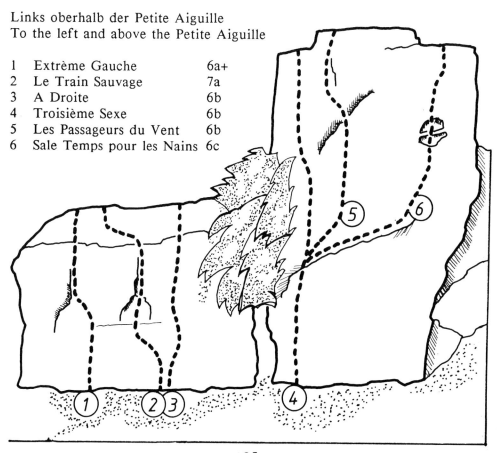

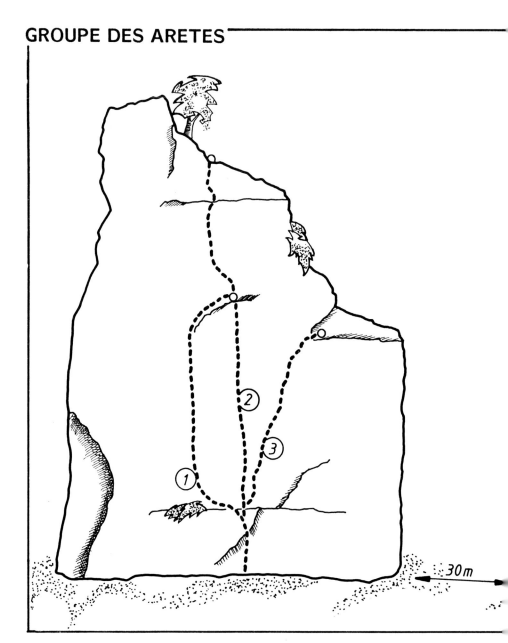

Die markanteste Route hier ist die zum Teil unterirdisch verlaufende "Grotte d'Ali Baba" (136).
The route with the best defined character herabout is the partially subterranean "Grotte d'Ali Baba" (136).

1	Yoghourt Acide 6c,	6b+
2	Venesse le Bienheureux	6b+
3	Mon Oncle d'Amérique	6c+

Ungefähr 30 Meter weiter rechts:
About 40 metres to the right:

4	Tyrolyse	6b+
5	Coyotte	6b
6	Dead Portos	6c+

und noch weiter rechts:
and even further over to the right:

7	Le Germain Bactérien	7a+

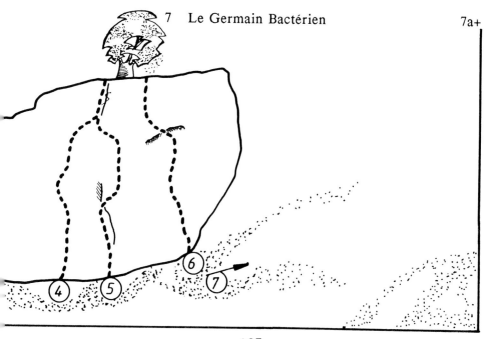

DOIGT DE DIEU

Rechts des Classics "Doigt de Diaeu Integral (143) - 6a - starten, direkt am Strand:

1	Isostar	6b
2	Weekend à Rome	7a+, 6c

ebenfalls in diesem Sektor:
also in the vicinity:

- Alzacotte   6c

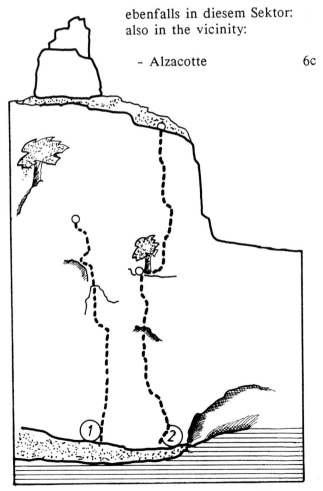
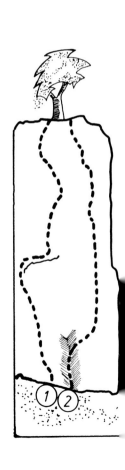

GROUPE DE PIOLET

Neue Routen unter dem "Refuge":
New lines below the hut:

Linker Teil - left side:

1	Moira	7c
2	Indianasteroid	7a+
3	A la Queue Leu Leu	5+
4	Space Rat	6a

Rechter Teil - right side:

5	Salaire de Sueur	6a
6	Not Cacau Today	6c
7	Aliboron	6c

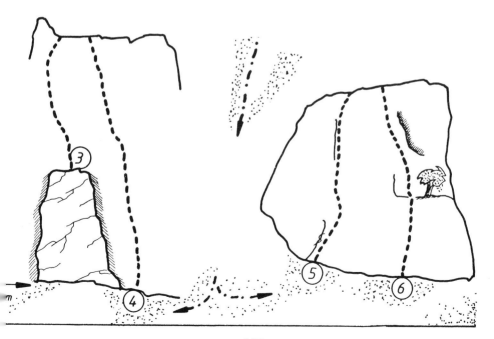

Die Klettergebiete um Toulon ~ The Toulon Climbing Areas

- (A) Le Baou
- (B) Le Cimaï
- (C) Mont Coudon
- (D) Tourris
- (E) La Piade

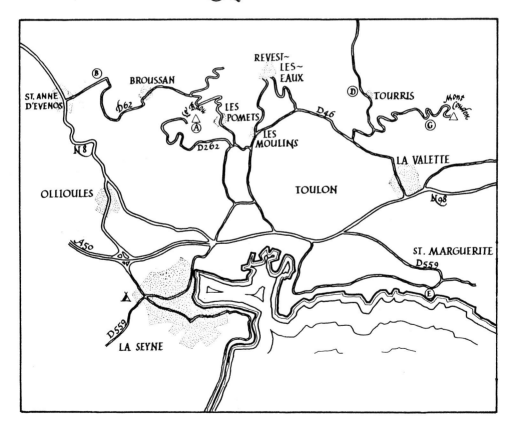

19. BAOU DE QUATRE OURO

Im Rücken die Einsamkeit und Wildnis der Provence - steinige Hochebenen, Pinienwälder und schroffe Schluchten - unter unseren Füßen die Großstadt Toulon - ein Gewirr von Hochhäusern, Straßen und Gärten, die von felsigen Hügeln und dem tiefblauen Meer eingefaßt werden. Irgendwo dort unten, in einer Vorstadt von Toulon, so erzählt mir Volker, sei sein Vater im Jahr 44 gefangengenommen worden. Es folgten dreieinhalb Jahre Kriegsgefangenschaft in der marokkanischen Wüste. Ob ich wüßte, daß sich hier im Hafenbecken von Toulon im Jahr 1942 die gesamte französische Flotte selbst versenkt hatte? Um nicht für den Rommel Panzer und Kanonenfutter transportieren zu müssen. Jetzt wirken die Leiber der Zerstörer und U-Boote, die unten im bedeutendsten französischen Kriegshafen vor Anker liegen, wie in einer blauen Lagune schlummernde Seeungeheuer - und wir hier oben in den sonnenbeschienenen Kalkplatten wie Kinder, die auf einem Vulkan spielen.

Die siebzig Grad steilen Platten und Pfeiler am "Fels der vier Winde", mit Bohrhaken gut bestückt, laden mit einer Vielzahl von Routen im 4. bis 6. Grad zur beschaulich-besinnlichen Nutzung ein. Hier verdiente sich ein gewisser Patrick Edlinger seine Sporen. Der Grund, daß heute jeder den Namen kennt, ist allerdings weiter rechts in der überhängenden, ca. 80 Meter hohen zentralen Südwand zu suchen. Dies erklärt vielleicht, warum - ganz und gar gegen die durchschnittliche Landessitte - hier die Hakenabstände mit steigender Schwierigkeit zunehmen. So lassen Routen wie "Paralyse", "La Capouera" und "Trémolo" die Probleme der "echten Welt", die drunten im Hafenbecken drohen, wenigstens bis zur nächsten Gipfelrast in Vergessenheit geraten.

Behind us lies the Provence in all its loneliness and wildness - rugged plateaus, pine forests, and gorges - at our feet, the city of Toulon - a maze of skyscrapers, busy streets, and gardens enclosed by the hills and the deep blue sea. It was somewhere down there, relates Volker, that his father was taken prisoner of war in 1944 to spend three years in labor camp in the Morroccan desert. Was I aware that in 1942 the French sank their entire fleet in the harbor of Toulon in order to prevent having to transport tanks and cannon fodder for Rommel? Now the hulls of the detroyers and submarines anchored in the most significant French war harbor seem like slumbering sea monsters in the blue lagoon below, and we up here on the sunny limestone slabs, like children playing on a volcano.

The 70 degree slabs and pillars on the "Rock of the Four Winds" is well equipped with bolts and sports a multitude of pleasure climbs in the grade 4 to 6 range. The reason for its reputation lies further to the right, however. One certain Patrick Edlinger cut his teeth here on the overhanging, 80 meter high central south face. This may explain why - in stark contrast to usual national custom - the distance between bolts increases in proportion to the difficulty of the route. For this reason the attempts of such routes as "Paralyse", "La Capoura" and "Trémolo" make you forget the problems of the "real world" that threaten in the harbor below, at least until the next rest on the summit.

ANFAHRT UND ZUGANG

Von Toulon auf der D 46 in Richtung le Revest bis am Rande der Stadt links die Straße nach le Broussan abzweigt. Wenig außerhalb des Ortes biegt links die Straße zum Baou de Quatre Ouro ab, die man ungefähr zwei Kilometer verfolgt, bis rechts ein sehr steiles Teersträßchen zum Sattel unterhalb der Wand führt. Vom Parkplatz beim Wasserreservoir erreicht man in ca. 10 Minuten die Einstiege.

ÜBERNACHTUNG

Da wegen der Großstadtnähe in den toulonesischen Klettergebieten fürchterlich geklaut wird, ist vom wilden Campen abzuraten. Unter den verschiedenen Campingplätzen schien uns "St. Jean" nahe beim Mammouth-Supermarkt in la Seyne am günstigsten. Er hat auch im Winter geöffnet, und man gelangt in 15-20 Minuten sowohl zum Baou als nach Cimaï.

VERSORGUNG

In der "Auberge de Cimaï" erhält man für 75 Ffr. ein Gourmet-Menu. Es ist besser, sich wegen der großen Nachfrage vorher anzumelden. Dies Schlemmerparadies liegt auf der Anhöhe gegenüber der Cimaï-Wand.

BESTE ZEIT

In allen Gebieten um Toulon wird praktisch das ganze Jahr über geklettert. An Mistral-Tagen geht man am besten nach Cimaï.

APPROACH

From Toulon take the D 46 toward le Revest till you get to a road at the edge of town which branches toward le Broussan. Just out of town take the road left to Baou and stay on it till you reach a very steep asphalt road leading to the saddle below the wall. The climbs are a ten minutes' walk from the parking spot at the water reservoir.

CAMPING

Due to the rampant theft in the proximity of the urban area of Toulon, it is not advisable to pitch a tent outside of guarded camping areas. Among the various campgrounds, St. Jean near the Mammouth supermarket in la Seyne seems to be the most advantageous. It is open in winter, and from here you reach both Baou and Cimaï in 15-20 minutes.

SUPPLIES

In the "Auberge de Cimaï" you can have a gourmet meal for 75 francs. It is safest to make reservations, as this glutton's delight is highly popular. You reach it by continuing on the road to Cimaï till you reach the rise opposite the crag.

BEST SEASON

You can climb the year round in all the areas around Toulon. On Mistral-days you are best off in Cimaï.

Le Baou de Quatre Ouro

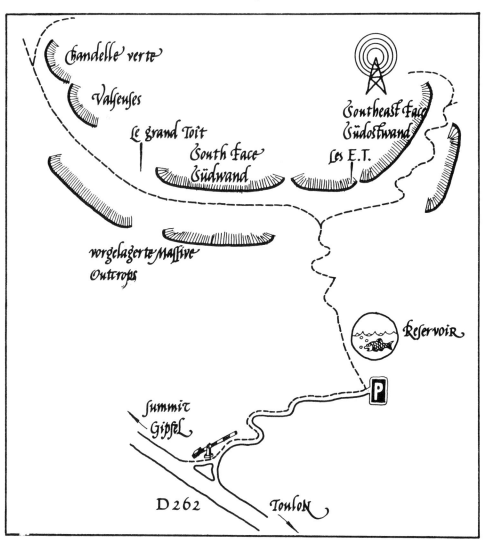

Da praktisch alle Routen am Fels angeschrieben sind, ist eine Orientierung anhand der Übersichtskarte und der Routenliste möglich.

As most routenames have been marked at the start of the climbs, orientation should be possible using our survey map and the following list of routes.

MASSIF CHANDELLE VERTE

Bibou de Gauche	6a
Bibou de Droite	6a
Direkteinstieg	7a
Diabolo Mente	5+
A Toit et moi	5+
Pétard Fumant	6a
Sorciers de Salem	6a
Tam-tam Voudou	6b
Chandelle Verte	6c-
Super-Pintade	5+

MASSIF VALSEUSES

La Nuit de Temps	6a
Valseuses	6a
Citron Pressée	6a+
L'Estron Sublime	6a
Les Peigne-Culs	5+
Dieu d'Eau	7a
Amour au Téléfone	6a+

In dem nach rechts anschließenden Wandteil, bis zum "Grand Toit", befinden sich folgende Routen:

On the wall to the right, that ends at the "Grand Toit", you'll find the following routes:

SÜDWESTWAND, RECHTER TEIL
SOUTHWEST FACE, RIGHT PART

Banana Blues	5
L'Ascenseur pour l'Echaffaud	5
La Marquisette	4
Les 3 Bananiers	4+
Quadrephonia	5+
Supermarquisette	4+, 1 Move 5+
Directe de Rotoplo	6b+
Rotoplo	6a
Fiston Rastèque	5+
P 74 Directe	5
La Jean-Marie	4
Rhinoféroce	5

ZENTRALE SÜDWAND (RECHTS VOM GRAND TOIT)
CENTRAL SOUTH.FACE (TO THE RIGHT OF THE GRAND TOIT)

Le Grand Toit	7c
Ricochet	5+
H, LM!	6c
Bataille de Sucre	6a
Ogoun Feraille	6b
Gllog	6b
Clochards Celestes	6c
Figolu	7a+
Bidis Stones	7b
Corto Maltese	7a
Over Paralyse	7a
Paralyse	7a
Les Chemins de Kathmandou	7b
Mahavishnu	7b
La Janny	6a+,6a,5
Tarte aux Cheveux	6c+
Capouera	6b+,6c,7a
Les Anges de la Rue	7b
Trémolo	7a
Kolyma (Var. l. of Quipour)	6c
La Quipour	5+,6b+,4+
Engatze (to r. of 2. SL of Qip.)	7c+
L'Aire du Temps	6c,6b,6a
La Boulmich	5+,5+,4+
La Gambille	4+,5+,4
Genzalco	6c

OSTWAND - EAST FACE

La Chappe	3
Septembre Noir	6a,5,6a+
Les E.T.	4,2,3,2
Le Genevrier	4+,4+,5-
Vaque à l'Ame	6a
L'Empire des Sens	6b,1 move 7a
Seven Up	7b
Le Jardin	4,3-,4+
Les Fils de Lumière	6b
(alt finish to "Le Jard.")	
Le Secret de Polichinel	6c+
Gagna	7b+
Walkyrie	6b+,6c,5-
Le Pilier	5+,6a+,5+,
Chrystal qui Songe	6c,6b,6c+
Les Trois Fadas	5,6a,4+
Right Variation	5, 4, 4+
Easy Rider	6b+,7a+ (Dach-roof)
Le Pilier de Phalange	6c/b+

ABSTIEG FÜR DIE OSTWAND

Bis zur Antenne aufsteigen, dann Geröllfeld bis auf halbe Höhe hinunter und nach rechts.

DESCENT FOR THE EAST FACE

Climb to the TV-Tower, descend the scree slope. Once you're down it halfway, head right.

20. CIMAI

Le Cimaï gleicht einer Welle aus Stein: wie im Brechen gefroren hängt der Kamm des sanft gewölbten Hügels über einem strukturlosen gelben Felskonkav von achzig Metern Höhe. Ihre furchterregende Neigung prädestinierte die erstarrte Wellenwand in der "Eisenzeit" zu einem Eldorado der Artifkletterei. Und noch aus der mittleren Entfernung zweifelt auch ein optimistisches Auge an der freien Bekletterbarkeit. Wer sich jedoch auf einen Meter Abstand heranwagt, entdeckt überall scharfe Käntchen und Noppen, manchmal auch Schlitze und Löcher. An diesen können sich Leute, die können, festhalten und sogar über längere Strecken emporbewegen. Trotz der guten Absicherung kommt es aber vor, daß Kletterer, die anderswo lässig einen Franzosensiebener flashen, in Cimaï von Selbstzweifeln überfallen werden. Im Bereich von 6a bis 6c sind die Bewertungen extrem hart. Wenn Cimaï heute auch berühmt ist wegen seinen überhängenden Hohlspiegelklettereien, so gibt es doch an den Felsstufen, die zu den Bändern unter die Wölbungen hinaufziehen, sowie entlang den zwischen den Überhängen eingelagerten Rinnen und Rissen eine Anzahl von Routen zwischen 4 und 6a.
In unsere Topos haben wir von den rund 100 Cimaï-Führen nur die markantesten aufgenommen. Da jedoch alle Routennamen an den Einstiegen angeschrieben sind, wird sich der werte Führerbenutzer mit Hilfe der Kurzbeschreibungen in der Routenliste ohne Probleme orientieren können.

ANFAHRT UND ZUGANG

Von Toulon auf der N 8 nach Ste. Anne d'Evenos. Hier rechts ab auf der D 62, die nach 1,5 Kilometern unter den Felsen vorbeiführt. Parkplatz rechts an der Straße.

Le Cimaï likens a wave of stone: as though frozen in breaking the ridge of a gently sloping hill is suspended above a structureless ochre rock vault. In the Iron Age of Climbing, its fearful inclination destined the petrified wall of water to become an Eldorado of aid climbing. Even a closer inspection from a short distance leaves doubt in the mind of the beholder as to the free-climbability of the structure. Only close scrutiny reveals the sharp edges, knobs, and sometimes even mini-cracks and holes. Those who are able, can use these for forward locomotion. But in spite of the high quality of the pro, it is not uncommon that climbers, who elsewhere flash French grade 7 with ease, are suddenly plagued by doubts about their climbing talents. The grading in the range from 6a to 6c is extremely stiff. Though the fame of Cimaï stems from the climbs on its overhanging concave mirror, there are, nonetheless, a host of possibilities in the 4 to 6a range on the rock belts leading to the terraces beneath the vaults, as well as in the cracks and gullies tucked in between the overhangs. We have included topos for only the most well-defined of the over 100 routes in Cimaï. However, since all the route names are marked on the climbs, the reader will have no problems finding the routes with the help of the short descriptions in the route list.

APPROACH

Take the N 8 to Ste. Anne d'Evenos. Turn right here onto the D 62, which takes you to the cliffs, 1.5 kilometers away. Parking is available on the right.

CIMAI

In Cimai haben wir nur die markantesten Führen in unsere Topos eingezeichnet und die übrigen aufgelistet. Da alle Routennamen an den Einstiegen angeschrieben sind, wird man sich so leicht orientieren können. Die Zahlen der Routenliste beziehen sich also immer auf die einzgezeichneten "Orientierungsführen", wo die ohne Ziffer aufgeführten zu finden sind, geht aus Kurzbeschreibungen hervor.

CIMAI
LINKER WANDTEIL - LEFT SIDE

1	Le Z	5+
2	Anal Plus	6a+,6a
	links vom SP nach der 1.SL:	
	to the left of belay 1:	
	- Résurgances	7a+
	- Tolérance	7a
	rechts von "2":	
	to the right of "2":	
	- Bains douches	7a
	nach rechts abzweigend:	
	branching off to the right:	
	- E =mc2	6c+
	von unten beginnend:	
	starting from the ground:	
	- Les Trois Chameliers	6c+,6a

3	Fredany	6c
	links, vom selben Band:	
	to the left, from the same ledge:	
	- Exil Intérieur	7c+
	- Rodeo	7a
	- Samizdat	8a
	rechts davon:	
	to the right:	
	- Danseuse Etoile	7b
4	Cheminée de Descente	4
	zwischen 4 und 5:	
	between 4 and 5:	
	- Green Peace	6c+,6b+
	- Fiu	6a
5	Escartefigue	7a+
	rechts davon:	
	to the right:	
	- Le Crapeau	6b+
	- Les Lauriers d'Apollon	6b+
	die Fortsetzung dieser Routen ist:	
	the continuation of these is:	
	- Si Vis Pacem, Para Bellum	7a

6	Dolomitum	7b+,6b
	links davon:	
	to the left:	
	- La Fille du Coupeur de Joints	6c
	- Simulacres	8b
	rechts davon, vom Band aus:	
	to the right, from the ledge:	
	- La Déchirure	7b
	- En un Combat Douteux	8a
	- Paradis Perdus	7b+
7	Syndrom Chinois	6b+,6c,6a+
	links fünf Führen bis zum Band:	
	to the l.five routes to the ledge:	
	- Nuit Exotique	5+
	- Equateur	6a+
	- Alice au Pays de Merveilles	5
	- Un Taxi pour que j' te Broute	6a
	- Estampe au Rabais	6b
8	Sous l'Oeil de Bouddha	6b,6a,6b+
	rechts davon 3 kurze Touren:	
	to the right three short routes:	
	- Tire-toi Minable	7b+
	- Les griffes de Satan	6c
	- Une Etrange Passion	6a+
9	Le Chat Huant	4,5,5
10	Boat Peoples	6b,7a

CIMAI
RECHTER WANDTEIL - RIGHT SIDE

9	Le Chat Huant	
	links davon	4,5,5
	to the right:	
	- L'Echo des Savanes	6c
	- Le Crépuscule des Idoles	6c
11	El Condor Pasa	5+,7a,7a
12	La Jean Bert	4,4+,4
13	La Philomène	4,5,5+,5+
	links davon, in einer gelben Wand:	
	to the right, in a yellow wall:	
	- l'Interlude	6b,
	- Contes de la Folie Ordinaire	7a+,7a
	- Terminus Amertume	7a
14	Le Piliers des Clodos	7b
	Fortsetzung/continuation:	
	- Pantomime	8a
15	Rêve d'un Autre Monde	6c,6c+,6b+
	rechts davon, am Sockel:	
	to the right, on the buttress:	
	- Mythe et Réalité	7c+
	- La Touffe	7b+
	- Sortilèges	8b
16	La Clodo	3,5
	vom Band, das leicht über die 1. SL von 7 erreicht werden kann: starting on the ledge, that can be reached via pitch 1 of 7:	
	- Over Nimbus	6b
	- La Moak	6a,5+
	- Grosse Pintade Technique	6a+,6a+
	- Cocktail Magique	7a
	- Le Hamster Jovial	6b+,5+
	- Alerte Cérébrale	7a

17	La Dédé	4,4+,3
18	Orange Mécanique	8a

to the left, from the ledge:
links davon, vom Band aus
- Hiéroglyphes   7c
- Ossuaire   7b,7b+

branching off to the right from 9:
von 9 zweigt rechts ab:
- Cathédrale   7c

19 Tropique du Cancer   6b,5
links davon:
to the left:
- Energie Douce   7b+
- Vive la Vie   6c

im Wandteil rechts von 10 sind:
on the wall to the right of 10
you'll find:
- Serum Philosophique   6a+,5
- Café Crème   6b
- Cul de Venus (pfui!) 7c
- Toutes des Chiennes   7b+
- T'es à l'Usine Eugène 7c
- L'Ange Exterminator
- Pensée Obscure   7a+

CIMAI
RECHTER WANDTEIL – RIGHT SIDE

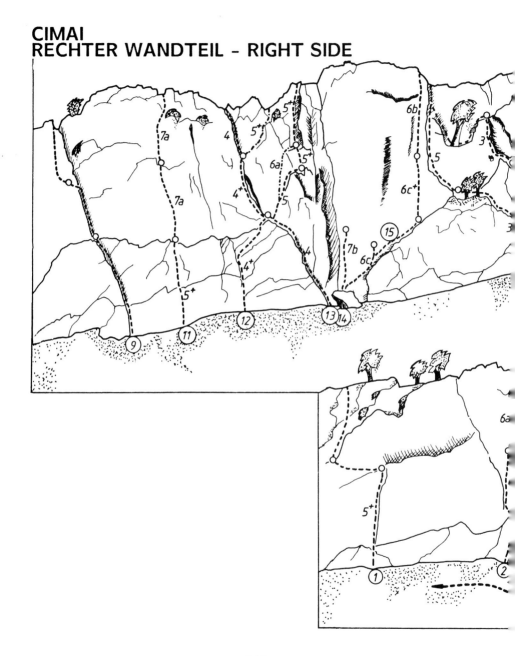

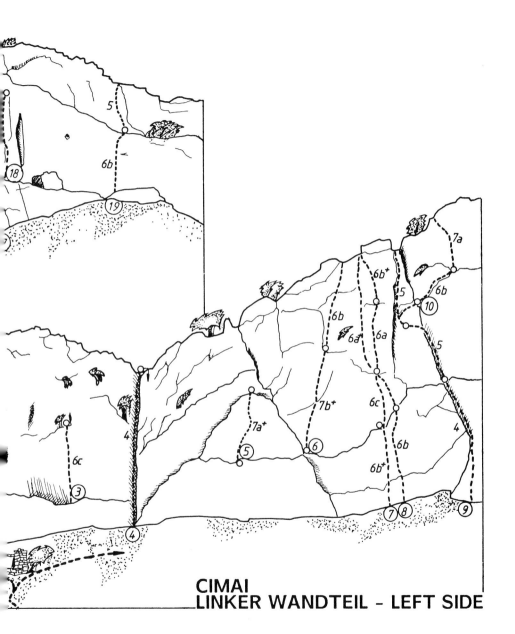

CIMAI
LINKER WANDTEIL - LEFT SIDE

21. MONT COUDON

Während drüben in Cimaï regenbogenbunte Glitzerhosen und T-shirts mit selbstbewußten Aufschrieben die Blößen der göckelesbraunen Götterleiber schmücken, trifft man am Mont Coudon noch auf Saurier mit Helm und Trittleiter sowie auf ein paar Urmenschen in Malerhosen und mit Stirnband über dem gefurchten Antlitz. Viele der knapp 50 Führen in den 20 bis 70 Meter hohen Wänden des Mont Coudon sind nämlich auch für Wochenendkrabbler zu haben, d. h. im Bereich zwischen 4 und 6b angesiedelt und mit "Spits" abgesichert.

Die 500 Meter lange Felswand teilt sich in drei im Charakter unterschiedliche Wandzonen. Während im rechten bis zu 60 Meter hohen Teil steile Wandklettereien im Grenzbereich zwischen Genuß und Extrem vorherrschen und man sich die niedrige mittlere Wandzone für die Zeiten aufheben sollte, an denen man keine Lust hat, "richtig" zu klettern, dominieren im linken Wandteil die Plattenschleicher. Es ist ein sinnlicher Genuß, nach den Raspelgriffen von Cimaï die Fingerkuppen in die glatten, hautsympathischen Felsdellen zu schmiegen, wenn einen die Böen des Mistrals nicht wiedermal aus den Reibungstritten zu pusten versuchen.

ANFAHRT UND ZUGANG

Von la Valette im östlichen Weichbild Toulons auf der D 46 in Richtung le Revest, bis ein Schild nach rechts den Weg zum Mont Coudon weist. Man folgt dieser Straße, der D 446, gut 6 Kilometer weit, bis in einer Linkskehre rechts der Straße am Fels in roter Farbe ECOLE D'ESCALADE angepinselt ist. Man befindet sich oberhalb der Ausstiege des zentralen Wandteils.

Whereas the visitor to the Cimaï will encounter only Kentucky fried peacocks sporting rainbow colored lycras and T-shirts with bold logos, the caller at Mount Coudon may stumble onto a few dinosaurs with helmets and etriers as well as several Neanderthal specimens in painter pants and headbands above deeply furrowed countenances. Many of the 50 or so routes on the 20 to 70 meter high cliffs of Mont Coudon are suited for the weekend recreational rock bumbler as well - that is, they range from 4 to 6b and are equipped with solid bolts.

The 500 meter long rock wall is divided into three zones, each with different characteristics. Whereas the right hand side of the crag is dominated by steep face climbs ranging from the pleasure to the extreme categories, and the low middle section is one that can be well reserved for days when you don't feel up to "proper climbing", the left zone sports mainly the renowned friction slabs. After the rough treatment by Cimaï limestone, the smoother rock here is balsam to thin skin (if you're lucky enough not to be caught by the Mistral trying to blow you off).

APPROACH

From la Valette, which bounds Toulon on the East, take the D 46 toward le Revest, until you reach the sign for Mount Coudon on the right side of the road. Take this road (D 446) for 6 kilometers until you reach a left facing bend on the right side of the road. Here ECOLE D'ESCALADE is painted in red on the rock. You are now above the exit of the climbs in the central section of the crag.

Linker und mittlerer Wandteil:
Vom Parkplatz erreicht man, sich schräg rechts haltend, nach 70 Metern den Beginn des markierten Abstiegs (Schwierigk. 1-2). Am Wandfuß kann man sich entscheiden, ob man linkshaltend die Einstiege des zentralen oder rechtshaltend die Routen des linken Wandteils ansteuern will.
Um zu den Einstiegen des rechten Wandteils zu gelangen, fährt man von der roten Felsanschrift noch ca. einen Kilometer in Richtung Coudon-Gipfel weiter bis zum Parkplatz nach dem Tunnel. Von hier rechtshaltend auf einem Weg hinab zu den Einstiegen.

ÜBERNACHTUNG, VERSORGUNG ETC.

Siehe Baou de Quatre Ouro.

Left and Middle Sectors:
If you continue from the parking spot diagonally to the right for 70 meters, you will reach the top of the descent (grades 1 and 2). At the foot of the descent you can decide whether to steer left towards the central part of the cliff or turn right to reach the left sector.

Right Sector:
To reach the climbs in the right section drive roughly one kilometer further in the direction of the summit to a parking spot behind the tunnel. From here head right on a trail that leads to the start of the climbs.

CAMPING, SUPPLIES ETC.

See Baou de Quatre Ouro

MONT COUDON
MITTLERER WANDBEREICH - CENTRAL PART

Gleich rechts des Abstiegs (im zu Tale blickenden Sinn) findet sich "Le Petit Surplomb" (4+). Geht man weiter in diese Richtung, kommt man zum LINKEN WANDTEIL. Links des Abstiegs beginnt der ZENTRALE WANDTEIL. Linkerhand (nun vor der Wand stehend) sind 10 Toprope-Routen (3 - 6b) mit Umlenkhaken. Rechts davon ist die 2 SL-Tour "Les Pompiers" (5+) und weiter drüben, in einer glatten Platte, "Curling" (6c). Rechts von Curling kann man ca. 15 Meter weit abklettern oder abseilen, um zu den Einstiegen des RECHTEN WANDTEILS zu gelangen.

To the right of the descent (facing downward) is "Le Petit Surplomb" (4+). Further over is the LEFTHAND PART of the Mont Coudon area. Just to the left of the descent is the CENTRAL PART beginning with 10 practice climbs, grades 3 to 6b with fixed toproping ankers. To the right of the toproping area (this time facing the wall) you'll find the two pitch route "Les Pompiers" (5+) and an almost vertical slab inhabited by "Curling" 6c). To the right of "Curling" you can downclimb 15 meters or rappel to reach the RIGHT PART of the cliff.

MONT COUDON
LINKER WANDTEIL – LEFT SIDE

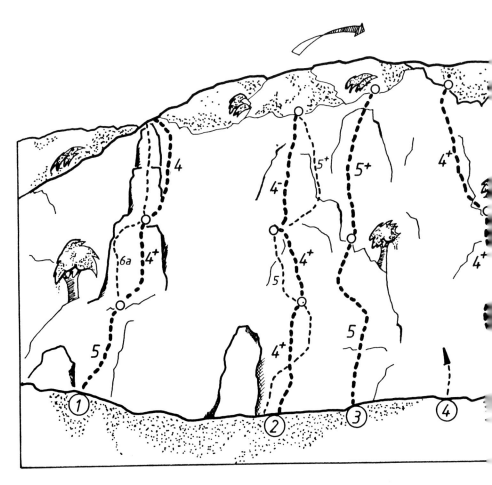

1	Les 3 Gouttes de H2O	5, Var. 6a
2	Salle de Bain	4+, Var. 5+
3	Saint Maclou	5+
4	Ne Touche pas mon Pof	6b+, 6b
5	Le Chêne	4
6	Melodie Aérienne	6a
7	Les Oliviers	5
8	Boëly	4+
9	Grand Toit	5+
10	Le Bal à Bougival	6a
11	Armaguedon	6a
12	Le Voleur Bagdad	5

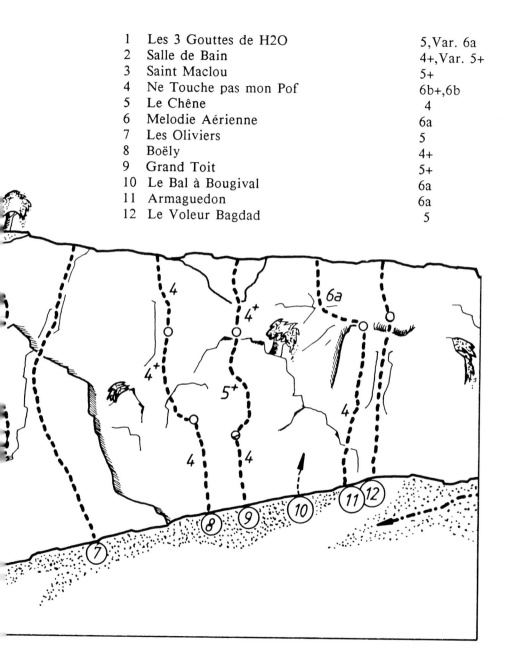

MONT COUDON
RECHTER WANDTEIL - RIGHT SIDE

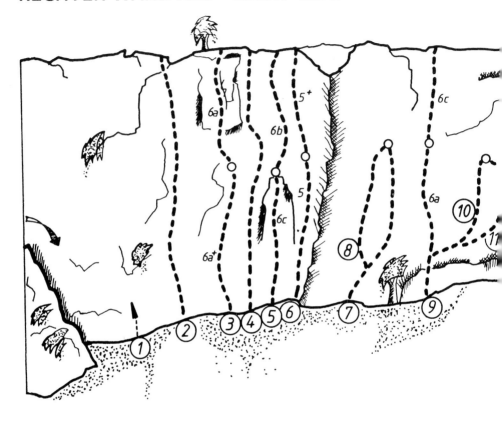

1	Le Soleil Couchant	
2	On se Calme	
3	Les Flirts du Mal	6a+
4		7a
5	Feeling	6c
6	Chronastro	5+
7	Les Malheures d'Emillie	5+
8	Le Paradis Perdu	5+

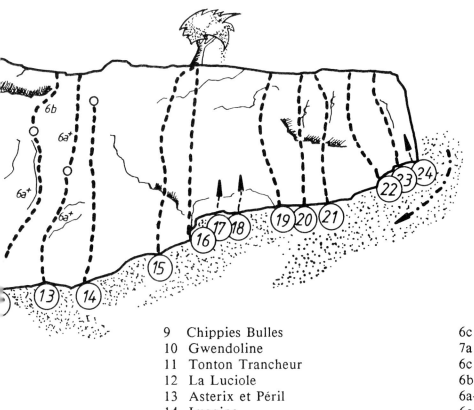

9	Chippies Bulles	6c
10	Gwendoline	7a
11	Tonton Trancheur	6c
12	La Luciole	6b
13	Asterix et Péril	6a+
14	Imagine	6c
15	Aziza	7a
16	Anais	6a
17	Toit à Jouer	6b
18	Les Hauts Ferrés	6c
19	Arc de Cercle	
20	Pyrrhacantax	
21	Gobovol	7b
22	Doux Frisson	6c
23	Jean Marie	5+
24	Violon Dinque	

22. LA PIADE

Der 800 Meter lange Meeresquergang unterm Fort de Ste. Marguerite hat inzwischen schon eine gewisse Berühmtheit erlangt. Er wird normalerweise als Boulderquergang ausgeführt. Je nach Routenwahl bewegt man sich im Vierer- bis 6b-Gelände, zwingend sind 5+-Teile. Falls einem die Umgehungsmöglichkeiten der Schlüsselpassagen zu interessant anmuten, weicht man einfach ins nasse Element aus. Bei starkem Wellengang sollte eine Begehung verschoben werden. Auf eine detailierte Beschreibung verzichten wir hier, da wir eurer Kreativität und eurem Pioniergeist keine Zügel anlegen wollen.

ANFAHRT UND ZUGANG

Von Toulon auf der D 42 und N 559 nach le Pradet. Bei der Bushaltestelle "Sainte Marguerite" biegt man, dem Schild CROSSMED folgend, nach rechts ab und überläßt das hoffentlich von allen Wertgegenständen geleerte Fahrzeug zweihundert Meter weiter vorn seinem Schicksal. Gleich gegenüber vom Parkplatz führt ein Straßenstummel zu Treppen, die zum Meer hinunterführen. Sich nach links wendend marschiert man ca. 500 Meter am Strand entlang bis zur Klippenkante.

ÜBERNACHTUNG, VERSORGUNG ETC.

Siehe Baou de Quatre Ouro.

The 800 meter long sea traverse beneath Fort de Ste. Marguerite has gained renown among the inhabitants of the northern spheres as well. It is normally listed as a boulder traverse. Depending on how you piece it together, it ranges anywhere from 4 to 6b (there are some unavoidable 5+ sections). If, at times, you find the detours around the difficult sections too interesting for your taste, you can escape by the sea route. If the breakers are battering the cliff all too wildly, you may prefer to postpone your attempt of the traverse. As the climb has an unlimited number of variations, in order not to put a cramp on individual creative expression, we will leave the route-finding to your own taste.

APPROACH

From Toulon take the D 42 and the N 559 to le Pradet. At the bus stop "Sainte Marguerite" turn right and follow the signs for CROSSMED. Leave your car emptied of all valuables and parked 200 meters further on. Just behind the parking spot a remnant of a road leads to stairs that descend to the sea. When you reach the bottom, turn left and hike 500 meters along the beach till you reach the edge of the cliff.

CAMPING, SUPPLIES, ETC.

See Baou de Quatre Ouro.

23. TOURRIS

Last und least stellen wir von den toulonesischen Kletterzentren das Toprope-Gebiet Tourris vor. Heute finden sich an der um die 20 Meter hohen und 200 Meter langen Felswand etwas über 20 Probleme mit Umlenkbolts. Einige Routen sind nun auch schon für den Vorstieg eingerichtet. Vor Ort wird sich der Leser wohl selbst zurechtfinden.

ANFAHRT UND ZUGANG

Von la Valette wie zum Mont Coudon vier Kilometer in Richtung le Revest und rechts ab wie gehabt. Nach gut einem Kilometer zweigt links von der Zufahrt zum Mont Coudon das Sträßchen nach Tourris ab. Man folgt ihm bis zu einem Päßchen, westlich von dem sich die Felsen befinden. Ein schwarz markierter Pfad beginnt gleich hinter dem Paß und führt in ungefähr zehn Minuten zum Ort des Geschehens.

ÜBERNACHTUNG, VERSORGUNG ETC.

Siehe Baou de Quatre Ouro

Last and least of the climbing centers of Toulon we would like to present the toprope area of Tourris. To date there are some 20 toprope problems equipped with belay anchors above the climbs on this 20 meter high and 200 meter wide cliff. The routes are gradually being equipped to be led as well.

APPROACH

From la Vallete follow directions for Mont Coudon (four kilometers toward le Revest, then right, etc.) After you have been on the road to Mont Coudon for about one kilometer, there is an intersection to Tourris. Take this road till you get to a pass. The crags are to the west of this pass. The trail with black markers starts just beyond the pass and leads to the cliff (10 minutes).

CAMPING, SUPPLIES, ETC.

See Baou de Quatre Ouro

24. BAOU DE ST. JEANNET

Schon in alten Chroniken werden die Calanques als Spezialkurort für im ewigen Gletschereis erstarrte Alpinsaurier wärmstens empfohlen. Der Baou de St. Jeannet blieb dagegen von teutonischen und angelsächsischen Berggeschädigten bis in die achziger Jahre hinein weitgehend verschont. Als dann aber auch im kontinentalen Europa das Freiklettern Mode wurde, verzeichnete das mittelalterliche Städtchen über der Bucht von Nizza eine sprunghafte Zunahme der Daunenjackentouristen, besonders, wenn droben im Verdon die Temperaturen unter den Sehnenzerrungspunkt fielen. Zwar sind die Führen an der "Grande Face", der gut 300 m hohen SW-Wand des Baou, was ihre Länge angeht, durchaus mit denen des südfranzösichen Maßklettergebiets vergleichbar. Aber nur drei der St. Jeannet-Führen, nämlich "Patience", "La Mafia" und "Bernard Etaint la Bougie" sind jenen Klassikern ebenbürtig. Eine Handvoll kommt ihnen was Ruhmträchtigkeit, Linienführung und Exponiertheit angeht bestenfalls nahe. Aber gerade die Tatsache, daß die Grande Face, besonders im zentralen Wandbereich, stark gegliedert und nahbar ist, hat es möglich gemacht, hier genußvolle Führen von mittlerer Schwierigkeit zu kreieren. Sie schlängeln sich, häufig begleitet von üppiger, jedoch niemals störender Vegetation, von Terasse zu Terasse dem Gipfelplateau entgegen.

Dies soll jedoch nicht heißen, daß der Baou für den modernen Topklimmer ein im Vergleich zu den bekannten Renommierklettergebieten zweitklassiges Ausweichziel wäre. Denn jenseits des brüchigen Südpfeilers, der die Grande Face rechts begrenzt, tut sich die Bilderbuch-Klettergartenwelt der "Ressauts" auf. Im silbergrauen Fels dieser vier in die Südostflanke des Berges eingelagerten Wandstufen können Fingernagelzerrer, Alpinisten in der Winterpause und geländegängige Hunde jeweils nach ihrer Fasson selig werden. Und auch im Januar heizt die gutmütige provençalische Sonne oft die Kulissen ausreichend auf, sodaß die Zuschauer beim Vertikalballett nicht auf den atemberaubenden Anblick der

Already ancient chronicles recommend the Calanques warmly as a watering place for alpinosaurs who have stiffened their joints in the ice of the Western Alps. In contrast to the Calanques, Baou de St. Jeannet was spared the onslaughts of the mutilated anglosaxon and teutonic veterans of the mountains until the l980's. However, as the free-climbing bug caught on in Continental Europe as well, the tourist information agencies noted a surge of down-clad visitors to the Bay of Nice, particularly when the temperatures in the Verdon approached the ligament pulling point. Though the routes of the "Grande Face", the 300 meter high SW Face of Baou, can compete in size with it's more prestigious opponent in la Palud, as far as the quality of climbs goes, only three of the routes, "Patience", "La Mafia", and "Bernard Etaint la Bougie", have the quality of Verdon classics. Another handful of the climbs in St. Jeannet may come close. The fact that the Grande Face, especially in its central part, is so highly structured and approachable has allowed the creation of a wealth of pleasurable routes in the medium difficulty range. These wind upwards from terrace to terrace (often interspersed with vegetation that is rarely bothersome) to the summit.

All this is not to say that the Baou is of little interest to the first rate climber or that the area is,, at best, a second class alternative to other recent developments. On the contrary, on the far side of the friable south pillar which forms the right boundary of the crag, the French climbers have developed a modern mini-paradise in the form of the "Ressauts". In the silver-gray rock of these crags inset into the four terraces of the south east flank of the mountain, fingertip hangers, alpinists in winter retreat, and skilfull dogs can all find their own particular brand of recreation. We have limited our selection of routes to the classics on the Grande Face and several of the most recommendable ones on the Ressauts, with particular emphasis on those of the second level. These should suffice to keep your muscles fit until the unbearable isolation of this

Heldenkörper der Akteure verzichten müssen. Damit auch garantiert keiner von ihnen verlorengeht, hat irgendein gutmütiger Mensch die Führen am Baou numeriert und diese Zahlen fürsorglich an die Felsen gemalt. Da die Ziffern aber nicht unserer Ordnung gemäß von West nach Ost den Fels versauen, sondern recht chaotisch geflickschustert wurde, führen wir sie nur nach dem Routennamen in Klammern auf. Unsere Auswahl an Führen beschränkt sich auf die Klassiker an der Grande Face und die besten Touren an den Ressauts, mit besonderem Schwerpunkt auf der zweiten Wandstufe. Dies sollte ausreichen, die Muckis in Form zu halten, bis euch die unerträgliche Einsamkeit dieses Altrheins der Freikletterei nach la Turbie hinübertreibt.

Vielleicht schaut ihr aber vorher mal im relativ jungen Klettergebiet von La Source vorbei, das der Grande Face südwestlich vorgelagert ist. Wie dort, unterscheidet sich der Fels in La Source deutlich von dem der Ressauts. Statt an rauhen, wasserzerfressenen Griffen zerrt man sich in den rund 100 Routen des neuen Klettergebiets an gelben Leisten und Käntchen dem Lichte entgegen - und freut sich mit geschwollenen Armen an den supersoliden Betonbolzen.

ANFAHRT UND ZUGANG

Von Vence auf der N 210 in nordöstlicher Richtung 6 Kilometer bis zur Abzweigung nach St. Jeannet. Am besten stellt man das Fahrzeug auf dem Parkplatz am Ortseingang ab, von wo man die Einstiege mit Hilfe der Zugangsskizze auf den Seiten 332 & 333 in 10 bis 20 Minuten erreicht.

backwater of free climbing areas drives you to seek the crowds in la Turbie.

Before you go, you might like to have a look at a new climbing area that lies southwest of the Grande Face, la Source. Here too, the rock is markedly different from the Ressauts. Instead of rough, water-worn holes, you pull on yellow bands and ridges in the some 100 routes of this area. The solid bolts make this a good place to give your forearms a good workout.

APPROACH

From Vence drive 6 kilometers northeast on the N 210 until you reach the intersection to St. Jeannet. In town it's best to park at the entrance to the upper part. From the parking lot here you can get to all the climbs in 10 to 20 minutes with the help of the map on pages 332 & 333.

CAMPING

The nearest campsite is "Les Cent Chênes" in St. Jeannet bas Village, some three kilometers below the upper part of town, toward Gattières. It is officially open from April until October, but so far noone seems to mind winter campers.

FURTHER INFORMATION

Michael Dufranc, ESCALADES AU BAOU DE ST. JEANNET, 1983, is out of print and thus hard to come by.

S. Biondi, LA SOURCE DE ST. JEANNET, 1986, published by the author, can be purchased in the "Tabac" shop opposite the Hotel St. Barbe.

ÜBERNACHTUNG

Der nächste Campingplatz ist "Les Cent Chênes" in St. Jeannet, Bas Village, ca. drei Kilometer vom oberen Ortsteil entfernt in Richtung Gattières. Der Platz hat nur von April bis Oktober geöffnet, bisher wurde aber noch niemand in den Wintermonaten vertrieben.

WEITERE INFORMATIONEN

Michel Dufranc, ESCALADES AU BAOU DE SAINT-JEANNET, erschienen 1983, vergriffen und deshalb nur noch ausnahmsweise auffindbar.

S. Biondi, LA SOURCE DE SAINT-JEANNET, 1986 im Selbstverlag, zu finden im "Tabac" gegenüber vom Hotel St. Barbe.

Setzt den... *JOKER*

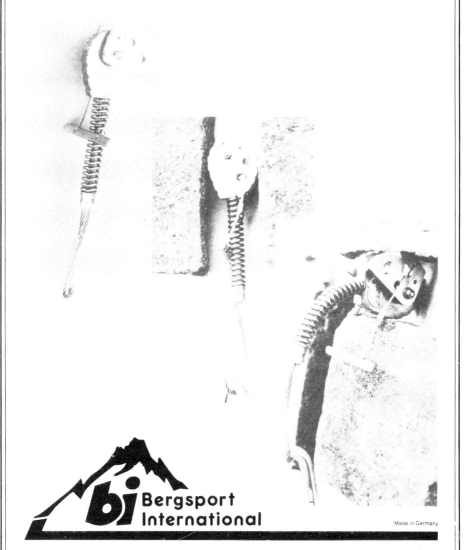

bi Bergsport International

Made in Germany

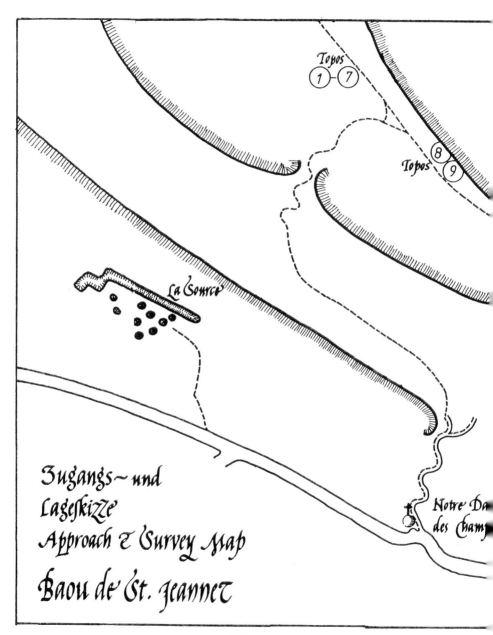

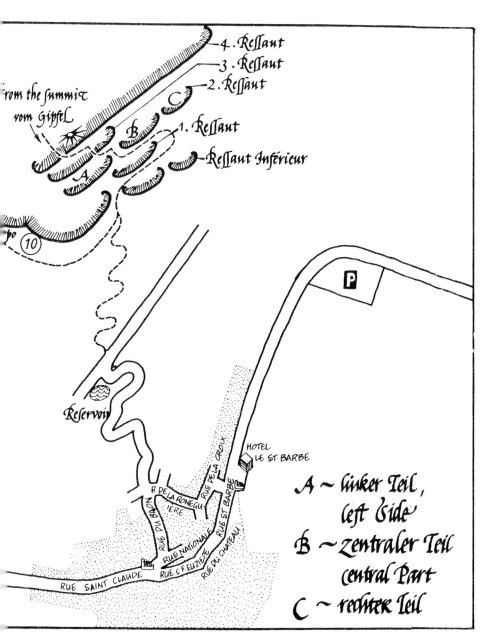

SECTEUR PERIL JAUNE/DIRECTISSIME

1	Délire (37)	7a
2	Le Péril Jaune (34)	6a
3	Directissime (33)	6a

SECTEUR DE LA MAFIA

4	Patience (36)	6b+
5	La Mafia (32)	6b+
6	Bernard Etaint la Bougie (44)	7a+
7	Le Jardin Suspendu (31)	5+

SECTEUR DE LA MALET LA TONTON WALKER

8 La Malet (21) 4+
9 Combination La Loco & La Proue de Navire (17 & 18) 6b+
10 La Tonton Walker (16) 6a

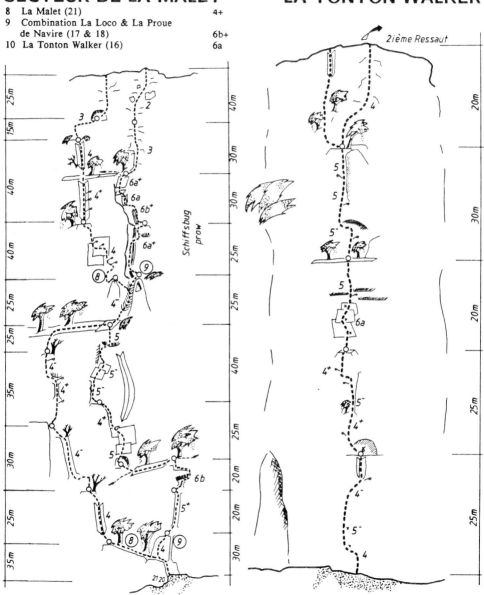

SPORT BERGLAND

7410 Reutlingen · In Laisen 11

DIE EXPERTEN FÜR BERGSPORT UND TREKKING

DEUXIEME RESSAUT
LINKER TEIL - LEFT SIDE

1	La Popeye (35)	6c
2	La Dalle a Dudu (139)	6a+
3	La Sésame (38a)	6b
4	Morgane de Toit	7b
5	Nabuchodonosor (142)	5,6a+
6	Les Parents Frustrés	7b
7	Mur Noir (39)	5,6a
8	Les Travailleurs (106)	6a,6a
9	Le Hongrois (40a)	6a,6b

10		6c+,6a
11	La Pie XII (40)	5+,6a
12		6b
13	La Voie Lactée (41)	5+
14		5+/6a
15		6a
16	L'Arête du Mur de sa Vie (43a)	5-
17	Le Mur de sa Vie (43)	4+/5-
18	Variante (43b)	4-

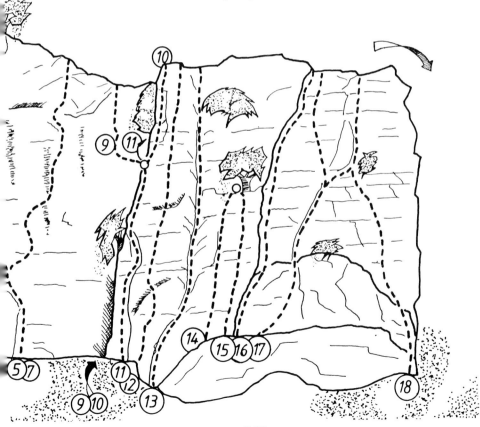

DEUXIEME RESSAUT
ZENTRALER TEIL - CENTRAL PART

1		5+
2	Gança	6a
3	Solexine	6c
4		
5	Les Temps Modernes (47)	6b
6	La Super-Tavan (48)	6b
7	La Tavan (49)	6a
8	Mephisto (134)	6b+
9	La Plantation (50)	6c+
10	Niagara (137)	7a
11	L'I (52)	6b
12	L'Ibis (138)	5+
13	Le Chameau (53)	6b+
14	La Dame (54)	5+
15	La Spinach (55)	5
16	Le Grand Chariot (135)	5+
17	L'Espoir (90)	6b
18	La Dalle à Daniel (91)	5

DEUXIEME RESSAUT
RECHTER TEIL - RIGHT PART

1	La Bouffique (155)	6a+
2	La Veuve (60a)	5
3	L'Ange (93)	6a
4	La Femelle (60)	6b
5		
6	L'Hypothénuse (58)	6a
7	L'Os du Grimpeur (59)	4
8	L'O.S. Dudu, Grimpeur (140)	6a+
9	Le Galérien (61)	6b
10	La Quebec (61a)	6a

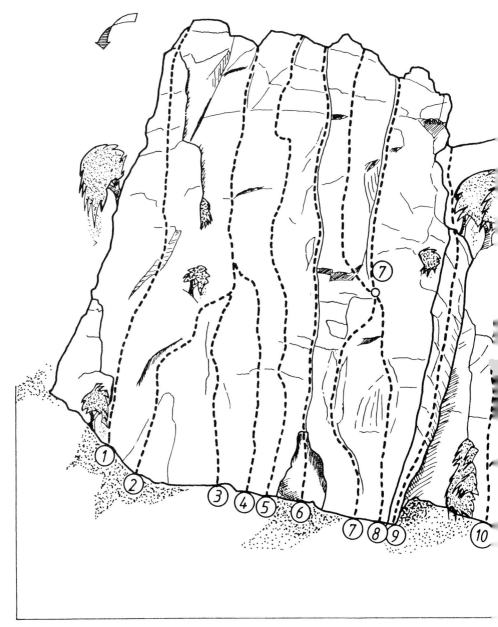

DEUXIEME RESSAUT
ZENTRALER TEIL – CENTRAL PART

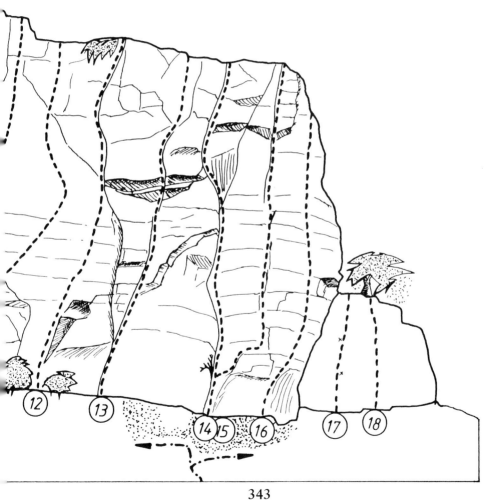

DEUXIEME RESSAUT
RECHTER TEIL – RIGHT SIDE

#	Route	Grade
1	La Bouffique (155)	6a+
2	La Veuve (60a)	5
3	L'Ange (93)	6a
4	La Femelle (60)	6b
5		
6	L'Hypothénuse (58)	6a
7	L'Os du Grimpeur (59)	4
8	L'O.S. Dudu, Grimpeur (140)	6a+
9	Le Galérien (61)	6b
10	La Quebec (61a)	6a

25. LA TURBIE

In Monaco kann man nicht nur sein Geld verlieren, sondern auch die Haut an den Fingerkuppen. Dies liegt nicht an irgendwelchen drakonischen Strafvollzugsmaßnahmen für Taschendiebe, sondern an den Erosionsgriffen droben an der Loubière und am Tête de Chien. Die "High Society", die sich hier auf senkrechtem Parkett trifft, steht jener unten an Klassenbewußtsein oder dem Drang dazuzugehören nicht nach. In den Felsen wie im Casino herrschen internationales Gedränge, regieren Spannung, Jubel und verunglückte Hoffnung.

Was die Lebensgewohnheiten angeht, lassen sich jedoch einige wenn auch unbedeutende Unterschiede aufzeigen zwischen den Glücksrittern drunten in Monte Carlo und jenen auf lichter Bergeshöh'. Nur wenige dort droben werden vom Nobelhotel vornehm duftend zum Ort des Geschehens chauffiert. Im Durchschnitt entkriechen sie vielmehr mit ca. zwölf Stunden Zeitverschiebung zum Dinestbeginn der Talschicht einer der Höhlen des Hundekopfs. Bald lassen die Sonne und etliche Tassen Pulverkaffee die Kopf- und Gliederschmerzen vergessen. Die Szene setzt sich in Bewegung. Nach einigem Anstehen findet jeder seinen Platz im Stadion, um sein Glück auf eine der über 300 an den Fels gepinselten Zahlen zu setzen. Nun kann jeder nach Herzenslust dem Kletterhimmel entgegensteigen. Denn der Traumfels über Monaco bietet zwischen dem Roche a Roche und der Ostwand des Tête de Chien so ziemlich alles, was auch ein verwöhntes Herz an genußvollen Zügen begehrt. Aus der Ferne ähneln die Felsen der Loubière bleichen Röhrenknochen , von bunten Ameisen flächig überkrabbelt. Nach rechts hin, wo die Wände des Tête de Chien lotrecht zu den Hochhäusern der Großstadt abzubrechen scheinen, wird die Population jedoch deutlich dünner. Nur relativ wenige derer, die an der Loubière am dritten Bohrhaken ihren Tagträumen vom zehnten Grad nachhängen, scheinen sich von der inzwischen schon berühmten

In Monaco you can lose not only your money, but also the skin off your fingers. This phenomenon is not a result of some medieval torture measures still applied to pickpockets, but directly related to the erosion pockets of the Loubière and the Tête de Chien. Both the crags and the casinos are dominated by an atmosphere of cosmopolitain bustle, excitement, high expectations and shattered hopes.

The differences, insignificant as they may be, between the soldiers of fortune below in Monte Carlo and above in la Turbie lie in their life styles. Only few of the guests of to the heights are chauffeured daily from posh hotels to the scene of action. Some twelve hours later than the night shift the dwellers of the heights creep from a cavern in the "dog's head". Soon the warm sunshine and large doses of caffeine make them forget head and joint aches. When the scenario finally gets moving all rush to secure their spots in the queue to place their bets on one of the roughly 300 numbers scrawled onto the rocks. From the distance the cliffs of the Loubière look like bleached shin bones crawling with colorful ants. To the right, where the walls of the Tête de Chien plunge towards the skyscrapers of the city, the population becomes noticeably thinner. Only few of those who hang their daydreams of the tenth grade on the third bolt of the Loubière feel the urge to try their luck on the photogenic slabs of the "Athos". The "Paroi du Fort" on the far eastern side of the cliff has even fewer vistors than the south face. The neglect of this section does injustice to the originality of "Big Ben", and the very stiff "Amuse Geule" and Jeux de Mains", for the quality of rock here is every bit as good as that of the Loubière.

Fotografierplatte von "Athos" herausgefordert zu fühlen. Ganz zu Unrecht erhält die "Paroi du Fort", ganz im Osten des Hundekopfmassivs, noch weniger Besuch als die Südwand. Und dabei bietet sie mit dem superoriginellen "Big Ben", der strengen "Amuse Geule" und "Jeux de Mains" Touren für jeden Geschmack, die hinsichtlich der Felsqualität kaum hinter der Loubière zurückstehen. An der Paroi du Fort ist darauf zu achten, daß man nicht über die Mauer der früheren Festung steigt und wandernd absteigt, sondern wieder über die Wand abseilt.

ANFAHRT UND ZUGANG

Von Nizza auf der N 7 nach La Turbie. Hier zuerst in Richtung Cap d'Ail und kurz vor dem Ortsausgang links abbiegend nach knapp einem Kilometer zum Parkplatz beim Tête de Chien. Wie man zu den verschiedenen Einstiegen gelangt, geht aus der Karte auf den Seiten 350 & 351 hervor.

ÜBERNACHTUNG & VERSORGUNG

Konnte man früher in den Cavernen des Tête de Chien nächtigen (siehe Text), so wurde dieser Möglichkeit durch die Unterbringung eines Reitstalles dortselbst jetzt ein Riegel vorgeschoben. Der Erfahrung gemäß duldet die Polizei ca. sechs auf dem Parkplatz oberhalb der Felsen über Nacht abgestellte Fahrzeuge, jedoch keine Zeltler. Der nächste Zeltplatz liegt am Col d'Eze, acht Kilometer von la Turbie in Richtung Nizza. Die nächsten Supermärkte findet man in Nizza.

WEITERE INFORMATIONEN

In TOPOS A LA CARTE dürfte das Klettergebiet von la Turbie derzeitig am umfassendsten dargestellt sein.

APPROACH

From Nice take the N 7 to la Turbie. From here go first toward Cap d'Ail. Just before the town exit, turn left and drive about one kilometer to the parking lot above Tête de Chien. To get to the various cliffs, see aproach map, pages 350 & 351.

LODGING

If the caves of the Tête de Chien earlier (see above) provided the ideal free lodging for climbers with thin pocketbooks, this alternative has today been eliminated through the establishment of riding stables here. The police seem to tolerate to a maximum of six cars parked overnight in the lot above the crags, but not tents. In la Turbie there are a few run-down hotels, the prices of which are roughly comparable to the price of a night in a Swiss alpine hut. The nearest campsite is at the Col d'Aze 8 kilometers toward Nice from la Turbie.

SUPPLIES

The nearest supermarkets are located in Nice.

FURTHER INFORMATION

The local guidebook is out of print. A new edition is not forthcoming due to the death of its author. Martin Lochner's TOPOS A LA CARTE provides the most complete information on the area.

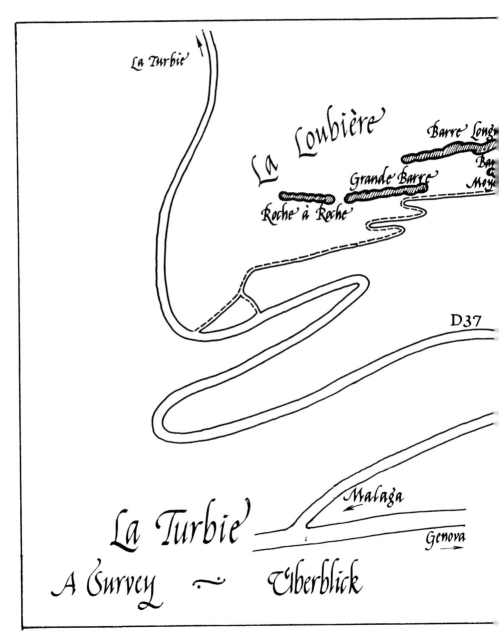

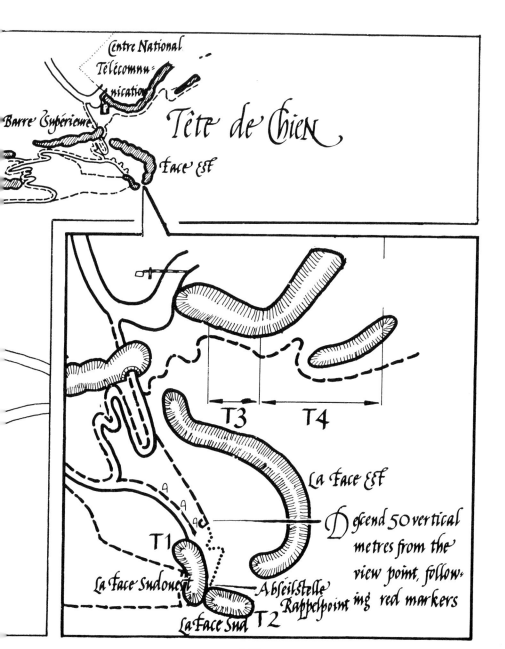

TETE DE CHIEN
FACE SUD-OUEST

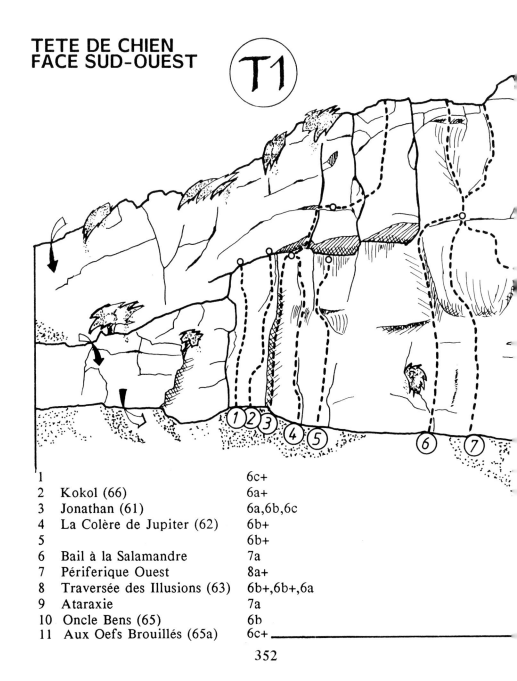

1		6c+
2	Kokol (66)	6a+
3	Jonathan (61)	6a,6b,6c
4	La Colère de Jupiter (62)	6b+
5		6b+
6	Bail à la Salamandre	7a
7	Périferique Ouest	8a+
8	Traversée des Illusions (63)	6b+,6b+,6a
9	Ataraxie	7a
10	Oncle Bens (65)	6b
11	Aux Oefs Brouillés (65a)	6c+

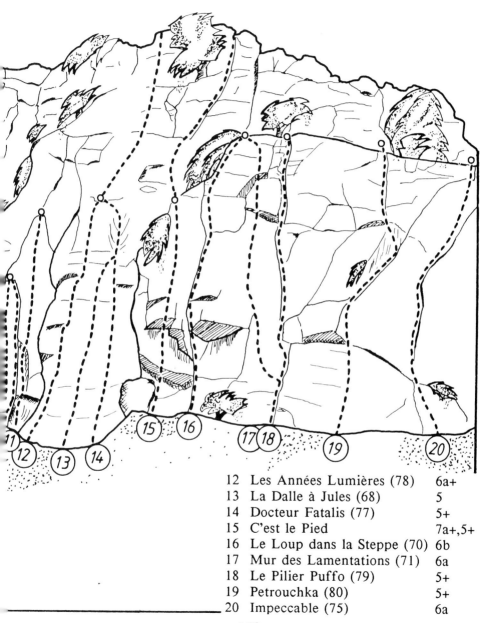

12	Les Années Lumières (78)	6a+
13	La Dalle à Jules (68)	5
14	Docteur Fatalis (77)	5+
15	C'est le Pied	7a+,5+
16	Le Loup dans la Steppe (70)	6b
17	Mur des Lamentations (71)	6a
18	Le Pilier Puffo (79)	5+
19	Petrouchka (80)	5+
20	Impeccable (75)	6a

TETE DE CHIEN
FACE SUD

1	Impeccable (75)	6a
2	Bleue (76)	7a
3	Sodome et Gomorrhe	6c+
4	Idées Noires	6c
5	Corto Maltese	6c+,6a
6	Les Passagers du Vent	6b+,6a
7	Papillon	7a+,7a,6a
8	Athos (81)	7a
9	L'Arrache-Coeur	7b+
10	Boudiou	7a,7a+
11	Gougoutte	6b,6c,6a
12	Dièdre d'Angle (110)	3,7b,6a,6c,5+
13	Ausstiegsvariante	5+

TETE DE CHIEN
FACE SUD

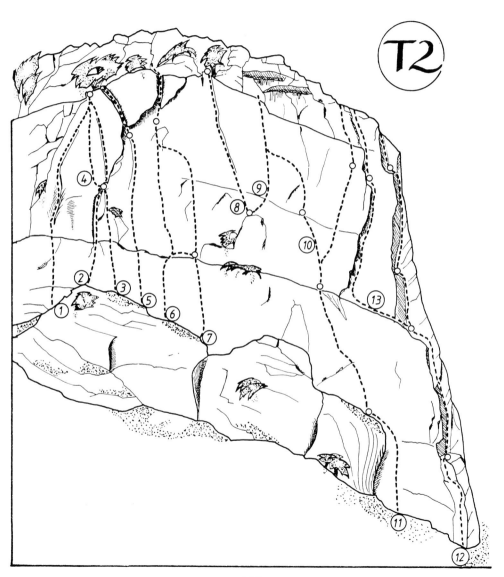

PAROI DU FORT
LINKE SEITE - LEFT SIDE

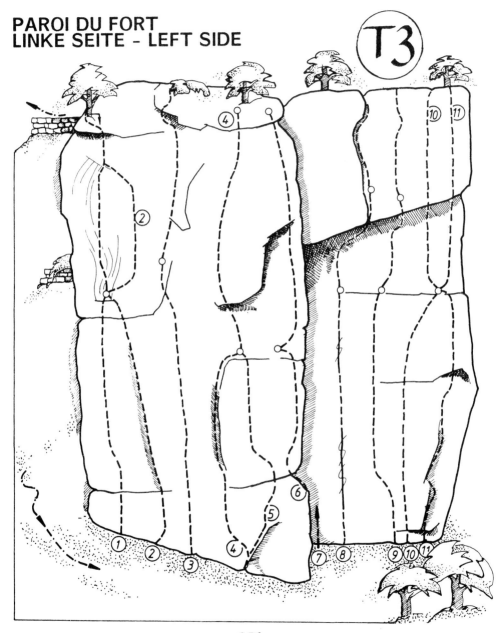

PAROI DU FORT
LINKE SEITE - LEFT SIDE

1	Jeux de Mains, Jeux de Vilains	6a+,6a+
2	Dit Merçi	5+,6a+
3	Sensa Balles	7a+,6a
4	Bulle de Savon	6b+,6b
5	Gwendoline	7a+
6	L'Araignée Mélomane	7a+,5+
7	Escartefigure	6a+,6b+,6b

in der schmalen Wand:
1. SL Riß, 2. SL Quergang nach links,
3. SL Wand
in the narrow wall:
pitch 1, crack, pitch 2, traverse left,
pitch 3, face

8	Carte Postale (106)	6a+,6c,6a
9	Coralie	6c,7a+,5+
10	Dislexie Cotationelle	6b,6b
11	Pas de Panique chez les Neurones	6c,6b

PAROI DU FORT
RECHTE SEITE - RIGHT SIDE

#	Name	Grade
1	Digitale	6c+,7a
2	Frénésie Bacchanale (101)	6a+,6c,6+
3	Yaourt Nature	6a,6a+
	rechter Ausstieg right hand finish	6a+
4	Mongolita	7b,6b
5	Le Retour de Roy Rogers	7b+
6	A Feu et à Sang	7a
7	Mibab	6c
8	Margoton	5+
9		6a
10		6b
11	Facile à Faire	7a
12	Que le Meilleur Perde	7b
13	Amuse Geule	8a+
14		6c
15	Big Ben - in the big cave in der großen Höhle	5,7a,6b+,6a

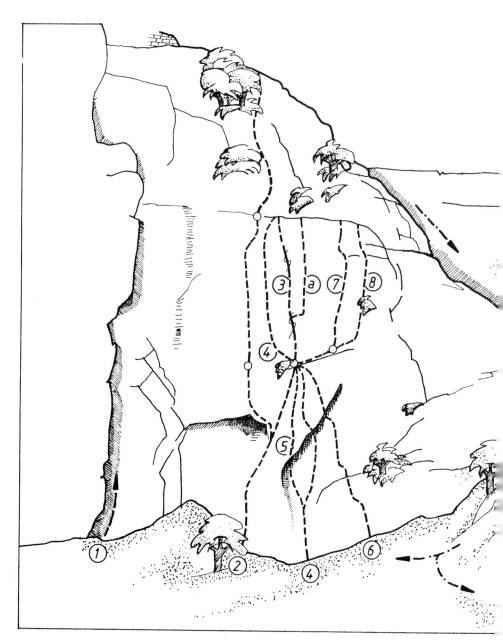

PAROI DU FORT   RECHTE SEITE - RIGHT SIDE

FOTO - UND VORLAGENNACHWEIS
PHOTO AND TOPO DIRECTORY

Seite/page

15 Eduard Burgada in "Prende la Tete" (7c). Can Gans Dionis, Siurana, Photo Dario Rodriguez.

19 Joan Caban in "Isadora donde estas?" (7b), Can Piqui Pugli, Siurana, Photo Dario Rodriguez.

45 Peter Schreibweis in "Espero Sur Central", Puig Campana, Photo Nicholas Mailänder.

79 Fco. Javin Orive in "Prende la Tete" (7c), Can Gan Dionis, Siurana, Photo Dario Rodriguez.

83 Liz Klobusicky in "La Fina" (5+), Toix East, Photo Nicholas Mailänder.

99 Peter Gomersall in "Cleoplaca" (7a/b), Mascarat Inferior, Photo Liz Klobusicky.

113 Yurso Riera in "Canto Gregoriano" (7b), Aguja de la Nuit, Chulilla, Photo Dario Rodriguez.

125 Volker Leuchsner und Guido Lammer in "La Polaca Ataca" (6c), Montanejos, Photo Nicholas Mailänder.

133 Fco. Javin Orive in "Pelix del'Oest (7b), Pared de la Yedra, Montanejos, Photo Dario Rodriguez.

139 Guido Lammer in der Pared Negra de la Maimona, Montanejos.

148 Fco. Javin Orive in "Lati Vansiao" (7b), La Plantxa, Siurana, Photo Dario Rodriguez.

165 Josep Batlle in "Asesinato Premeditado" (7b+), Montserrat, Photo Dario Rodriguez.

171 David Tarrago in "Alli Baba" (8a), Montserrat, Photo Dario Rodriguez.

179 Pep Boixados in "Sesion Continua" (7c+), Tocho del Macana, Montserrat, Photo Dario Rodriguez.

267 Irmgard Braun in "6ième Métatarsien (6b/c), Mont Ste. Victoire, Photo Volker Leuchsner.

284 Volker Leuchsner in "La Polaca Ataca" (6c), Montanejos, Photo Nicholas Mailänder.

309 Stefan Glowacz in "Rodeo", Cimai (6c+), Photo Uli Wiesmeier.

317 Irmgard Braun in "Curling" (6c), Mont Coudon, Photo Volker Leuchsner.

359 Stephan Glowacz an der Athosplatte, Tête de Chien, Photo Nicholas Mailänder.

Die folgenden Topos in diesem Buch basieren auf Originalen von:

The following topos are based on originals by:

Seite/page

78	Desnivel
122	Desnivel
132	Desnivel
134	Desnivel
149-157	Juan Chaporro
166-67	Armando Ballart
168-185	Nacho Ganzedo
186	Armando Ballart
188-191	Armando Ballart

Notizen